THE WOODVILLE REPUBLICAN

MISSISSIPPI'S OLDEST EXISTING NEWSPAPER

Volume 1: December 18, 1823-December 14, 1839

Compiled by
O'Levia Neil Wilson Wiese

HERITAGE BOOKS
2007

HERITAGE BOOKS
AN IMPRINT OF HERITAGE BOOKS, INC.

Books, CDs, and more—Worldwide

For our listing of thousands of titles see our website
at
www.HeritageBooks.com

Published 2007 by
HERITAGE BOOKS, INC.
Publishing Division
65 East Main Street
Westminster, Maryland 21157-5026

Copyright © 1990 O'Levia Neil Wilson Wiese

All rights reserved. No part of this book may be reproduced or transmitted in any form or by any means, electronic or mechanical, including photocopying, recording or by any information storage and retrieval system without written permission from the author, except for the inclusion of brief quotations in a review.

International Standard Book Number: 978-1-55613-365-7

This book is dedicated to the memory of Captain JOHN SOUTH LEWIS, grandfather of John South Lewis, Publisher Emeritus, and great grandfather of Andrew J. Lewis, Publisher/Editor of The Woodville Republican.

Capt. JOHN SOUTH LEWIS, CSA
Editor -- 1879-1900
Capt. Co. K, 16th Miss. Regiment
Longstreet's Div., Lee's Army No. VA

Other Heritage Books by O'Levia Neil Wilson Wiese:

Cemetery Records of Greene County, Alabama, and Related Areas

A. F. Carl Wiese Descendants

The Woodville Republican: Mississippi's Oldest Existing Newspaper:
Volume 1: December 18, 1823 - December 17, 1839
Volume 2: January 4, 1840 - October 30, 1847
Volume 3: January 8, 1848 - January 9, 1855
Volume 4: June 22, 1878 - December 25, 1880
Volume 5: January 1, 1881 - December 22, 1883
Volume 6: January 5, 1884 - December 26, 1891

CD: *The Woodville Republican, Volumes 1-5*

TABLE OF CONTENTS

Rand, McNally & Co.'s New Map of Mississippi, 1895	Inside front cover
Dedication	iii
History of *The Woodville Republican*	vii
Introduction	ix
Abstracts	1
December 18, 1823	1
January 1, 1824	1
January 4, 1825	9
January 10, 1826	17
January 1, 1827	25
January 5, 1828	36
January 3, 1829	45
January 2, 1830	55
January 15, 1831	72
(No 1832 issues)	
January 5, 1833	89
January 4, 1834	108
January 3, 1835	137
January 2, 1836	161
January 7, 1837	186
January 6, 1838	208
January 5, 1839	232
Index	255

THE WOODVILLE REPUBLICAN

On Thursday, the eleventh day of December, 1823, *The Woodville Republican* made its appearance in the town of Woodville. The oldest newspaper still in existence in the state of Mississippi, it has been in the Lewis family since Captain John S. Lewis, the grandfather and great-grandfather of the present owners, purchased the paper on June 7, 1879.

Throughout the years, many illustrious and influential citizens came from Woodville and Wilkinson County, and many of their activities since December 1823 have been reported weekly in *The Woodville Republican*.

No complete file of *The Woodville Republican* now exists, since many of the early volumes burned years ago. Nevertheless, hope remains that in the future additional issues may be discovered.

The founder and first editor of the newspaper was Mr. W. A. A. Chisholm. Throughout the following years, *The Woodville Republican* chronicled the lives and activities of the community during the formative years of the county.

Mr. Chisholm was editor for approximately twenty years. In 1842, the paper was owned and published by William A. Harris and Company. William J. Keller was editor during the beginning of the Civil War until its close, but the copies published during the war carried no names of the editor, publisher, or owner.

In commenting on the era between 1869 and 1876, Mr. John W. Bryant, publisher, gave this account: "In 1869, *The Republican* fell into the hands of the Republican Party, and for a few years advocated their odious principles...."

During this period of reconstruction, the paper was edited by Henry W. Noble, a Wilkinson County Republican who also held the office of sheriff. In 1876, Col. J. H. Jones assumed editorship. Prior to 1876 Col. Jones edited the *Woodville Sentinel*, which was the voice of the Democratic Party.

J. W. Shattuck and H. F. Simrall served as editors until 1879, when

Captain John S. Lewis bought the newspaper and edited it until his death in 1900. Under his editorship, the paper not only kept its influenial standing, but soon took its place as one of the leading exponents in the advocacy of Democratic Party principles. His son, Robert Lewis, succeeded his father as editor and held that position until his own death in 1934.

Robert Lewis published the Centennial Edition in 1924, and following his death, his widow assumed the editorship of the paper while his daughter became associate editor.

Robert Lewis's son, John S. Lewis, graduated from the University of Mississippi in 1935 and replaced his sister as associate editor until 1938 when he was elevated to the position of editor. At that time he was Mississippi's youngest editor of the state's oldest newspaper. He continued in this position until his son, Andrew J. Lewis, became the editor; at that time John S. Lewis assumed the title of Publisher Emeritus.

The history of this newspaper and that of the surrounding area are so closely tied together that it is difficult, if not impossible, to separate the two. In a recent letter to me, Mr. John S. Lewis enclosed two brief histories of the paper, one written by him and the other by his father. These articles describe the attributes of illustrious citizens who were instrumental in forging the state of Mississippi.

Today there are 173 other weekly papers that are over one hundred years old, and only forty-five of them are older than *The Woodville Republican*. Furthermore, of this number, only eight were established in 1800 or earlier.

On February 26, 1831, Editor G. D. Boyd remarked, "Deaths and marriages and other remarkable events belong to the history of a country, and ought to be recorded in the public journals within their vicinity...." This has certainly been accomplished in *The Woodville Republican* weekly newspaper.

O'Levia Neil Wilson Wiese
Waco, Texas

INTRODUCTION

In researching Wilkinson County, Mississippi, for information on my mother's people, I realized that much of the needed information could not be found in court records but was recounted in the back issues of the oldest newspaper in the state, *The Woodville Republican*.

Given were the announcements of Masonic Lodge celebrations, legal notices and rewards for runaway slaves, lists of available patent medicines given along with their usages and recipes for various concoctions. Throughout the issues, foreign news and humorous jokes made up much of the paper, along with marriages and deaths, religious and community activities, court proceedings and legal disputes, personal estate and tax sales, military and public office elections, deaths from epidemics, illness, murders, and suicides. There were accounts of river boats and river traffic, the building of the Mississippi's first railroad, the West Feliciana, and so forth.

These are the genealogical items which constitute the substance of this book. The abstracts of the issues contain only information that is deemed necessary for further research. The few extractions merely illustrate the times and the style of writing; for example, there was indiscriminate use of capital letters, and often what we now consider to be compound words, they separated into two words. The comments enclosed in parentheses reflect my own personal knowledge and family research.

I have taken great care to make this book both interesting as well as useful to those who are engaged in ongoing research.

Good hunting!

THE WOODVILLE REPUBLICAN

Publisher: William A. A. Chisholm

December 18, 1823

Estate sale of EDWARD RANDOLPH.

Died in this town on Friday last, WILLIAM F. NOLAND.

Died in Port Gibson on Dec. 10, JAMES A. MAXWELL M. D. 45 yrs, leaves wife and six small children. He was ill several months.

Washington City, Nov. 22: Capt. WILLIAM BARROW, 60 years, respectable and wealthy, from Feliciana Parish, La., leaves a daughter Mrs. Benoist, who is a widow, a younger daughter in Philadelphia, and a son and nephew at Columbian Collage near this city. On the way home, he was taken ill of Typhus.

Proposal to publish in St. Francisville La., a weekly newspaper; THE LOUISIANA JOURNAL.

January 1, 1824

The Rev. Messas. KING & MCLEOD, of the Presbyterian order will perform divine service on Sunday, next 4th inst.

The President has appointed CHARLES M. NORTON Esq., of Adams county for Marshall for the Mississippi District.

Married Monday last by Rev. Mr. FOX, Maj. A. M. FELTUS to Miss ELIZA ANN VENTRESS, dau. of the late Mr. LOVICK VENTRESS.

Married evening of 24th inst. by Rev. MARK MOORE, Dr. JESSE SAUNDERS, of Alabama to Miss MARIA DAVIS of this city.

Married on the same evening, SAMUEL DAVIS, Esq. to Miss MARY WILLIAMS, both of this county.

Murdered yesterday morning, Dr. DGAHAN, lately from Baton Rouge, by a man named Carlisle.

Died the 29th, WM. A. RICHARDSON, Esq. after a wasting illness of more than two years.

FRANCES NELSON, adm'rx., & WM. M. LINDSEY, adm'r., of the HUGH NELSON estate

January 6, 1824
BENJAMIN ECCLES, exec'r., of Dr. JOSEPH Y. SMITY's estate.

JOSEPH HUNTER's 120 acres land to be sold; east by heirs of E. RANDOLPH, west by N. HUNTER, and north by JOHN BELL.

January 10, 1824
Land belonging to the estate of JOHN COULTER Esqr's., is to be sold.

FUQUA land to be sold. 303 acres bounded on north by WILLIS JOHNSON, east & south by DAVID BATTERSON and JAMES RICHARDSON, and on the west by Dr. ROACH and Wm. DUNBAR.

January 15, 1824
Married at Port Gibson Friday the 9th instant by JAMES CORNELL, Esq'r., Mr. JOHN BRENT, formerly a citizen of this town, to Mrs. HARRIET SHAW.

200 Arpens of land belonging to NARSWORTHY HUNTER to be sold, north by JOHN BELL, east by JOSEPH HUNTER, and south by SAMUEL W. LEWIS.

January 20, 1824
Trustees of the Poor Report: ISAAC CHALMER, BENJ. ROLLINS, THOS SCOTT, THOMAS CASON, JNO. S. LEWIS, W. M. LANDSEY, R. EWELL, J. Y. SUTTIN, E.T. FARISH or (PARISH), REUBEN RUELL, A. M. MCCARNEY, and JAMES MARTIN.

Lands sold for taxes: DAVID W. COOK, FOS. FUQUA, DRURY SPURLOCK, estate of STEPHEN AMBROSE, GEORGE CONSTANTINE, JAMES BOYCE, THODODRE DORSETT, JOHN HUGES' estate, HUTSON ALFORD estate, Mrs. ANN SMITH, ABSALOM HAMMETT, WM. DUNBAR's estate, J.M. MCCOMAS, H. CHOTARD, and ROBERT COCHRAN.

January 27, 1824
RALPH ELLINGTON's 3 acres of land is to be sold, bounded east by DUDLY RUTLEDGE, and west by JOHN KEITHLEY, and located in the town of Woodville.

February 3, 1824
PRISSILAH CLAMPITT, adm'rx., of SAMUEL CLAMPITT's estate

JNO. MCALPINE, exec'r., of PETER MCGRAW's estate

A town lot located in front of FRANCIS KELLER and belonging to B. H. & W. T. LEWIS, is to be sold.

JESSE H. CARTWRIGHT's land that is to be sold is bounded on the south by MOSES LIDDELL, west by CALLEHAN, north by JOSEPH J. SCOTT, and east by JAS. SHAFFER.

February 10, 1824
ANDERSON GLOVER, dec'd, one item, "Laura" for sale

February 17, 1824
CHAUNCEY PETTIBONE's land, known as "RICHLANDS", to be sold

HUGH C. MILLS of St. Francisville, was murdered by JOEL LEWIS.

The land certificate of JOHN LOVE of Amite is in the possession of GEORGE HUFF who wishes owner to claim same.

Died Tuesday the 10th, in this town, THOMAS ASPINAL, merchant.

February 24, 1824
RICHARD WAMACK's land is to be sold.

Estate of THOMAS ASPINALL, deceased

J. G. RICHARDSON, exec'r., of the WILLIAM ARTHUR RICHARDSON's estate

March 2, 1824
Died in this town, after a short and severe illness, Mrs. MARY E. DAVIS, consort of Mr. ROBERT DAVIS. Funeral at Mr. WM. STAMPS

Died at Woodville on the 22nd, HEZEKIAH B. HULL, Esq., Counsellor at Law, 36 years of age. Mr. Hull was from Connecticut amd a graduate of Yale.

March 9, 1824
Married the 2nd, by THOMAS DAWSON, Esq., Mr. HENRY T. THOM to Miss MARY DAWSON, all of this county.

Died in this town on the 6th, CATHERINE GILL, infant daughter of R. M. GILL, Esq.

March 16, 1824
Z. McCARSTLES deceased, two quarters of land to be sold, north by heirs of James Dixon, east by Goodrich and Marshall, south by public land, west by a fractional section deeded to Z. McCARSTLES heirs and by John S. Lewis. SARAH McCARSTLE, exec'x

Lands to be sold. AGNUS PATTERSON, JOSEPH HUNTER, RICHARD WAMACK and HARVEY WRIGHT, L. PITCHER, B. H. & W. LEWIS, and WM. STEWART.

March 23, 1824
Notice: All accounts of B. F. PALMER are placed in the hands of R. M. GILL, Esqr., for settlements.

March 30, 1824
Died at his residence on the 25th, Mr. ROBERT BETHEY HAMMETT, a respectable planter.

JOHN BUNCH, adm'r., of the JACOB BUNCH's estate

HELEN CARR, widow of JOS. W. CARR will petition court for her dower in land known as a part of a certain tract of land granted to THOMAS FOSTER. Same tract conveyed by CASANDRA & EPHRAIM FOSTER, to said JOSEPH CARR, by deed January 16, 1819.

ELIZA W. NICHOLSON, widow of SAMUEL NICHOLSON will apply for dower to lands in Wilkinson Co.

April 6, 1824
NANCY ELLSBERRY's land is to be sold. 194 acres.

WILLIAM HUNTER's land is to be sold. 500 acres.

JNO. L. BRUCE, adm'r., of the WILLIAM G. BRUCE's estate

Lands to be sold: WM GRAYSON, ROBT. GRAYSON, JON A. COMBS, JOHN YERBY, JOHN YEISER, and JOSEPH MARLOW.

April 13, 1824
April 20, 1824
NATHAN E. RAYMOND 's land is to be sold. 395 acres.

Board of Medical Censors licenced to practice Medicine & Surgery: JOHN BARNES MD, Wilkinson Co., ROBERT W. WALKER MD, Amite Co., AYREE MERRILL MD, JOSEPH WILLIAMS FREIOT MD, & JOHN S.CORNEL MD, Adams Co., JOHN HATHORN SAVAGE MD, Jefferson Co., GEORGE F. JAQUESS MD, THOMAS B. MAGRUDER MD, Claiborne Co., SAML. ADOLPHUS CARTWRIGHT MD,and

JAMES AUGUSTUS McPHEATERS MD, Adams Co.

April 27, 1824
May 4, 1824
JESSE H. CARTWRIGHT, adm'r., for the LANDON DAVIS' estate

May 18, 1824
May 25, 1824
JOEL GLASS, adm'r., for the JOSHUA GLASS' estate

WILLIAM YERBY 's land is to be sold.

June 1, 1824
MARIA S. HULL, widow of HEZEKIAH B. HULL, will petition the court for her right of dower.

ELLEN CARR, widow of JOSEPH W. CARR, will petition court for her right of dower. Land 550 acres.

Married: Mr. ROBERT K. FLEMING late editor of the "Republican Advocate", to Miss LUCINDA LELAND in Illinois.

Married in Bowling Green, Mr. TENERCE CONEY, editor of the "Green River Correspondent", to Mrs. JANE FOSTER.

June 8, 1824
June 15, 1824
Doctor MICAJAH FRAZIER died last Sunday.

Died in this place, yesterday, MATILDA, infant daughter of the late Doct. WM. LANGLEY.

Died at Elmsley, this morning, Mrs. BETHIA LIDDEL, consort of MOSES LIDDELL, Esq'r.

Died in the Parish of Feliciana, the 11th, Capt. JEDEDIAH SMITH, a respectable planter.

June 22, 1824
Notice: GEORGE H. GORDON Esq., will attend to the settlement of WILLIAM T. LEWIS's business in his absence.

Married in Natchez the 20th, by Rev. BENJ. M. DRAKE, Mr. WILLIAM C. GRISSAN to Miss ZIPPORAII that city.

MOSES LIDDELL, adm'r., of the RICHARD SINGLETON's estate

June 29, 1824
ISABEL KNIGHT, adm'rx., & GEO MORRIS, admr., of the HENRY KNIGHT's estate

July 6, 1824
MARY HAMMETT & LEMUEL PREWETT, adm'rs., of ROBERT B. HAMMETT's estate

July 13, 1824
T. DEVALCOURT, formerly senior editor of the "Baton Rouge Gazette", has commenced the publication of a new journal, "Louisiana Republican".

Election locations to be held: Mount Pleasant, JESSE DELOACH's, upper Homochitto, VALENTINE C. GROOMS', lower Homochitto, Fort Adams, and Woodville.

July 24, 1824
Married at Natchez by Rev. Mr. Pilmore, the Hon. GERALD C. BRANDON, of this county, to Miss BETSY STANTON of that city.

WM. MATTHEWS, adm'r., of GEORGE MCDUFFIE estate, asks that all attend the residence of deceased to settle claims, as Matthews does not live in Wilkinson county.

WILLIAM REID, adm'r., of the HUGH REID's estate

July 27, 1824
NANCY ELLSBERRY, widow of JOSEPH ELLSBERRY, 1 tract of land SE 1/4 No. 17, T2, R1, 163 A. and SE corner of a 1/4 section purchased by CHARLES CASON of Jacob Ellsberry. Intersects with JOSEPH ELLSBERRY's land and same 35 acres purchased of Charles Cason.

August 3, 1824
BARBARA LOVELACE, exec'x., of the THOS. LOVELACE's estate

JOSEPH PATTERSON, adm'r., of the JARED C. BEASLEY's estate

August 18, 1824
August 27, 1824
ABRAHAM LANEHART, adm'r., for ADAM LANEHART's estate

Died the 23rd., PENELOPE CAGE, infant daughter of H. CAGE, Esq'r.

Died at his residence near Washington on the 20th, the Hon. LOUIS WINSTON, Judge of the 2nd Judicial

District.

JOHN KING, adm'r., for the ISAAC CARTER's estate

NANCY ELLSBERRY, admr'x., of JOSEPH ELLSBERRY's estate. 194 acres of land to be sold to settle debts of estate.

September 2, 1824
September 7, 1824

Commissioners appointed by the Orphans' Court of Wilkinson County for Dr. JOSEPH SMITH's estate: JOHN STEVENS, JOS. CALLENDER and JOHN CONNELL.

CAKER THERREL's land is to be sold. 300 acres

Capt. C. LAURET, captain of the steam boat, RAMAPO, leaves Bayou Sarah Landing for New Orleans every Friday.

September 14, 1824

Major JEREMIAH NOLAND and GERALD C. BRANDON, Esq., are candidates for Colonel, to fill the vacancy occasioned by the resignation of Colonel JOS. J. SCOTT of the 5th Regiment, M. M.

The admr's., of SAML. REILEY's estate, H. CAGE & J. Y. REILEY, will sell 600 acres of land, north & east by MOSES GORDON, south by JESSE EDWARDS, and west by heirs of DUNCAN STEWART.

JAMES BEUFORD, exec'r., of the PETER PRESLER's estate

Died in Pinckneyville, Mr. GEORGE F. RANDOLPH, Jnr. One day later, his consort, Mrs. RACHEL RANDOLPH followed him. (Rachel Stockett)

September 21, 1824

Commissioners appointed by Probate Court for the THOMAS ASPIN estate: JOHN STEVENS, FIELDING DAVIS, and JOHN CONNELL.

T. DAWSON's land is to be sold, 20 acres on Pearce Creek, bounded south by lands of Woodsides, and north by P. G. PARHAM.

THOMAS CASON, Snr. and LEWIS CASON's land is to be sold. 160 Acres, north by MURDOCK MCCRANEY, east by THOS CASON, and south by WM CASON.

CAKER THERREL's land is to be sold. 300 acres on Pearce Creek.

September 28, 1824

Candidates for Colonel to fill vacancy of Col. JOS. J. SCOTT are Capt. J. S. WAIDE, Major M. M. HOLLIMAN, and GERALD C. BRANDON Esquire.

BRS. SOJOURNER, exec'r., of WILLIAM SOJOURNER's estate

Died at residence of Mr. M. F. DeGRAFFENREID near this place on the 25th instant, Major CHAPMAN WHITE.

October 5, 1824

Died in Feliciana Parish, the Rev. MARK MOORE at the home of Mr. THOMAS S. CHEW.

ROBT. WISEMAN's land is to be sold. 160 acres north-east by JNO. GERMANY, south by THEODORE DORSSETT, and east by McCARTNEY

October 12, 1824

JAMES CRAWES's land is to be sold.

JESSE H. CARTWRIGHT's land is to be sold.

Death of Rev. MARK MOORE, age 59, and pastor of the Methodist Episcopal Church

C. E. HALL & J. G. YOUNG, executors of GEO. F. RANDOLPH Junr. 's estate

WILLIAM ALEXANDER's land is to be sold. 80 Acres, north by EDWARD McGEHEE, east by WILLIAM GOULDING, south by THOMAS KELLER, & west by ARCHIBALD McGEHEE

October 19, 1824

BRS. SOJOURNER, adm'r., of the estate of GABRIEL SOJOURNER and the estate of WILLIAM SOJOURNER Both deceased

October 22, 1824
October 26, 1824
November 2, 1824

ISAAC D. SHELBY, adm'r., of EVAN SHELBY's estate

November 9, 1824

THOMAS BELL's land is to be sold   1600 arpens

November 16, 1824

JOHN BUNCH, adm'r., of WESTLY FARMER's estate

November 23, 1824

Married by HOWELL MORELAND, Esqr., Mr. LEVI PREWETT

of this place, to Miss MILLBERRY HAMILTON, of Feliciana Parish.

Fort Adams: JOSEPH ROURKE was robbed of various notes while visiting Shippingport, Kentucky. All persons warned not to trade for said notes as payment has been stopped.

November 30, 1824

FRANCIS BAKER, Esq.,of Natchez, was murdered in Maysville, Ky., on his route to New Jersey.

December 11, 1824

SAML V. BRADLEY, exec'r., of IVESON G. LEA's estate in Amite County

Died, FRANCIS BAKER, Esq.,late senior editor of"The Mississippian", about 40 years of age, was assassinated. He was born in Delaware and has been separated from there for eight or ten years.

Died, Sat. 27th at his residence near Pickneyville, Colonel WILLIAM YERBY, 47 years of age, leaving a widow and orphans. He had served for several years in the legislature of his native state of Virginia. At the period of his death, he was a representive from Wilkinson County.

December 18, 1824

MARTHA DOVE, exec'x., of the WILLIAM DOVE estate

COL. WILLIAM YERBY, Representative to the General Assembly has died. Election is to be held to fill that vacancy.

December 25, 1824

D. COOPER, exec'r., of the JOHN COULTER, Esqr.'s estate, will sell 500 acres of land.

The land of the JAMES McDOWEL and J. SCARLETT's estates will be sold.

The land of JOHN B. HORTON & JEREMIAH DOWNS is to be sold.

1825
January 4, 1825

Married at the residence of William Eacles, Esq. by the Rev. Mr. Fox, Mr. JOSEPH SEVERSON to Miss JENNETT CARRAWAY.

MARY NETTERVILLE, adm'x., of the JEREMIAH NETTER-

VILLE estate

MARY FRAZIER, adm'x., of MICAJAH FRAZER's estate

ROBT. E. LOVE, adm'r., of MATTHEW McCULLOCK's estate

DANL. D. ANDERSON, ex'r., of WM. ANDERSON's estate

<u>January 11, 1825</u>
<u>January 18, 1825</u>

N. WADDELL, & N. NORWOOD, admr's., of JOHN HODGES's estate

ELIZABETH YERBY, exec'x., of Col. WILLIAM YERBY's estate

FELIX STEPHENS, adm'r., of ELIJAH PHIPPS's estate

<u>January 25, 1825</u>

D. COOPER & SARAH McCARSTLE, adm'rs., of ZALMON McCARSTLE's estate

<u>February 1, 1825</u>

The Rev. Mr. DARES of Nashville will preach at St. Francisville on the first Sunday in February, on Wednesday at Sharon, on Thursday at the Red house of Maj. JOSEPH JOHNSON near the line, on Friday at Woodville, and on Saturday and Sunday at Bethel.

<u>February 9, 1825</u>
<u>February 15, 1825</u>

BATON ROUGE GAZETTE: Duel between Mr. DUHY, editor of the "Merchantile Advertiser", and Mr. CRUZAT, editor of the "Argus" took place. First fought with pistols, then small swords--both dreadfully wounded.

Miss ELIZABETH ANN WESBROOK intends opening a school for small boys and girls. Terms: "Reading and Writing, per quarter, English Grammer, plain sewing, needle work and marking, $6.00 per quarter."

Commissioners appointed for JOSEPH CARR estate; WILLIAM BELL, C. EVANS HALL and J. A. MUMFORD.

REMOVAL: The office of the WOODVILLE REPUBLICAN has been removed to the west end of the house fronting the Public Square, formerly occupied by the late T. ASPINAL as a store, and at present by

Capt. JAMES MARTIC.

February 22, 1825
March 1, 1825
March 15, 1825

MARY OGDEN, adm'rx., for ISAAC E. OGDEN's estate

JOHN C. SIMS, adm'r., of PETER PRESLER, Snr.'s estate

Commissioners appointed for estate of WILLIAM YERBY dec'd., WM. HAILE, JAS S. WAIDE, and LEMUEL PITCHER.

Amite County Orphans'Court ordered all persons interested in the real estate of IVESON G. LEA, deceased, to appear.

March 22,18 25

"Nashville Republican": Married Tuesday the 13th by the Rev. LEVIN EDNEY, Mr. SAMUEL FOREHAND to Miss SALLY M. M'PHARISON.

March 29, 1825

JONATHAN COMB's 50 acres of land is to be sold.

WILLIAM H. BENTON, Editor of the late "Mississippi Republican" published at Natchez, has removed the office to Vicksburg, Warren county, and commenced the publicatian of a new paper under the title, "The Republician".

Died, on the 26th instant at the residence of her mother, Mrs. MARY COLLIER, consort of G. B. COLLIER Esqr., of this town.

April 5, 1825

Died, on Thursday the 21th March at the residence of A. M. FELTUS, Esqr., Mrs. ELIZABETH VENTRESS, relict of the late LOVICK VENTRESS, Esqr., in her 55th year of age.

JANE KELLER, & G. W. KELLER, were appointed adm'rs., of GEORGE KELLER's estate.

April 12, 1825

JNO. L. BRUCE, curator of JOHN ANDERSON's estate in East Feliciana

JOHN KAIGLER & ESAIAS KAIGLER, appointed ex'rs.,of the ANDREW KAIGLER's estate.

MOSES LIDDELL & JOS. CALLENDER, were appointed admr's., of the JOHN HENRY POST's estate.

April 19, 1825

Married in Jackson, La., on Thursday evening last, by BENJAMIN ECCLE, Esqr., Mr. HENRY RICHARDSON to Miss LOUISA KELLER.

Notice by ZACH SMITH: "All persons are hereby cautioned against trading with MARGARET SMITH as she has left my bed and board without any provocation---therefore I shall not pay any contract that she may make on my account."
(Her rebuttal appeared on May 14).

April 27, 1825

Married at Fort Adams on the 19th, Mr. WILLIAM RICHARDSON to Mrs. ELIZABETH CURTS.

The citizens of Wilkinson and Adams Counties are requested to meet at the Court House in Woodville on the first Monday in May next, for the purpose of contributing aid in the improvement of the road through the HOMOCHITO SWAMP & LOVE's FERRY.

May 4, 1825
May 14, 1825

Married on Thursday evening last, Mr. GEORGE NIMON to Mrs. MARTHA B. MAY, both of this place.

J. JOOR, appointed adm'r., of JOSEPH BOOTH's estate

JOSEPH SEVERSON, was appointed adm'r., of the CHARLES RICE's estate.

CATHERINE EDWARDS, was appointed exec'x., of the EDMUND EDWARDS estate.

SAMUEL V. BRADLEY, ex'r., of the dec'd., IVESON G. LEA's estate will sell house and lot in Liberty.

May 21, 1825

JAMES BAILEY, ex'r., of the HUMPHREY DRURY's estate

May 28, 1825

In St. Francisville, HENRY MILLER, a blacksmith, was shot by HENRY GASTIN, a journeyman printer and employer.

Commissioners appointed for ISAAC WILLIAMS estate;

JOHN STEVENS, FIELDING DAVIS and Wm. T. HAYES.

Land known as "Foleo', old Field Tract" to be sold & divided among heirs of MARTHA DAVIS. Sale to be held at the house of Dr. N. E. RAYMOND which ajoins said lands.

June 4, 1825
June 11, 1825

This office will be removed next week to the house lately occupied by Mr. JAMES SHAFER.

Married at Sligo, on Thursday evening the 16th, by the Rev. JAMES A. FOX, Mr. TIGNAL JONES STEWART to Miss SALLY ANN RANDOLPH, eldest daughter of JUDGE RANDOLPH.

Married at Ashley place, on Wednesday evening the 15th, by the Rev. J. A. FOX., Mr. LEMUEL PITCHER and Mrs. MARY STARK.

Married at Cherryfield, on Thursday evening the 16th, by the Rev. WILLIAM WINANS, Mr. SAMUEL TUELL to Mrs. HUGHES. (Wilkinson County Marriage Book states, Mrs. MARY B. HUGHES)

Died on the 13th, MARTHA, youngest daughter of Mr. HUGH CONNELL.

June 25, 1825

MOSES GORDON, Senr., adm'r., of the WILLIAM HORTON, estate.

Died in this town, on the 21st, LOUISA, infant daughter of Mr. REUBEN L. BONNEER.

July 2, 1825

Baton Rouge. JOHN BANYAN of Kentucky was killed. Verdict of manslaughter was returned on THOMAS O' CONNOR.

Died in this town on the 27th., EMOCH, infant son of Mr. ELISHA GOWER.

July 9, 1825

JAIL PRESLER, widow and relict of PETER PRESLER petitions the court for permission to sell 1800 acres surveyed by ELIJAH POPE.

July 16, 1825
July 23, 1825

Married on Thursday evening last, by the Rev. JAMES A. FOX, Doct. DAVID HOLT to Miss JULIA

WHITE, both of this place.

JOSEPH WALLER refuses responsibility of MARY WALLER's debt.

July 30, 1825
D. COOPER, the adm'r., of ZALMON McCARSTLE, dec'd., will sell land.

JOHN M. WILSON, was appointed exec'r., of RICHARD KIDD's, late of Pickneyville, estate.

August 7, 1825
August 13, 1825
Died on the 10th instant, WILLIAM R. BRUCE, infant son of Mr. JOHN L. BRUCE.

A Post Office has been lately established at Fort Adams and Mr. C. EVANS HALL appointed Post Master.

VICTOR N. HARRIS, adm'r., of the VICTOR HARRIS estate.

August 20, 1825
August 27, 1825
Died in Monroe Co., on the 17th, Dr. BARTLET C. BARRY. Died about the same time, his brother-in-law, JOHN B. RAZER, a Merchant and Post Master at Columbus.

Commissioners appointed for estate of ROBERT BRADEN: DAVID IRWIN, DAVID COON, and DANIEL SLACK. (Mount Pleasant)

September 3, 1825
Commissioners for estate of ROBERT BRADEN will meet to receive claims at house of DANIEL McGANEY at Mt. Pleasant.

G. D. BOYD, appointed, adm'r., of the JOHN A. BAMBER's estate.

September 10, 1825
Died at Ashwood Place on Wednesday morning, THOMAS POINDEXTER, Esqr., formerly of Fredericksburg, Va.

JOEL GLASS, ex'r., & SUSANNAH BENTHAL, exec'x., both appointed for the THOMAS BENTHAL's estate.

September 17, 1825

Married at Hollywell on Thursday the 15th, by the Rev. JAS A. FOX, Mr. FIELDING DAVIS to Miss MARY DAVIS.

Married on the same evening by the Rev. GEN. A. IRION, Mr. VICTOR N. HARRIS to Miss ANN NETTERVILLE.

September 24, 1825
Died at Washington Ms., on Tuesday morning, the 20th, Dr. WILLIAM P. FOSTER, Editor of the "Ariel", published in the city of Natchez.

JOHN RICHARDS, adm'r., of the JAMES MILES's estate

October 1, 1825
October 8, 1825
Married in Port Gibson on Sunday evening the 2nd by the Rev. RANDAL GIBSON, Mr. ABRAM GREEN to Mrs. ANN MAXWELL, relict of the late Dr. JAMES A. MAXWELL.

Died Sunday the 2nd, at the residence of HOWELL MOSS, Esq., in the vicinity of Natchez, Mr. JAMES HUGHES, the editor of the "Mississippian".

Died on Wednesday last at Washington, Mrs. ANN MARIA EVENS, 25 years of age, wife of Mr. WILLIAM EVENS, and the eldest daughter of COLONEL ANDREW MARSCHALK.

Died Thursday in Natchez, Mr. WILLIAM MURRAY, printer.

October 15, 1825
Married on Thursday the 13th by the Rev. J. A. FOX, Mr. John CARRAWAY to Miss MARY FRAZIER, eldest daughter of the late Dr. MICAJOB FRAZIER; all of this county.

October 25, 1825
There was a yellow fever epidemic in Washington (Ms.) and Natchez. In the newspaper, ARIEL, "....that we have a morbid or infected atmosphere there can be no doubt. Of thirteen physicians, three of them were taken sick last week, viz... Doctors CORNELL, HUNT, and WALKER"..."The news from Natchez respecting the sickness is truly melancholy. Numbered among those who have died since the last ARIEL was printed are the names of SAML. POSTLETHWAITE, President of the bank, Maj. N. PERKINS and Dr. CORNELL."

October 29, 1825
Died at Natchez, on Monday 24th, of the prevailing Epidemic, Mr. WILLIAM LORING CALLENDER, formely of this place. He was 25 years of age and a native of Wilmington, N. C. and emigrated to this state about two years since.

November 5, 1825
Married in Kentucky on the 22d Sep., by the Rev. THOS. CLELAND, Mr. FRANCIS R. RICHARDSON, formerly of this county and Miss SARAH M., the daughter of Mr. B. MAGOFFIN of Harrodsburgh.

November 12, 1825
Married on Thursday evening last, by JACOB CHAMBERS, Esqr., Mr. GREEN B. MORRIS to Miss ELIZABETH EILER, both of this county

November 19, 1825
November 26, 1825
Married on Thursday the 17th instant, by the Rev. J. A. FOX, Mr. CHARLES PENNIMAN to Miss LUCETTA A., daughter of Dr. SAMUEL ROBINSON, both of Pickneyville.

Married on Thursday the 24th instant, by the Rev. GEO. A. IRON, Major GEORGE H GORDON to Miss MARY CALLIHAM, daughter of Mr. DAVID CALLIHAM, all of this county.

Married lately at St. Francisville, Mr. THOMAS C. ADAMS to Miss ALSENATH WALLER, both formerly of this county.

Died at the residence of the late Col. WILLIAM YERBY, Mrs. FRANCIS YERBY age nearly 97 yrs.

December 3, 1825
A. DANIEL, ex'r., of the THOMAS ASPINALL's estate

Married on Thursday evening, by Benj. Eccles, Esqr., GEORGE B. COLLAER, Esqr., to Miss SARAH CLARKSON, both of this county.

Murdered on Sunday last, Mr. THOMAS JACKSON.

December 10, 1825
Married at Sligo on Sunday the 4th, by Benjamin Eccles, Esqr., Doctor GEORGE A. BEDFORD to Miss SARAH B. COBB, both of the Parish of Feliciana, State of Louisiana.

Died at his residence in the county on Wednesday, REESE EFLEESON, Esqr., former cashier at the bank.

December 20, 1825

The second volume of this paper has been completed. WM. A. A. CHISHOLM retires and turns over the publication to Mr. SAMUEL T. KING.

Married on Thursday evening, by the Rev. J. A. FOX, FRANCIS GILDART, Esqr., to Miss JUDITH BAILEY, all of this co.

MARY SHELBY, adm'x., of the ISAAC SHELBY's estate

LEMUEL PREWETT, adm'r., of the ROBERT B. HAMMETT's estate

WM. CARSON, adm'r., of the JAMES COLEMAN estate

1826
January 10, 1826

Died at the residence of WM BUCKNER in this county on the 7th, Rev. BENJAMIN DAVIS, 44 years of age, Minister of the Baptist Church.

January 24, 1826

NANCY PINSON, admr'x., & JOHN O. WILLIAMS adm'r., for the DANIEL B. PINSON estate

JOHN G. YOUNG & C. EVANS HALL appointed exec'rs., of the Gen. F. RANDOLPH estate

February 7, 1826

MARY S. OGDEN, adm'rx., of the DAN OGDEN estate

J. JOOR, exec'r., of the JOHN NORWOOD estate

February 14, 1826

JOHN TISON refuses all debts of "...wife PHEBE".

WM. ANDERSON, adm'r., of the JAMES EWELL estate

February 21, 1826

JOSEPH A. FOSTER, adm'r., of the THOS. JACKSON estate

Married on Thursday evening last by the Rev. JAMES A. RANALDSON, Dr. EDWARD T. FARISH to Miss ELIZA SMITH.

February 28, 1826

ELEANOR BURTON, admr'x., of the WILLSON BURTON estate

March 7, 1826

Married on Wednesday evening by the Rev. GEORGE A. IRON, Mr. WILLIAM W. YERBY, Attorney at Law of Amite County to Miss THIRSA ANN HADLEY, of this county.

March 18, 1826

MATILDA FLEESON is the widow of REESE E. FLEESON.

Married on Sunday evening, Mr. JOHN ILER to Miss Mary RUTLEDGE, daughter of Mr. DUDLEY RUTLEDGE, all of this county.

JAMES MEEK, adm'r, of the JOHN WILKINSON's estate

March 25, 1826

ROBERT DAWSON, adm'r, of THOMAS W. DAWSON's estate

WM. H. HANNA, appointed guardian for JAMES HANNA, minor heir of H. HANNA.

April 1, 1826

WM. M. LINDSEY, adm'r., & FANNEY NELSON, admr'x., of the HUGH NELSON estate, will present their claims to the Orphans Court.

April 8, 1826

WILLIAM F. NOLAN's land is to be sold.

Married on Thursday the 6th, Mr. EDWARD FELTUS, merchant to Miss SARAH W. MARSHALL, both of this place.

April 15, 1825

Died on Saturday morning the 1st, at Berry Hill, near Fort Adams, Mr. THORP PARROT, in the 91st year of his age.

Died on the 9th at the house of Mr. JESSE CRAFT in Pike Co., Major THOMAS CREWS, of this county.

PETER SMITH, Adm'r., of the NATHANIEL JONES estate

April 22, 1826
April 29, 1826

R. H. SPEARS & A. SPEARS appointed adm'rs., of the AUSTIN SPEARS estate

PRESTWOOD SMITH, adm'r., of THOMAS KELSEY's estate.

Commissioners appointed to received claims against the ISAAC DILLAHUNTY estate: WM HAILE, F. DAVIS, JOHN CONNELL and JOHN STEPHENS.

May 6, 1826

Married on Thursday the 27th by the Rev. WM. WINANS, Mr. RICHARD SPEARS of Amite County to Miss MARTHA McGAMEY of this county.

May 13, 1826

Married on Thursday the 4th, by JAMES BEUFORD, Esqr., Mr. WILLIAM CHURCH to Miss JANE WILSON, all of this county.

JESSE BROWN, adm'r., of the estate of BENJAMIN THERRELL, THOMAS CREWS, and EDITH CREWS, his deceased wife.

May 20, 1826

Acting Executor of the PATRICK FOLEY estate, GERALD C. BRANDON, releases executorship.

Administrator GERALD C. BRANDON holds final settlement of ROBERT E. BRANDON's estate.

May 27, 1826

Appointed Commissioners, H. D. KELLOGG, ARTHUR DANIEL, and CHAUNCY S. KELLOGG, for the JOSHUA GLASS's estate

LOUISA LIGON, adm'x., & WM. JOHNSON, adm'r for the JOHN LIGON's estate

JOSEPH JOHNSON , adm'r., for the Rev. BENJAMIN DAVIS' estate

June 3, 1826
June 10, 1826

Married on Thursday the 1st by JOHN BRICE, Esqr., Mr. JAMES FANNER to Miss MARY ANN ROACH all of this county.

Married on Wednesday, by BENJAMIN ECCLES, Esqr. Mr. WM L. CASON to Miss JANE COOK, all of this county.

Candidates for office: WILLIAM HAILE of Wilkinson County, ADAM L. BINGAMAN of Adams County, RICHARD STOCKTON JR., MAJOR JOSEPH JOHNSON, COL. ABRAM M. SCOTT, M. F. De GRAFFENREID, and C. P. SMITH.

JOHN McALPINE, ex'r., & DRASILLA LARKSTON, exec'x., for the estate of JOSEPH P. CLARKSTON.

DR. THOMAS LYNE is a physician in Woodville.

June 17, 1826
ISAAC WILLIAMS's estate declared insolvent.

D. B. THOMPSON requests that all who owe money to estate of RICE PIERCE to pay. THOMPSON is leaving the country.

Land belonging to the estate of CHAPMAN WHITE, deceased, is to be sold.

JESSE BROWN, adm'r., of the estate of BENJAMIN THERRELL, THOMAS CREWS and EDITH CREWS, his deceased wife

PETER M. LAPICE vs. MATTHEW BETHANY. Land sold

June 24, 1826
Claims received against estate of RICHARD KIDD.

Dissolved partnership between E. T. FARISH and J. G. GUIGNARD

FELIX GRUNDY's land is to be sold.

Interest in a lot belonging to THOMAS KIRKHAM is to be sold.

July 1, 1826
CAGE & HENDERSON of Woodville opened a law office.

ANDREW McCARTNEY, adm'r., of ANDREW B. McCARTNEY'S estate

BENJAMIN ROGERS, adm'r.,of JOHN ROGERS's estate

July 8, 1826
BRIDGES SOJOURNER, adm'r., of the JACOB CURTIS estate

July 15, 1826
Died, June 7, at his residence in Buckinham, EDWARD PATTERSON, aged 70. He was a Revolutionary soldier and left an aged widow.

July 22, 1826
Died in Washington, February 26, 1826, Senator JOHN GAILLARD.

Married July 13, ZACHARIAH CANFIELD to JULIA P. JONES.

Died July 16, Mrs. MARY HAMMETT, consort of WILLIAM HAMMETT.

July 29, 1826
Died in Natchez July 24, JAMES STEEN, a native of Antrem in the North of Ireland.

Died in Amite county, July 18, age 71, Captain JACOB BUCKHOLTE, a soldier of the Revolution.

DAVID BERRY, adm'r., of ANDERSON BERRY's estate

JESSE SIBLEY, adm'r., of THOMAS HILL 's estate

Married July 29, EDMOND GINN to Mrs. ELIZA ANN HARRISON.

L. BERRY THOMPSON, adm'r., of JOHN TANNER'S estate

Copartnership of SAML W. LEWIS and WILLIAM MONKS

J. JOOR, exec'r., for the J. NORWOOD estate

DAVID DAVIS, exec'r., for the DUNCAN SHAW's estate.

August 5, 1826
Doctor JAMES R. OGDEN, a native of New York died Tuesday morning at Mr. Wm. Bush's residence.

August 12, 1826
The accounts of DAVID ARMSTRONG, in Woodville, are in the hands of T. R. DOWNING.

DAVID BERRRY refuses to pay debts of his wife, MARTHA BERRY.

NATHAN MANSFIELD & J. G. RICHARDSON, were appointed admr's., of the WILLIAM MANSFIELD estate.

JARED C. BEASLEY is declared insolvent.

Claims are accepted on Doctor JOSEPH Y. SMITH's estate.

August 19, 1826
Capt. WILLIAM LEIBY of Circleville, Ohio, died on the 5th, due to injury from firing at the Jubilee celebration.

Died at sea, Mrs. SARAH FOX, consort of the Rev.

JAMES A. FOX, and left affectionate husband and dear little children.

It is assertained that in 1820, there were more than five hundred inhabitats of the town of Nantucket bearing the name of COFFIN, all probably descendants of TRIISTAN COFFIN who settled in this country about the year 1644, and who was the first to visit America. (Originally from the "Nantucky Enquirer")

Died in Baton Rouge on August 12, ANTHONY PENNISTON, 27 yrs old and a native of Petersburg, Virginia. He was killed by JOHN B. POTTS.

JOHN ABSHEAR murdered by JOHN DAY, both citizens of Simpson Co. (Originally from Russelville, Ky.,)

August 26, 1826
Mr. WM. B. FISHER rented a house belonging to Col. JOHN S. LEWIS, directly below the dwelling of Mr. D. BASS, where he carries on Hat Manufacturing, Silk Dying and etc.

September 2, 1826
Married at Judge Hampton's in this county, on Thursday, the 31st by BENJAMIN ECCLES, Esqr., Mr. THOMAS S. HERBERT and Miss SUSAN F. HUGHES, daughter of the late Capt. JOHN HUGHES.

Land to be sold for debts, bounded on north by WILLIAM L. CASON, west & south by U.S. and east by lands of JOHN JOOR.

September 9, 1826
W. W. YERBY permanently locates law office in Woodville.

A public auction is to be held at JOHN McCRADY's plantation.

J. H. MILLER of Fort Adams declares assertions made by THOMAS CLAY are lies. Character substantiated by Doctor D. T. ORR, near Sligo, Kentucky.

Married on Tuesday last, by the Hon. THOMAS H. PROSSER, FREDERICK A. BROWDER, Esqr. of the Parish of Feliciana to Mrs. HARRIETT HOOK of this county.

Died at the Elysian Fields, Amite County, Mrs. MARY DAVIS, in the eighty-fifth year of her age.

THE REPUBLICAN AND WILKINSON WEEKLY ADVERTISER
September 16, 1826

Land granted by Spanish Government to HUGH DAVIS (650-A) to be sold. Same property of the JAMES BOYCE estate, lying in Wilkinson County, Ms. JAMES FOSTER vs. ROBT. BOYCE adm'r., of JAMES BOYCE's estate.

HARRIS ANDERSON, adm'r., of the WILLIAM ANDERSON's estate.

Died, RICHARD C. ANDERSON, Esqr. of Kentucky, at Carthagena on July 28, on his way to the Congress of Panama.

Married on Thursday, Capt. WILLIAM L. BRANDON to Miss GEORGIA ANN C. DAVIS, daughter of Mrs. Susan Davis, all of this county.

Died on Tuesday, Mrs. SARAH BRUCE, consort of JOHN L. BRUCE of this county.

Died Thursday, Mrs. ----SLACK, consort of Mr. DANIEL SLACK. (Wilkinson County Marriage Book states, DANIEL SLACK m. RUTH G. BRUCE on January 20,1823)

September 23, 1826

J. H. MILLER withdraws his accusations against THOMAS H. CLAY.

September 30, 1826

GERALD C. BRANDON desires release from being adm'r., of the ROBERT E. BRANDON and PATRICK FOLEY estates.

G. D. BOYD, adm'r., of the JOHN A BAMBER estate.

RICHARD SEAGARS, adm'r., of JOHN LAMMOND's estate

October 7, 1826

BYTHEL HANES, a Revolutionary Soldier

PRESTWOOD SMITH, adm'r., of THOMAS KELSOE's estate.

October 14, 1826

Married on Thursday by LEMUEL MILES, Esq., Mr. ELISHA HODGES to Miss CATHARINE COMBS, all of this county.

Married by the Rev. GEORGE A. IRION, Mr. ROBERT

NORWOOD to Miss LEVICE SOJOURNER, all of this county.

Married by Benjamin Eccles, Esqr., Capt. AMMON BURR to Miss CLARRISSA M. KEITH, all of this county.

Died on the 2nd., ELIZABETH FELTUS, daughter of Major A. M. FELTUS.

Died on 12th, HENRY JAMES FELTUS, son of Major A. M. FELTUS.

Died in Philadelphia on September 9, WM. H. RUFFIN, Esqr., of this city.

Massacre in Louisville last Friday! HOWARD STONE, EDWARD STONE of Bourbon, DAVID COBB of this place, and JAMES GRAY. The fifth victim was a Mr. Davis, a passenger on the boat.

October 21, 1826
October 28, 1826
Died in this county on the 27th, Mr. T. R. DOWNING

November 4, 1826
Died Thursday morning, the 12th., Mrs. ELIZABETH ISLER, consort of Mr. PETER ISLER, leaving a husband and six children.

November 11, 1826
PETER QUIN, adm'r., of JOHN W. FERIS's estate

SARAH DAVIS, adm'x., of ZACHEUS DAVIS's estate

ANTHONY M. PERRYMAN vs. JOHN CARTWRIGHT

November 18, 1826
Died in Port Gibson last Sunday, Col. JOSEPH S. GIBBS, aged 28 yrs.

DELILAH HART, adm'x., of GEORGE HART's estate

November 25, 1826
Judge T. H. PROSSER grants application of ALLEN CAIN to have land divided into seven equal parts. Land bounded on north by DAVID F. COON, east by estate of DANIEL WILLIAMS, dec'd, south by LOVEC VENTRESS, dec'd, and west, the estate of NATHANIEL SCUDDER, dec'd. JOHN H. DAVIS, HARRY ANDREWS, and THOMAS LESTER to divide 750 acres.

FRANCIS & CHARLES RATCLIFF, admr's., of the PETER RATCLIFF's estate in Amite County.

Died, Doctor ALBERT HENRY PROSSER, 24 yrs. at the residence of his father, Judge THOMAS H. PROSSER, of Wilkinson County.

December 2, 1826
LEWIS DAVIS's heirs vs. PATRICK FOOLEY's heirs

WM & NOLAN STEWART, exec'rs., of Capt. JOHN STEWART's estate

ROBT. SMITH & SAM'L M. NESMITH, admr's., of JOHN NESMITH's estate

LEWIS CASON, ex'r., of THOMAS CASON's estate

December 7, 1826
SUSAN HAMPTON, adm'x., of HENRY HAMPTON's estate

December 18, 1826

1827
January 1, 1827
THOMAS MEREDITH, JNO B. BURKE & SAMUEL B. MARSH of Amite County, Ms.

Note lost by JOSEPH FANNER, Sen'r & JAMES FANNER, payable to CURTIS EMRY, guardian of GEORGE THIRLKILL. Note left with JOS. THOMPSON

January 8, 1827
Appointed, ANNA F. RUFFIN, exec'x, & MOSES LIDDELL, exec'r., of WILLIAM H. RUFFIN's estate

The final account of BRIDGES SOJOURNER, adm'r., of GABRIEL SOJOURNER and WILLIAM SOJOURNER's estate will be presented.

JAMES JONES & JOEL GLASS, admr's, of THOMAS R. DOWNING's estate

In Pinckneyville, JOHN M. & JAMES WILSON's partnership has been dissolved.

C. EVANS HALL has been released as exec'r., of GEORGE F. RANDOLPH's estate

MARGARETTA P. FOLEY, adm'x., of JAMES W. FOLEY's estate

DAVID COOPER's final sttlement as administrator of JOHN COULTER, RICHARD DAVENPORT, and ZALMAN McCASTLEs' estates.

January 15, 1827
JACOB SEEBER, adm'r., of URIAH McGRAW's estate

January 23, 1827
Married Thursday 4th, Mr. JESSE BELL to Miss ELIZABETH ANN JONES, daughter of Mr. ISAAC JONES of this county.

Married the same evening, Mr. JAMES VARNELL to Miss THIRSA ANN McGRAW. Both marriages by Benjamin Eccles, Esquire.

February 2, 1827
Married Thursday by Rev. JACOB CULATH, Mr. JOHN DUNBAR to Miss ANN CALLAHAN, all of this county.

Died Wednesday at his residence, Judge JOHN P. HAMPTON.

The final account of MOSES GORDON, adm'r., of WM. HORTON's estate will be presented.

The final account of JOHN KING, adm'r., of ISAAC CARTER's estate will be presented.

February 10, 1827
EDWARD FELTUS vs. JOEL F. RANDOLPH   (estate)

WILLIAM SMART vs. JAMES PEARCE

February 17, 1827
Do not trade for promissory note signed by R. H. SPEARS, W. H. RAMSEY and JOHN COLLINS, payable to ALETHA SPEARS, admr'x., of AUSTIN SPEARS's estate.
    Notice by RICHARD H. SPEARS

Do not trade for notes of HENRY HUMBLE.
    Notice by HUGH McDRAINE.

WM. L. CASON refuses debts of wife, JANE CASON, as she has left his bed and board without cause.

R. M. NEWMAN refuses to pay note to WILLIAM H. ERWIN.

February 24, 1827
March 3, 1827
Married Thursday by Bishop J. CREATH, Jr., Col.

WM. T. LEWIS to Miss VIRGINIA E. MARSHALL, both of this place.

March 10, 1827
Married on Sunday the 4th, Mr. WILLIAM D. ALLEN to Miss MARTHA SCOTT LANDERUM of this county.

Died in Amite County on the 21st, Rev. MATHEW BOWMAN, 63 yrs., a Methodist Episcopal minister.

JOEL BROOM's land is to be sold.

HENRY W. PATTREY vs. JOEL F. RANDOLPH

March 17, 1827
Died on the 16th, Doctor WILLIAM P. TRASK of this county.

Married Thursday by the Rev. WILLIAM WINANS, Doctor FRANCIS A. McWILLIAMS to Miss JENNETTE S. NESMITH.

MICHAEL AMMENS, adm'r., of JOHN AMMENS's estate

JAMES L. REED, adm'r., of RICHARD ALLBRITTEN's estate

SARAH RICHARDSON, adm'x., & HENRY QUIN, adm'r., of HENRY RICHARDSON's estate

WILLIAM MELLON, adm'r., of SAMUEL MELLON's estate

MARY ANN FAIRCHILD, exec'x., of the LOFTED FAIRCHILD estate

March 24, 1827
1640 acres of WILLIAM HAZLIP's land to be divided.

80 acres of JAMES SHROPSHIRE's land to be sold.

ELIZABETH McCULLOUGH, admr'x., of the JAMES McCJULLOUGH estate

Wm Crory vs. BERNARD McCROSSON

JACOB COON, adm'r, to GEORGE GOLLIFER's estate

Appointment of VINCENT GARNER, adm'r, & ELIZABETH MARTIN, adm'x., of DERRELL H. MARTIN's estate.

F. A. BROWDER, in right of his wife, late executrix of MOSES HOOKE, dec'd, will present his claims to Orphans' Court.

WILLIAM MATHEWS, adm'r., of GEORGE McDUFFIE's estate

WM. MONKS, adm'r., of JOHN YEIZER's personal estate

April 5, 1827

Married Sunday the 25th, Mr. JAMES BAILEY of this county and Mrs. CLARA THROOP of Baton Rouge.

C. EVANS HALL, adm'r., of SAMUEL PICKENS's estate

DAVID BERRY, guardian of minors, HIRAM BERRY, SARAH BERRY, ELVIA BERRY, ELIZABETH BERRY and PAMELIA BERRY.

April 14, 1827

CHARLES W. HARRIS of Pike County, adm'r., of DAVID HADEN's estate

Furniture purchased by Wm. W. YERBY of the dec'd., Captain JOHN STEWART's estate, is to be sold.

J. L. TRASK, ex'r., & HARRIET TRASK, exec'x., of Dr. WILLIAM P. TRASK's estate

JNO. KAIGLER & ESAIAS KAIGLER, ex'rs., of ANDREW KAIGLER's estate

JOHN RICHARDS, adm'r., of JAMES MILES's estate

April 21, 1827

Married in West Feliciana Parish on Thursday evening, Mr. JESSE DAVIS to Miss ANN MARLEY.

April 28, 1827

JAMES DUKE refuses to honor note payable to BARNABAS CURRY.

Married Thursday 29th by Rev. Mr. Borrella, Mr. T. DeVALCOURT to Miss FELONISE GUIDAV, all of St. Martinsville, La.

May 5, 1827

Married on Thursday, by the Rev. James A. Fox, the Hon. WILLIAM HAILE to Miss NANCY JOOR, eldest daughter of Major General JOHN JOOR, all of this county.

MARY CARROLL, admr'x., of JOHN CARROLL's estate

May 12, 1827

Married Sunday by Rev. GEORGE A. IRION, Mr. JOHN KING to Miss JEMIMA G. HARRIS all of this county.

Married Sunday the 29th by Rev. JOHN WURTS CLOUD, Colonel JOSEPH CALLENDER, cashier at the Branch Bank to Miss SARAH REAZEALE, all of Port Gibson.

Died on the 8th, Mrs. MARTHA ROACH

Died on the 9th, Mr. DAVID I. GRAY

THOMAS S. HERBERT Jr., adm'r., of JNO. P. HAMPTON's estate

B. A. LANDRUM paid note of $65 to MARK ANDERSON.

May 19, 1827

Rev. ALBERT A. MULLER, Rector of Trinity Church in Natchez, will preach in St. Paul Episcopal Church on Sunday, the 20th.

Real estate of RICHARD ALLBRITTAINDEN to be sold

May 26, 1827

Died Sunday 20th, Doctor W. C. SMITH leaving a widow and children. He was buried with Masonic honors.

Married Tuesday 22d, Mr. SAM N. RATCLIFF to Mrs. NANCY HAYES.

Rev. JACOB CREATH will preach at the Baptist church.

June 2, 1827

Died Wednesday 30th, Capt. STEWART COLE

Died this morning, Mr. DANIEL HART

Died in New York, April 29th, Mr. RUFUS KING, 73, late Minister to England.

Died April 23rd, near Malanzas, Island of Cuba, where he had retired for his health, ISRAEL PICKENS, late Governor of Alabama.

Died June 1, Miss JEMIMA EDWARDS, and on the 4th, her sister, Mrs. SARAH DAVIS, having devised effects to the amount of more than a thousand dollars to the children of her sister, ELIZABETH DUNN, living somewhere in the state of Miss.
(This notice was requested by THOMAS EDWARDS of Columbia City Ga., April 10, 1827)

Married Thursday 31st, by Rev. THOMAS BROWN, Mr. WALTHALL BURTON to Miss TERRESA ANN THERRELL, all of this county.

SUSAN GARFLEY, adm'x., & JOSEPH JOHNSON, adm'r., of Mrs. MARTHA ROACH's estate.

June 9, 1827
C. EVANS HALL, adm'r., of S. C. HEADY's estate

Died the 8th, from being wounded at his saw mill near Caledonia Springs, Mr. CALEB WILCOX.

June 16, 1827
Pike Co., ROBERT BURTON, MOSES GREER vs. JOHN CARTWRIGHT

WRIGHT ELLINGTON, adm'r., of WILLIAM MELTON's estate

R. ROACH states that during his absence, Letters of Administration were granted to SUSAN GARTLEY and JOSEPH JOHNSON by the Orphans Court on MARTHA ROACH's estate. He now forbids sale of property under penalty of the law.

June 23, 1827
Married Thursday, Mr. LORENZO D. BROWN to Miss SARAH STOCKET.

Died Sunday 10th, Mrs. MARGARET RICHARDSON, consort of Col. JOHN G. RICHARDSON of this county.

Any person disposed to purchase the land near Woodville on which JOS. I. SCOTT resides, commonly called the race tract, would do well to apply early to MOSES LIDELL.

June 30, 1827
The Copartnership of JOHN S. LEWIS & LOZ. D. BROWN is dissolved.

Married Thursday 28th, by the Rev. B. PIPKIN, the Rev. THOS. C. BROWN to Mrs. ELIZABETH BINGAMAN of Louisiana.

Married on the same evening, Mr. JOSEPH P. HENLEY to Miss ELIZABETH A. WESTBROOK, all of this county.

DORCAS KNIGHT, exec'x & ELISHA SOWER, adm'r., of WILLIAM E. KNIGHT's estate.

W. N. HARRIS, adm'r., of VICTOR HARRIS's estate

July 7, 1827
July 14, 1827

Election will be held at several Election Districts in Wilkinson County, to wit: DAVID BERRY'S on Percy Creek, N. E. RAYMOND's, JESSE DELOACH's on the Homochito, Mount Pleasant and at the Court House in Woodville.
Signed by JOHN CONNELL, Sheriff.

GIDEON FITZ, announced that Mr. F. G. HOPKINS has opened a school in the Mississippi Academy.

JESSE DELOACH, appointed adm'r of the DANIEL WHITAKER's estate

July 21, 1827

G. L. LOVELACE, adm'r., of THOS. SHEPPARD's estate

1,028 arpents of land belonging to BERNARD McCROSSON is to be sold.

WM S. LEWIS is commissioned as an Auctioneer in Wilkinson County.

July 28, 1827

Doctor WM A. ARDREY, has established his office at his brother, ALEXANDER ARDREY's, 3 miles south of Woodville.

WM HAILE, et al vs. HENRY DORSHE

LEM. PITCHER, H. D. KELLOGG, and BENNETT LEA were appointed as commissioners to receive claims against the JOHN LIGON estate.

JAMES S. WAIDE, ARTHUR DANIEL and D. B. THOMPSON were appointed as commissioners to receive claims against REESE E. FLESON's estate.

August 4, 1827

ELIZABETH SMITH, adm'rx., of Doctor WM. C. SMITH's estate

Rev. PEYTON S. GRAVES, late Missionary of New Orleans, will perform Divine service in the Methodist Episcopal Church.

L. PITCHER, adm'r., of JAMES DICKSON's estate

August 11, 1827
August 18, 1827

Married Thursday 16th, by JAMES S. CARRAWAY,Esq., Mr. JOSEPH POURSH to Miss SALLY ARMSTRONG, both of this county.

August 25, 1827

Died Thursday night, the 23rd of a short illness, SARAH BELA D. CLARKSON, age 7, and MARY S. CLARKSON age 9, daughters of Mr. CHARLES S. CLARKSON of Greenwood, 12 miles west of Woodville. They were taken ill and died within an hour of each other.

Claims against the estate of EDITH THERILL, alias EDITH CREWS, dec'd., who intermarried with THOMAS CREWS, dec'd., will be accepted by LEA, SIMS, and LEWIS, Commissioners.

Kidnapped! JOHN MILLER, U. S. Army in Baton Rouge, La., states that a man called JUANQUIN CAPEZ, alias JUANQUIN PELARA, kidnapped Miller's son, MARTIN MILLER, 10 years of age, on July 18, 1827. Miller followed Pelara as far as Woodville, then lost tract of same. Advertisment placed in papers in the states of Ms., La., and Ala.

September 8, 1827

Married on Thursday the 6th, Mr. ROBT S. MORRIS to Miss SUSAN KNIGHT of this county.

Died at the resident of his father near Pinckneyville on Saturday the 1st, of a short but violent illness, Mr. THOMAS M. DELOACH, about 30 years of age. "In the loss of this gentleman society has to deplore one of its most estimable members, and his family and friends a most amiable and beloved relative and friend, he had reached the age of maturity, beloved, and respected by all who knew him, but just when all the excellent qualities of his heart had fully developed themselves, he was snatched away from the enjoyment of all sublunary things and taken to what bourne from whence no traveller can return." (Obituary of Ruffin Deloach's son, Thomas.)

Died in Amite County on the 23rd, DODLEY JONES son of MARY JONES, and D. JONES, 4 years, 4 months & 13 days old.

September 15, 1827

Attorney JULIUS M. CLARKSON settles in Woodville.

Died on Saturday near St. Francisville, Mrs. SOPHIE BRADFORD, wife of JAMES M. BRADFORD,

Attorney and Counsellor at law.

September 22, 1827
DANL. SLACK, adm.r., of STEWART COLE's estate

G. L. LOVELACE, adm'r., of THOMAS SHEPHERD's estate

Attachments placed on estate of HENRY BARNES, deceased.

Married on Thursday, Mr. WILLIAM T. MAYES to Miss EMILY MERSEILLES, all of this county.

Married the same evening by Rev. W. WINANS, the Rev. PEYTON S. GRAVES to Miss AURELAY G. BRUCE, of this town.

Died Monday last, Mrs. H. BUSH, consort of the late Capt. ISAAC BUSH.

September 29, 1827
October 6, 1827
Married Thursday by Rev. GEORGE A. IRON, Mr. WILLIAM DOWTY and Miss MALISSA M. SMITH, daughter of Mr. Z. SMITH.

Died Friday 28th at Cold Springs, Mrs. R. RAYMOND, consort of Dr. N. E. RAYMOND, aged 40 years. She was a member of the Presbyterian Church, and left an affectionate husband and six loving children.

October 13, 1827
ABEL WADDILL & G. W. KELLER, adm'rs., of the NOEL WADDILL estate.

JESSE BELL, guardian for ELIZA McGRAW, infant heir of the estate of PETER McGraw, deceased. September, 1827.

MARY BRUCE, admr'x., files a final account of CHARLES BRUCE's estate.

Died on the 8th, JOHN H. DAVIS, Esquire.

Died in West Baton Rouge on the 4th, Mr. PETER L. VICTOR, Surgeon Dentist.

Died October 11th in Natchez, after a severe illness of eight days, Mr. FELIX G. STIDGER, a printer, of Bardstown, Kentucky.

Died Sunday last, Mr. JOHN BASSETT, Printer.

October 20, 1827

Married on Thursday 18th, by HOWELL MORELAND, Esqr., Mr. DANIEL SLACK to Miss HARRIETT BUSH, daughter of the late Capt. ISAAC BUSH.

Married on the same evening by JOHN McGEE, Esqr., Mr. WILLIAM CONNOR and Miss MARTHA LEATHERMAN, daughter of DANIEL LEATHERMAN.

Died Monday in the 16th year of age of bilious fever, Mrs. MARY DOROTHY TEMONS, consort of Mr. JOHN H. TEMONS, and daughter of Mr. PETER CONRAD.

October 27, 1827

J. P. GILBERT, adm'r., of THOMAS DAWSON, Senr,'s estate.

J. BIRMINGHAM wishes to be released as guardian for WM. T. JONES.

E. SMITH & G. A. IRION, adm'rs., of WM. C. SMITH's estate

November 3, 1827

Duel between Mr. FREDERICK WILLIAMS, of East Baton Rouge, and Mr. EDWARD RANDOLPH of this county. Both wounded.

Died the 20th, the Lady of Judge EDWARD McGHEE in Montgomery, Alabama.

Died the 2nd, in this county, Mrs. ELIZABETH J. GRAY, consort of the late Mr. DAVID I. GRAY.

Died in St. Francisville on the 24th, Mrs. ANN O'DONALD, consort of Mr. CHARLES O'DONALD.

D. COOPER, adm'r., of JOHN COULTER's estate

JAS. Y. McNABB, ex'r., of MICHAEL MORRIS's estate

November 10, 1827

THOS. FOSTER Adm'r., of THOMAS FOSTER, Senr.'s estate, states: "No person can trust HENRY R. NERSON's to a share of the Negroes conveyed by Thomas Foster Senior, in a Deed Gift to ELEN CARR, during her life, and then to heirs as Nerson has already received more than his share."

EDWARD TURNER vs. SOPHIA GILDART

FREDERICK A. BROWDER vs. HENRY HAMPTON, adm'rs.

CHARLES McMORRIES, adm'r., files final settlement of JAMES B. HAYES

Died October 20th, Mrs. HARRIET A. R. McGEHEE, wife of EDWARD McGHEE, Esqr., of this county.

The deceased, DAN'L B. PINSON's property is to be sold.

November 17, 1827

ELIZABETH SMITH, admr'x., and widow of Wm. C. SMITH, asks for her dower rights.

The land of CHARLES McMICKEN & DANIEL McGAHEY is to be sold for taxes.

Died in this county the 14th, Mr. ROBERT B. BEASLEY

ADAM ANDREWS opens a school for an "English Education".

Land known as "Clarkesville Plantation" to be divided into five shares or parts by Commissioners CHARLES S. CLARKSON, FREDERIC A .BROWDER and JOHN M. WILSON. Heirs of Capt. Benj. Farrar, dec'd., one infant son, Benjamin Farrar, Dr. R. C. RANDOLPH in right of this wife, ANN RANDOLPH, late widow of Capt. Farrar, Dr. Wm N. MERCER in right of his wife, ANN MERCER, ELIZA YOUNG, and BENJAMIN F. YOUNG.

N. HUNTER, adm'r., of NARSWORTH HUNTER's estate.

November 24, 1827

WILLIAM JOHNSON & W. W. WHITEHEAD have formed a copartnership in the practice of law.

December 1, 1827

Married the 20th by L. Miles Esqr., Major J. W. JETER of Adamsville to Mrs. SUSAN PORTER, all of this county.
(Wilkinson County Marriage Book states: I.W. JETER)

December 8, 1827

Married 29th by JACOB CHAMBERS, Esq., Mr. THOMAS BENTHAL and Miss CYNTHIA JACKSON, all of this county.

PETER W. SMITH, adm'r., of WILLIAM MELTON's estate and also deceased ABRAM M. WADE's estate.

Sale by Trustees of MARTHA ROACH'S estate

December 15, 1827
Married at the Cottage on the 13th, ROBERT L. DUNN Esq., of Amite County and Mrs. ELIZA W. NICHOLSON.

December 22, 1827
Sale by JOS. JOHNSON, adm'r., of Rev. BENJAMIN DAVIS's estate

Married, EDMOND H. WAILES, Esqr., and Miss JANE B. NEWELL, eldest daughter of Mr. GEO. B. NEWELL of this county.

Sale by DANIEL SLACK, adm'r., of ISAAC BUSH's estate

Disagreement settled between JESSE BELL AND WILLIAM ELLIS. Referees chosen to serve: Dr. J. W. JETER, GEO. B. COLLIER, Esqr., HUGH CURTIS and JOHN McGEE.

December 29, 1827
Commissioners for dec'd., GEO F. RANDOLPH Jr.'s estate: L. R. MARSHALL, JNO. CONNELL and BENJ. ECCLES.

ELIZABETH BROOKS, adm'rx., of WILLIAM BROOKS's estate

ELIZABETH HINSON, adm'rx., of JOHN HINSON's estate

ELIZABETH McCULLOCH, admr'x., of JANE WOMACK's estate

ADAM HOPE, adm'r., of NATHANIEL D. HOPE's estate

S. T. KING, guardian of JAMES W. JONES. (DAVID JONES, dec'd.)

JAMES WILSON, adm'r., of EDWARD RANDOLPH's estate

1828
January 5, 1828
Mouse colored mare taken up by EBENEZER WILLIAMS

Tax sale of WM. H. PHILLIPS's land

Commissioners for JOHN LIGON's estate; LEM.

PITCHER, H. D. KELLOG, & BENNETT LEA.

Commissioners for THOMAS R. DOWNING's estate: ARTHUR DANIEL, H. J. POWELL & JAMS S. WAIDE.

January 12, 1828
NANCY HINSON, adm'x., of JOHN HINSO estate

ELIZABETH THOMAS, adm'x., of DANIEL THOMAS's estate

GEORGE MORRIS, adm'r., of ROBERT B. BEASLY's estate

The land of the dec'd., DAVID JONES, is to be sold by S. T. KING, guardian of James W. Jones.

Commissioners were appointed for the REESE E. FLEESON's estate.

Final settlement of WILLIS MURPHREY's estate

JOSEPH A. CLAYTON, adm'r., of THOMAS N. FRAZER's estate

January 19, 1828
Married 13th, Mr. DANIEL WOOKARD to Mrs. MARY FRAZIER all of this county.

Died at his father's residence in Kentucky, 15 th of December, JULIUS M. CLARESON, Esqr., 24 yrs. and late of this place.

JANUARY 29, 1828
JAMES RANDOLPH, adm'r., of EDWARD RANDOLPH's estate

Lost, a red Morocco Pocket Book containing sundry papers and accounts against F. R. RICHARDSON, HENRY HAMPTON, ELISHA GLOWER & CHARLES McMORRIES. Signed by JOSHUA RUTLEDGE

February 9, 1828
Died on the 23rd, Mrs. MARY L. RICHARDSON, consort of Col. JOHN G. RICHARDSON of this county. Age 28 yrs.

Land belonging to the estate of STEPHEN AMBROSE is to be sold.

February 16, 1828

Appointment of ELIZABETH DAVIS, as admr'x., and H.

CONNELL as adm'r., of the deceased JOHN H. DAVIS.

LOUISA L. WOOLFOLK & G. R. ROUNTREE are the sole heirs of the deceased AUSTIN WOOLFOLK.

The Rev. JACOB CREATH, Jr. will preach in the Baptist Church.

HARRY CAGE, Esqr., was elected Judge of the Third Judicial District, over his opponent, GEORGE WINCHESTER, Esqr.

JNO L. WALL, adm'r., of LOTT ROBINSON's estate

Lost or mislaid, a note drawn by JOHN W. GILDART

Married the 7th, Mr. WILLIAM C. S. VENTRESS to Miss AUGUSTA M. RANDOLPH, daughter of Hon. PETER RANDOLPH.

Died on the 4th, Col. HORATIO STARK, 31, formerly of the U. S. Army, leaving a devoted family.

Died on the 14th, Mrs. MARY DAVIS, consort of Mr. FIELDING DAVIS.

March 18, 1828

Sale by ABEL WADDILL & GEORGE W. KELLER, admr's., of N. WADDILL 's estate

Died at the house of Mr. E. GINN on Friday the 7th, Mrs. JANE MARTIN, consort of the late Mr. JAMES MARTIN.

Died the 10th, Mr. DANIEL REYNOLDS

Died the 13th, Mr. BENJAMIN N. RODGERS

The Rev. JACOB CREATE, Jr. will preach a funeral sermon, on the death of Mrs. DRUCILLA CLARKSON at Percy's Creek Meeting House on the last Sunday in this month.

JOHN M'CREDY forwarns anyone not to buy land and Negroes from COLIN C. M'REA as M'CREDY has been defrauded.

March 21, 1828

SAMUEL JAYNE vs. JAMES C. McSHEE

Deed of trust sale executed by JESSE REA, May 16, 1825. Sale title taken by JOHN C. WHITE.

O. J. ORMSBY forwarns anyone trading for a note given to him by ISSAC B. RATCLIFF & SAMUEL N. RATCLIFF.

The copartnership is dissolved between WM. A. A. CHISHOLM and SAML. T. KING.

April 8, 1828
Died on 30th, Mrs. JEMIMA G. KING, 28, consort of Mr. JOHN KING.

Commissioners appointed for CHARLES HENDERSON's estate: JOS A FOSTER, ARTHUR DANIEL & D. B. THOMPSON

April 15, 1828
(Extract of a letter from R. C. LANGDON to H. TOOLEY dated Alexander, La. April 3, 1828). Lost child of Mrs. HULDAH CLARK identified by his mother. THOMAS TUTTY alias EDWARD H. MORRIS was the kidnapper.

Land of JAMES DUKE to be sold

April 22, 1828
JOHN PRICE wishes to sell land before returning to Ky. Land will be shown by Mr. FREDERICK LEAK.

Married near Natchez on Thursday, the Hon. MOSES LIDDELL of this county to Mrs. ANN MORRIS, of Adams County.

JOHN HENDERSON, adm'r., of Dr. Wm. C. SMITH's estate

April 29, 1828
JOHN Y. REILY, ex'r., of WILLIAM R. REILY's estate

A Regimental Court Martial will convene in the town of Woodville.......The Court will consist of Major GEORGE H. FORDON, Capts. MOSES GINN, Wm. JONES, THOS. BRANNON, CHARLES NETTERVILLE, JAMES VARNELL and Lieuts. SYLVENES WALKER, B. W. FINCH, JACOB HUFF, and JOHN H. LEWIS.

MARTHA SPEARS, admr'x., of RICHARD H.SPEARS's estate

May 6, 1828
A note was lost,given by Maj. GEO A. IRION to JESSE MOORE.

Deed of Trust Sale: S. B. PENNIMAN and HENRY BENNETT

ROBERT P. STUART, exec'r., of TEMPLE STUART's estate

ELIZABETH STARK, admr'x., of HORATIO STARK's estate

May 13, 1828
Commissioners appointed for THOMAS SHEPHERD's estate; SAML. HARRISON, J. S. WAIDE, and WM. D. MAYES.

ELIHU CARTER, adm'r., of ROBERT CARTER's estate and also MICHAEL O'CONNER's estate. The land is to be sold.

Married Thursday evening, by Wm. T. LEWIS, Esqr., Mr. STEPHEN JOHNSON to Mrs. MARGARET WALLER, all of this county.

May 20, 1828
Dead. CHIEF RED BIRD Died in prison at Prairie du Chien on the night of 16th. Wau-nig-scot-h-kaa-w or the Red Bird, a Winnebago Chief of note.

Married at Natchez the 14th, Mr. THOMAS G. ELLIS of this county and Miss MARY ROUTH, youngest daughter of Mr. ROB ROUTH.

Married in the Parish of West Feliciana on Thursday evening by Rev. WM. R. BOWMAN, to Miss HARRIET FLOWER, daughter of HENRY FLOWER, Esqr., all of that parish.

May 27, 1828
WILLIAM JOHNSON & W. W. WHITEHEAD have formed a copartnership.

June 3, 1828
ELEANOR BURTON, adm'rx., of WILSON BURTON's estate presents the final settlement.

June 10, 1828
AMOS WILSEY, adm'r., of JOHN BECK's estate

Request by JOHN TYSON for renewal of Land Certificate in favor of WYATT WILKINSON

The Post Office now is located in the store of JOSEPH RIDDLE.

JESSE PHIPPS requests permission to be discharged as administrator for JAMES PHIPPS, deceased.

Woodville Female Seminary teachers: HANNAH BURROUGH, CORNELIA A. BURROUGH, and CAROLINE M. BURROUGH.

Commissioners for JOHN P. HAMPTON's estate: C. S. KELLOG, J. W. GILDART, and L. R. MARSHALL.

June 17, 1828

Shooting match will be held at Percy's Creek at the store of J. W. JETER.

Married the 12th, by WM. T. LEWIS, Esqr., Mr. THEODORE MOLLEMANS to Miss MILEY ELLSBERRY, all of this co. (Note: No record of this marriage found in published marriage records of Wilkinson County, Ms.)

Died on the 15th, ELIZABETH ELEANOR BURR, infant child of AMMON BURR.

June 24, 1828

Settlement of estate by L. B. THOMPSON, adm'r., of JOHN FANNER's estate

Commissioners for CHARLES HENDERSON's estate: JOS. A. FOSTER, ARTHUR DANIEL, and D. B. THOMPSON.

July 1, 1828

Married 12th of June in Wilkinson Co., WM A. LANE Esq, Professor of Ancient Languages, Louisiana College, to Miss MARY C. C. TISON, daughter of Mr. JOHN TISON.

NOLAN STEWART & T. JONES STEWART, exec'rs., of the BENJAMIN N. ROGERS' estate

July 8, 1828
July 15, 1828
July 22, 1828

Fort Adams. Encounter between Mr. ROBERT JIMASON and Mr.-----CARROLL which terminated in the death of the latter.

LAZARUS DRAKE vs. JESSE SAUNDERS

Lost, note to SAMUEL WRIGHT from Dr. D. O. WILLIAMS

July 29, 1828

Died 23rd, Mr. HORATIO NELSON, 27, youngest son of Captain FRANCIS GILDART, dec'd of Wilkinson Co, at the residence of his mother, Mrs. SOPHIA GILDHART. He has left a doting and disconsolate mother and wife, a female infant, and brothers and sisters to lament his loss.

Died suddenly at his home near Pinckneyville on the 24th, Major SAMUEL HARRISON, 40 yrs, leaving a wife and four infant children.

Died at the Mansion House yesterday morning, the Hon. JOSHUA CLARK, Chancellor of the State of Ms.

JOHN McVEA and JOHN C. MORRIS dissolves their partnership.

August 12, 1828

Commissioners for WILLIAM MANSFIELD's estate: ARTHUR DANIEL, DAVID ARMSTRONG & JOSEPH A. FOSTER.

The personal property of the deceased, WILLIAM CALLIHAN, is to be sold.

September 6, 1828

DICK H. EGGLESTON, adm'r., of HORATIO N. GILDART's estate

Note lost, written by JOHN B. POSEY to JOHN H. COLLINGS

Died on the 1st, at Mrs. Carr's on Percys Creek, Mr. JOSEPH M. LIGON, of Fort Adams.

PETER VEAL has taken up a grey filly, 3 yrs old.

CHARLES KING has taken up a flee bitten grey mare.

PERCYS CREEK POST OFFICE has been established 12 miles west of Woodville, and J. W. JETER, Esqr., is the appointed Post Master.

DAVID POOL, adm'r., of JAMES SMITH's estate

September 13, 1828

THOMAS O. JONES, adm'r., of WILLIAM C. DAVIS's estate

The Rev'd JAMES A. FOX will preach the funeral sermon of the late HORTIO N. GILDART, at Ashly, the residence of his mother, on the 3rd Sunday the 25th, of this month.

H. MORELAND, trustee, to sell land. Deed of trust by SAMUEL TURBEVILLE to HOWARD MORELAND. Note to RICHARD D. GRAVES

GEO. B. COLLIER, exec'r., of DRUSILLA CLARKSTON's estate

N. CALLIHAM & J. H. REID, admr's., of WILLIAM CALLAHAM estate

September 20, 1828
Note lost. Drawn by JOHN B. POSEY to JOHN H. COLLINGS

September 27, 1828
E.OLDS, admr'x., of THOMAS OLDS's estate

Manslaughter! Capt. PRESTWOOD SMITH killed by Mr. A. M. WILSON. Capt. Smith left a wife and a large family of children.

September 30, 1828
WILL L. BRANDON, adm'r., of SAMUEL HARRISON's estate

Married in Amite, Mr. JOHN JONES of this county and Miss SARAH HAYGOOD, of the former.

Died near this town on Friday night last, at the advanced age of 76 yrs. of age, Mr. WILLIAM CONNELL, formerly Sheriff of Wilkinson County, Ms.

October 7, 1828
Married on the 6th, Mr. SETH C. PLATNER at Natchez, to Miss EMILY A. FRAZIER of this county.

October 14, 1828
October 21, 1828
October 28, 1828
Died the 8th on his farm near Thompson's Creek, in this Parish, Mr. WILLIAM DUNBAR, aged 37 yrs. 6 months and a native of Maryland, Worchester County, leaving a wife and three childen. (Orginally from the ST. FRANCISVILLE CRISIS)

November 4, 1828
November 11, 1828
Married on Thursday, by JOHN Y. REILY, Esqr., Mr. LEMUEL PREWETT to Miss CELIA McGRAW, all of this county.

JNO. STEVENS, adm'r., of THOMAS RICE's estate

COTESWORTH P. SMITH, adm'r., of PRESTWOOD SMITH's estate

November 18, 1828
One bay horse taken up by BENJAMIN KILLGORE

Married in East Feliciana, La., on Thursday the 6th of November, by CASWELL SMITH, Esqr., Mr. H. J. POWELL, of this county and Miss CAROLINE HOLLOWAY, of East Feliciana.

November 25, 1828
December 2, 1828
Married the 20th, the Honorable PETER RANDOLPH, Judge, to Miss ElZABETH LEATHERBERRY. (Originally from the SOUTHERN GALAXY)

Died the 26th, Mrs. ELIZABETH GRAYSON, consort of Mr. LEWIS GRAYSON of Alexandria, La. at ROBERT GRAYSON's in this co.

The property of Mrs. JOSEPHINE VAHAMONDE, is to be sold in the Parish of Iberville.

Married the 4th, by Wm. T. LEWIS, Esqr., Mr. JOHN O. RUTLEDGE to Miss POLLY NETTERVILLE, daughter of the late JEREMIAH NETTERVILLE, all of this county.

December 16, 1828
Married 16th, Mr. NICHOLAS NORWOOD to Miss SARAH C. LOVELACE daughter of the late THOS. LOVELACE, all of this county.

Married the 18th by Rev. JOHN C. BURRUS, ALFRED T. MOORE, Esq.,of Franklin county, to Miss MARY SINGLETON, daughter of the late RICHARD SINGLE-TON, of this county.

Married last Thursday in West Feliciana, JOHN HERFORD, M. D. to Miss CATHERINE MARY STERLING, eldest daughter of LEWIS STERLING.

Married on the same evening, JOHN L. LONDELL, Esq. to Miss ANN MATILDA STERLING, second daughter of LEWIS STERLING, Esquire..

Married lately in Providence, N. H., Mr. CHARLES LOVE Jr. to Miss MARY TRIPP.

Died the 9th at his residence on Percy's Creek, Mr. ELIJAH THERRILL, leaving a disconsolate wife.

December 30, 1828

Married 23rd, Mr. ELISHA BELL to Miss____HUNTER, daughter of Mr. NASWORTHY HUNTER. (Wilkinson County Marriage Book states: MARTHA I. D. HUNTER).

Married in Woodville on the 29th by Wm T. LEWIS, Esqr., Mr. JOHN JOSEPH LABARTHE to Miss DELEINE LANDLY, both of the Parish of St. Martin, La.

1829
January 3, 1829

Married on the 31st, Mr. JOHN HORGOOD to Miss HARRIETT R. HARVIN of East Feliciana Parish.

Married the 1st, Mr. JOHN LOYD to Miss SARAH LUSK of West Feliciana Parish.

Married the 1st, Mr. JACOB HUFF to Miss MARTHA GLOVER, daughter of Mr. Wm. GLOVER, all of this county.

JANE THERRIL, exec'r., of ELIJAH THERRIL's estate

NANCY SCUDDER, adm'rx., of NATHANIEL SCUDDER's estate.   Land Certificate

January 10, 1829

Mr. THOMAS NETTERVILLE, WILLIAM T. LEWIS, Esqr. and Mr. D. B. THOMPSON are all candidates for sheriff.

Married, the 1st, Mr. JACOB W. EDWARDS to Miss PROVIDENCE MARGARET OGDEN, second daughter of Mr. JOHN OGDEN, all of this co.

Married the 16th, in the Parish of West Feliciana, La., WM. W. WHITEHEAD, Esq., of this place to Miss ELIZABETH DAVIS of the former.

January 17, 1829

Two small packages of papers were lost belonging to H. B. MAXWELL.

January 24, 1829

ABRAM ILER gives notice to forwarn all his heirs or any persons from settling any of his business without his consent.

JOHN L. BRUCE, FIELDING DAVIS, WILLIAM T. MAYES, JOHN SLADE and JAMES REID are all additional canidates for sheriff.

Died at his residence at Laurel Hall, West Feliciana Parish, WM. ALEXANDER.

January 31, 1829
Gold Safe Chain found by I. L. LINEBAUGH on Fort Adams Road

February 7, 1829
Married the 1st, Mr. JOSHUA RUTLEDGE to Miss MARY ILER, daughter of Mr. ABRAM ILER.

Additional candidates for Sheriff are JAMES ARNELL, Dr. DICK H. EGGLESTON and CATO C. WEST.

JOHN KAIGLER & ESAIAS KAIGLER, ex'rs., will present their final settlement for ANDREW KAIGLER's estate.

ABRAHAM LANEHART, adm'r., will present the final settlement for ADAM LANEHART's estate.

February 14, 1829
DANIEL BASS was appointed as Justice of Peace in Woodville, and LORENZO D. BROWN as Justice of Peace in the Whitestown beat.

JAMES F. CONNER vs. Wm. H. PHILLIPS:

Died the 12th, at the residence of her mother, Mrs. PENELOPE STEWART, Mrs. CATHERINE CAGE, consort of the Hon. HARRY CAGE.

Married the 8th, by W. T. LEWIS, Esqr., Mr. THOMAS R. SIDEBOTTOM to Miss SARAH ANN NETTERVILLE.

Married the 12th by Wm. T. LEWIS, Esqr., Mr. THOS. B. NETTERVILLE to Miss ELIZABETH B. DELOACH, daughter of Mr. JESSE DELOACH.

February 21, 1829
Land of JAMES MEEK lost for nonpayment, now reclaimed under the act of Congress of the 23rd of May, 1828, entitled "An act for the relief of purchasers of Public Lands that have reverted for non payment of the purchase money".

The lands of the following were also reclaimed under this same act: WM. MATTHEWS, JOHN JONES, HENRY ANDREWS, H.CONNELL, and EIZABETH DAVIS & H. CONNELL, administrators.

HARRIETT C. GILL, exec'rx., of ROBERT M. GILL's

estate.

Married the 15th, Hon. EDWARD McGHEE to Miss MARY H. BURRUS, daughter of the Rev. J. C. BURRUS, all of this county.

Died on the 19th, MARTIN B. COOK, aged 9 years and 9 months, son of Mr. BELA COOK.

February 28, 1829

Sheriff's Sale: GROW & ARMSTRONG vs. JOHN H. MACKEY, JAMES C. WILKINS vs. SOPHIA GILDART, HORATIO N. GILDART, FRANCIS GILDART, and ROBT. (ROST.) S. GILDART, & ROBERT H. ADAMS vs. JAS DUKES.

Commissioners for the WILLIAM C. DAVIS's estate: JAMES S. WAIDE, DAVID ARMSTRONG & JOSEPH A. FOSTER.

Commissioners for the JAMES R. OGDEN's estate: ARTHUR DANIEL, JOSEPH A. FOSTER and D. B. THOMPSON.

J. JOOR, exec'r., of JOHN NORWOOD's estate will sell land known as the place where Col. JOSEPH J. SCOTT resided.

Married the 22nd, by JOHN MAVES, Esqr., Mr. RANDOLPH FOSTER to Miss LUCY HUNTER, all of this county.

March 7, 1829

C. B. HAYNES, adm'r., of DAVID SIX's estate

Reward of $10 offered by THOMAS GIBSON for return of his sorrel horse.

Married the 4th, ROBT. COLFAX, Esqr., to Mrs. NANCY RUSSELL, both of West Feliciana Parish.

Married the 26th, Mr. PETERSON G. PARHAM to Mrs. SARAH A. KELSEY, all of this county.

Married the 4th, Mr. ROBERT GERMANY of Feliciana to Miss MARGARET COSBY of Wilkinson.

March 14, 1829

Rev. Mr. WINANS will preach the funeral sermon of Col. R. M. GILL, late of this county, in the Methodist Church.

HARRIET C. GILL, exec'rx., of ROBERT M. GILL's estate

March 21, 1829

Married the 10th, by G. D. BOYD, Esqr., Mr. JOSIAS P. SAUNDERS to Miss ELLEN D. FRAZIER.

Died the 14th, Mrs. JANNETTE SEVERSON, consort of Mr. JOSEPH SEVERSON, of this place.

Died at the Navy yard, Washington City, Feb. 23, Commodore THOMAS TINGEY, aged 79 years.

ABRAHAM LANEHART, adm'r., for JESSE ENLOW's estate

March 28, 1829

Final settlement of JOHN BERAVER's estate by PETER RANDOLPH, administrator.

Land claimed under act of May 1828 by JOHN G. RICHARDSON.

Died on the 24th after a long illness, Mrs. ELIZABETH BURRUS, consort of Rev. Mr. Burrus.

Married the 25th, Capt. THOMAS SCUDDER to Mrs. MARY ANN ELIZABETH ALLEN, both of this county.

Married the 11th by Rev. JOHN C. BURRUS, CHARLES M. SHEPHARD, Esqr. of Golden Grove, La., to Miss MARGARET A. HOOKE of Salisbury Hall, Miss. (Wilkinson County Marriage Book states that CHARLES SHEPHARD m. March 9, 1829 to MARGARET BOOK)

Commissioners for RICHARD SPEARS estate: A. DANIEL, T. B. J. HADLEY & J. C. McCONNELL.

APRIL 4, 1829

WM. M. LINDSEY, adm'r., of HUGH NELSON's estate

MARTHA SANDERS will apply for a lost land certificate.

MARY A. LEEK, admr'x., for FREDERICH LEEK's estate

Land claimed under act of May 1828 by JOHN PAXTON

Final settlement of dec'd., JOHN BELL's estate.

Personal estate of dec'd., A. M. WILSON to be sold

Married in this county, April 2nd, Capt. JOHN W.

LEATHERMAN to Mrs. ARAMINTA BEASLEY.

Final settlement of dec'd., JARED C. BEASLY's estate

A. DANIEL wishes to be released from executorship of the deceased, THOMAS ASPANALL's estate.

Trustee sale for the benefit of JOHN M. & JAMES WILSON

Heirs of JOHN KETCHUM vs. heirs of JAMES P. SMITH Partition property that exist in common between heirs.

JACOB CHAMBERS, exec'r., of ROBERT WHITE's estate

April 11, 1829

Commissioners for dec'd., DAVID I. GRAY's estate: WILLIAM T. LEWIS, JAMES S. WAIDE, & THOMAS H. OSWALD

Final settlement of BENJAMIN THERRILL's estate

Married the 29th March by J. W. JETER, Esqr., Mr. BENJAMIN DALLEY to Miss LEVICE HERRINGTON, all of this county.

Died April 3rd, at his residence near Beaver Creek Meeting House, Mr. NEEDHAM H. BRYAN, leaving a family.

Died the 8th at the residence of WILLIAM STAMPS, Esqr., in the vicinage, Mr. ROBERT M. BEECH, 20 years. Member of the Wilkinson Guards and buried with military honors.

Land claimed under Act of May 1828 by CHARLES HESTER

April 18, 1829

Married the 8th, Dr. RICHARD ANGELL to Miss HONOR, daughter of Mr. SAMUEL GOODRICH, all of this county.

Married the 15th, by JOHN BRYCE, Esqr., Mr. JOHN B. GOWER to Miss FERRIDAY SAPP, all of this county.

Died the 9th at her residence in this county, Mrs. MARY S. BUSH, consort of Capt. Wm. BUSH and leaves a husband and family.

Land claimed under the Act of May 1828 by FRANCIS GILDART, assignee of LEM'L PITCHER, assignee of JOHN BRATCHER.

April 25, 1829

Funeral Sermon of the late Mrs. JANET SEVERSON will be preached in the Episcopal Church, Sunday, May 3rd.

May 2, 1829

JAMES Y. BRYAN, adm'r., of NEEDHAM H. BRYAN's estate

May 9, 1829

Tax sale. THOS. S. HERBERT will sell land of SAMUEL McCUTCHIN.

Married on Thursday last, Mr. JOHN OGDEN to Miss JANE JONES, all of this county.

Married on the same evening, Mr. WILLIAM BOYD to Miss SUSAN GLOVER, all of this county.

Land claimed under Act of May 1828 by Wm. J. BOATNER, assignee of EZRA COURTNEY.

Land claimed under the same Act by JAMES CAIN

May 12, 1829

Major General JOHN JOOR orders an election to fill the vacancy of Brigadier General WILEY P. HARRIS who has retired.

Died the 11th at the residence of her brother, Capt. JAMES S. WAIDE, Mrs. _____ AILES, leaving amiable children.

Land claimed under Act of May 1828 by HARRIS ANDERSON, adm'r., of ROBERT ANDERSON, dec'd., & Assignee of PETER GLOVER.

May 19, 1829

On Sunday, 31st, Rev. J. C. Burrus will preach the Funeral Service of JNO W. BRUCE and his sister, Mrs. AURELIA G. GRAVES.

May 26, 1829

Land claimed under Act of May 1828 by JACOB THOMLINSON

Land claimed under the same Act for HIRAM SINGLE-TON, assignee

June 2, 1829
June 9, 1829
June 16, 1829

Married 11th by DANIEL BASS, Esqr., Mr. JOSEPH BEIDLER to Miss MARY BENTHALL.

Married 11th, Mr. WM EVANS to Mrs. MARY MAGDALENE AVERS.

Married 14th, Mr. JOSEPH BEIDLER to Mrs. CATHARINE GREENLIES, both of Louisiana.

Land claimed under the Act of May 1828 by ARCHIBALD McGHEE, assignee of THOMAS KELLER.

June 23, 1829

Died in this town, on the 21st, Mr. SAMUEL FOSTER.

Doctor LESLEY will devote his attention entirely to Medicine and Surgery. He may be consulted at all times, except when absent professionally, at the residence of J. W. JETER, Esqr., at Percy's Creek.

Taken up by JAMES LEECH, a dark sorrell mare

H. CONNELL, adm'r., of WILLIAM CONNELL's estate

Commissioners were appointed for the deceased, BENNETT LEA's estate.

June 30, 1829

Commissioners were appointed for the deceased, SAMUEL HARRISON's estate.

July 7, 1829

A red roan horse was taken up by Mrs. ELIZABETH NORMENT.

July 14, 1829

DICK H. EGGLESTON, JOHN L. BRUCE, and WRIGHT ELLINGTON, decline as candidates for sheriff.

July 21, 1829

Land sale. Wm. H. RUFFIN vs. THOMAS KIRKHAM

Married at Natchez the 5th by JAMES CARSON, Esq., Mr. ASA KIMBALL of this place and Miss ANN GREEN of the former.

July 28, 1829

We are happy to perceive that our young friend, ROBERT PERCEY SMITH, a native Mississippian, is

-51-

second in his class at the Military Academy, West Point.

Rev. F. R. CHEATHAM will preach in the Methodist Church.

Married the 15th, LOUIS M. GARRETT, Esqr., to Miss SARAH D. SINGLETON, daughter of Mr. HIRAM SINGLETON, all of this county.

Married the 16th, by JOHN BRYCE, Esqr., Mr. JAMES C. LANGFORD to ELIZABETH HERSON, all of Wilkinson.

Died the 21st at the residence of his father-in-law, near this town, Mr. J.W. EDWARDS.

Died the 22nd, MARIA LOUISA, daughter of Mr. EDWARD FELTUS.

JOHN SLADE withdraws as a candidate for Sheriff.

DANIEL WOODARD, guardian of ELLEN D. SAUNDERS; formery ELLEN D. FRAZIER, will present his final account.

August 4, 1829
Final settlement of NATHANIEL D. HOPE's estate

Final settlement by JOHN L. WALL, the adm'r., of LOTT ROBERTSON's estate.

August 11, 1829
Died at Pinckneyville, the 27th, ELIZA AMELIA, aged 10 months, daughter of JAMES WILSON.

Died the 2nd at the residence of her mother's, Mrs. ELIZA RATCLIFF, 18 years of age, consort of Mr. ALLEN RATCLIFF.

Died in this town yesterday morning, Mrs. FOSTER, consort of Mr. JOB FOSTER.

August 18, 1829
L. P. McCAULEY requests that the following item be published. "Three children, DAVID BONE, CHRISTEANN BONE, and MARY BONE, forcibly taken (abducted) from their mother, WINNY BONE. One man arrested but children not located. David 12, Mary 2, and CHRISTEANN, 5 yrs old has large burn scars on her back and hips--now scarcely well. All are of light yellow complexion. Dated Clinton, July 30th,1829."

August 25, 1829
September 1, 1829
ELIZABETH STARK, admr'x., to Col. HORATIO STARK's estate

September 8, 1829
LEWIS W. COON & JOHN McNEELY, ex'rs., of CHARLES A. COON's estate.

Died the 2nd after a short illness, ANNE, only child of Col. JOHN S. LEWIS of this village.

Died the 3rd, Mr. JAMES BAILEY.

September 15, 1829
Final settlement of dec'd., WILLIAM G. BRUCE's estate.

September 22, 1829
CLAIBORNE TICKELL, adm'r., of SUSANNAH TICKELL,'s estate

Land of the deceased, CHAPMAN WHITE to be sold

Died the 2nd at Benton in Yazoo County, Rev. JOSEPH SLOCUMB, 57 years old. (Baptist)

Married the 13th, Mr. JAS DUNCKLEY to Miss EMILY H. KING, daughter of Mr. JOHN KING, all of this county.

Married the 13th, Mr. WM ARBUTHNOT to Miss _____WOODSIDES. (Wilkinson County Marriage Book states her name as SARAH WOODSIDES.)

The Rev. ISAAC SMITH will preach at the Methodist Church.

September 26, 1829
Died Aug 18th, at Belmont near Pinckneyville, the 8th, FRANCES ANN, infant daughter of JNO P. GILBERT.

Died the 24th at the residence of Dr. JAMES E. PHELPS, in Pinckneyville of fever, Mr. JOSEPH THEODORE YERBY, 20 yrs.

October 5, 1829
Died the 24th at the residence of Judge Chinn, West Baton Rouge, JOHN M. WILSON, Esqr., 32 yrs., formerly of Pinckneyville.

ANNA OWINGS, admr'x., of THOMAS OWINGS's estate

Commissioners appointed for the deceased, STEWART COLE'S estate

October 12, 1829
Died from a wound to the head, received from the trunk of a tree when leaping from his carriage as it overturned; Governor PETER DERBIGMY, of this state. (Originally dated from New Orleans, Oct.7)

October 20, 1829
Married the 6th by JNO. W. JETER, Esq., DANIEL ALTER to Mrs. MARY ANN WOODRUM, all of this county.

November 3, 1829
Died the 2nd, HELEN ANN, eldest daughter of Mr. Wm. A. A. CHISHOLM.

MARY HARSON, adm'x., of JOSEPH HARSON's estate

November 10, 1829
Note found, payable to SAM'L GOODRICH, signed and endorsed by JOHN ANDERSON.

November 17, 1829
November 24, 1829
Married near Mount Olympus the 10th, JULIUS C. M'CONNELL, Esqr., of Wilkinson, to Miss CORDELIA GIRAULT of the former place.

Died at the residence of Wm. T. MAYES near Buffalo, Mr. JOSIAH NICHOLSON. Leaves adopted Mother, relatives and friends

School section of land to be leased out where Captain TIMOTHY CHAMBERS now resides. DICK H. EGGLESTON.

LEWIS CASON, adm'r., of Dr. SAM'L WRIGHT's estate

December 1, 1829
Married the 26th, Mr. JOHN SMITH to Miss AMANDA DIXON, second daughter of Mrs. ELIZABETH QUICK, all of this county.

JESSE BROWN, adm'r., of JAMES BAILEY's estate

Commissioners continue to meet for WILLIAM CALLIHAM's estate.

Doctor DICK H. EGGLESTON, 5 miles below Woodville on the St. Francisville road, continues to offer his professional services to the public. He will also sell medicines at the lowest retail prices.

J. L. STEVENS will open a singing school in the Episcopal Church. He has on hand a number of music books.

December 8, 1829

The firm of CHAS NETTERVILLE, Sr. & A. McFADEN has dissolved.

ROB'T WHITE Jr., adm'r., of ROBERT WHITE, Sr.'s estate

December 12, 1829

Died on the 8th at Fort Adams, Mr. WILLIAM MONKS

Our Senator to Congress, THOMAS B. REED, died the 26th.

REUBEN HATCH of Ft. Adams will close his business.

December 19, 1829

SARAH BURNET, adm'x., for LUCAS BURNET's estate

December 26, 1829

Died at his residence in this county on the 22nd, JACOB CHAMBERS, Esqr., late representative of this county.

1830

January 2, 1830

Married the 12th, Mr. ANGUS CLARK to Miss LUCINDA McNEELY, daughter of Mr. JAMES McNEELY.

Married the 27th, Mr. ANDREW BRYANT to Miss ELIZABETH QUINE, all of this county.

Married the 28th, Mr. STEPHEN D. PLATNER to Miss BETHIA FRAZIER.

Married the 28th, Wm. S. LEWIS to Mrs. HARRIETT C. GILL.

Married the 30th by Rev. Wm. E. MATTHEWS, HENRY VOSE, Esqr. Jr., Editor of the "WOODVILLE REPUBLICAN, to Miss ANN H. N. OGDEN, daughter of DANIEL OGDEN, all of Woodville.

Married the 31st, Mr. MYRON S. BURNELL to Mrs. SUSAN N. VAUGHAN, all of this county.

January 9, 1830

Land of Mrs. CLARISSA MITCHELL is to be sold for taxes. Taxes due, $4.44 on 500 acres of land

Final settlement of WILLIAM BELL's estate. JESSE BELL & THOMAS BELL, executors

January 16, 1830

"I, THOMAS SCOTT, will apply for a Certificate of frofeited Land Stock, entered on Dec. 6, 1810 by ZALMON McCARSTLE and forfeited for nonpayment, agreeably to law, now claimed by me under the act of May 23, 1828. Dated Jan. 9, 1830. "

January 23, 1830

Claim against T. B. J. HADLEY was placed only as a matter of form. (The "Poor" Report)

LEWIS W. COON, adm'r., of CHARLES A. COON's estate, presents the final settlement.

DAVID CALLIHAM has established a blacksmith shop.

JACOB HUFF needs to employ a good sober blacksmith.

E. A. MONK appoints JOHN I. (L) WALL of Fort Adams as agent to settle estate of WILLIAM MONKS.

GEORGE B. COLLIER, ex'r., of DRUCELLA CLARKSON's estate

J. JOOR, adm'r., of JOSEPH BOOTH's estate, will sell land

SARAH BURNETT, adm'rx., of LUCAS BURNET's estate

WM. T. LEWIS, G. D. BOYD & JAMES S. WAIDE were appointed as commissioners for the estate of A. M. WILSON, deceased.

January 30, 1830

THOS. H. OSWALD, JAS. S. WAIDE & FRANKLIN WHITE, were appointed in the February term, 1829, as commissioners for the estate of WILLIAM CALLIHAM.

Commissioners appointed for the estate of RICHARD H. SPEARS will continue to meet at the store of ARTHUR DANIEL.

Departed this life, on Tuesday, 26th, at his residence, Col. MICHAEL HOLLIMAN, in the thirty ninth year of his age. He has lived in this state for eighteen years.

Died on Thursday, the 28th, WRIGHT ELLINGTON.

JAS. S. WAIDE, adm'r., of NATHAN KIMBALL's estate

February 6, 1830

Commissioners were appointed for the estate of RICHARD SPEARS, deceased.

Land to be sold by JOHN P. GILBERT, adm'r., of the estate of THOMAS DAWSON, deceased.

Copartnership dissolved; WRIGHT ELLINGTON ill

JOSEPH A. FOSTER & T. NETTERVILLE copartnership is dissolved.

February 13, 1830

Commissioners are appointed for estate of STEWART COLE, deceased.

February 20, 1830

JEREMIAH NOLAN, adm'r., of HENRY W. LEWIS's estate

Tax sale of land belonging to heirs of BENJAMIN KILGORE

Tax sale of land belonging to estate of PATRICK FOLEY

Dissolvment of firm of JOHN LEWIS & Wm. S. LEWIS

The partnership of SAM'L W. LEWIS & WM MONKS who has died, is dissolved.

Trustees of school in Township N. 3 of Range 3 West: JAMES BUFORE, W. T. MAYES, HENRY SCOTT, WILLIS HUNTER & H. H. BELL.

February 27, 1830

Plantation for sale located on the road from Woodville to Natchez. 950 acres. P. W. FARRAR

RHODA COLLINGSWORTH, formerly RHODA LINDSAY & her children, BLUFORD, CRESEY, & POLLY IRVINE LINDSAY, all under 21, & her friend, the late REBECCA LINDSAY vs. JOHN BRYCE, BLUFORD BROOKS, the administrator of the late Wm. BROOKS, NAZRA POOLE and his wife, NANCY POOL, formely, NANCY BROOKS, widow of Wm. BROOKS deceased.

Married the 25th by Wm. T. LEWIS, Esqr., Mr. MICHAEL WOODS to Miss SUSAN H. M'ALPINE, daughter of JOHN M'ALPINE, Esq., all of this county.

WM RABB, adm'r., of PETER RABB's estate seeks releasment as administrator.

Final settlement by WM. HAMMETT, adm'r., to estate of CHARLES HENDERSON, deceased.

March 6, 1830

Tax sale. Lands of WILLIAM W. YERBY, WEST GOODRICH, heirs of JOHN BECK, land of JAMES BRADSHAW, heirs of ISAAC CARTER, estate of JNO CUNNINGS, land of JOHN HENDERSON, JAMES K. COOK, JOHN HENDERSON, HENRY NICHOLSON, WILLIAM F. PARKER, NIGEA POOLE, and land of ERASMUS WATKINS.

Doctor DICK H. EGGLESTON has moved five miles below Woodville, on the St. Francisville road.

W. W. WHITEHEAD Attorney & Counsellor at Law

Died Saturday the 27th, Miss EMILY L. SINGLETON, daughter of HIRAM SINGLETON of this county, aged 14 years.

Died this morning at 10 o'clock, Mrs. ELIZA A. FARISH, consort of Dr. E. T. FARISH of this town.

Circuit Court attachment to recover $61. Mentions WILLIAM DILLAHUNTY, JOSEPH STOCKILL and RACHAEL STOCKILL

JAS WILSON vs. ELISHA BELL. 350 acres bounded by lands of GERARD C. BRANDON, R. (Ruffin) DELOACH, RANDOLPH, and heirs of JOS. HUNTER.

Circuit Court attachment to recover $90. Mentions CATO C. WEST, ARCHIBALD HAROLDSON and FRANKLIN WHITE

Tax sale of land of JOHN HUDRY and also land of TURNANN's heirs.

March 13, 1830

REBECCA LEWIS will accept genteel boarders for $12 per month.

Married the 9th, by Wm. W. YERBY, Esqr., Mr. DUDLEY B. STEWART to Miss MARY CARRAWAY, all of this county.

Horrible Disaster! The steamboat HELEN McGREGOR with about 410 passenagers aboard was destroyed. While leaving the landing, one of her boilers burst. Among those identified as killed were: RICHARD HANCOCK from Louisville, Ky., A. VAN METER of Hardin County, Tenn, JAMES BLEDSOE, Ky., ED. P. BEADLES, Clark County, Ind., J. DUNN, East Tenn., G. B. GILES, Cincinnati, EPHRAIM GOBLE, Brookville, Ind., WILLIAM STOCKWELL, Salem, Ind., Wm. EWING, Clark County, Ind., J. REAVES, Harrison County,Indiana,and LEWIS YOUNG, a black fireman. (List also included wounded)

Partnership dissolved between RILEY TOLLES & JAMES VARNELL

Circuit Court attachment of $84.62, mentions L. D. BROWN & ELEANOR BURTON and also DANIEL T. ORR

March 20, 1830
March 27, 1830
CHARLES S. COSBY, adm'r., of the JAMES O. COSBY estate

Circuit Court attachment of $150, mentions GEORGE W. PIPES vs. FREDERICK S. CABLE

April 3, 1830
Final settlement of GAVIN JAMES's estate

A list of General and Field Officers in the Revolutionary Regular Army from N. H., Mass., R. I., Conn., N. Y., N. J., Penn., Del, Ma, Va, N. C., S. C.,and Ga.

April 10, 1830
JULIUS C. M'CONNELL, attorney, permanently settles in Natchez.

Died 2nd of April, Mrs. SALLY RANDOLPH at the residence of her son, the Hon. PETER RANDOLPH, age 69. She moved from Va. along with her son and his family in the autumn of 1822. She leaves a son and daughter to deplore their loss.

The partnership between Dr's J. H. REED & RICH'D F. FLOYD has been dissolved.

Dr. J. H. HARRIS, Surgeon-Dentist
April 17, 1830
Rev. JAMES A. RANALDSON will deliver a discourse in memory of Dr. DAVID COOPER, deceased.

JOHN STRONG, adm'r., of JAMES BIRMINGHAM's estate, will make his final settlement.

April 24, 1830
May 1, 1830

Died the 24th in the 25th year of her age, Mrs. ELIZABETH BELL, consort of H. H. BELL of Wilkinson County.

May 8, 1830

HAMILTON M. ORR, was appointed adm'r., of estate of SAMUEL ORR, deceased.

Mr. JOHN A. SCOTT elected to the board of Trustees of Wilkinson Academy to replace Mr. SOLON HILL.

May 15, 1830

Died the 12th, WILLIAM M'GEHEE, the youngest child of the Hon. E. M'GEHEE of this vicinage.

May 22, 1830

Attorney JOHN M. MAURY, has taken an office in Natchez.

May 29, 1830

THEODOR MOLLEMAN, adm'r., of WRIGHT ELLINGTON's estate

JOHN HENDERSON appointed SAMUEL S. BOYD as his agent.

June 5, 1830

WILLIAM HAMMETT claims land once owned by ROBERT B. HAMMETT. (Act of congress May 23, 1828)

Mr. JOHN L. BRUCE has been appointed to take the census of our county, and we hope, he will do it effectually. The heads of the household are expected to answer ages of family, slaves, qualities and number.

June 12, 1830

B. MARSHALL & H. P. DATER 's firm is dissolved by mutual consent.

GEORGE H. GORDON, candidate for the legislature

Married the 1st by Rev. J. C. BURRUS, Mr. DANIEL PECK to Miss LOUISA H. LIGON of Wilkinson.

F. A. BROWDER, adm'r in right of his wife, of the estate of MOSES HOOK, deceased. Final settlement

June 19, 1830
W. M. BROWN will re-survey the "DAVID ROSS tract" of land, now owned by FREDERICK A. BROWDER, Esqr. Mentions Dr. JOHN F. CARMICHAEL and the "CHARLES PERCY tract".

BARBARA LOVELACE, adm'x., of THOMAS LOVELACE's estate, will present the final settlement.

June 26, 1830
Final settlement by CHARLES M'MORRIS, adm'r., of the estates of JAMES B. HAYS & RACHEL M'MORRIS, both deceased.

Final settlement by HIRAM A. BERRY, ex'r., in right of his wife, late JANE THERRILL, late executrix of the last will of ELIJAH THERRILL, deceased.

July 3, 1830
We heard this morning of the decease of ROBERT M. ADAMS, Esq., late Senator from this state to congress.

JONES H. SMITH, adm'r., of JOHN KEITHLY's estate

July 18, 1830
Copartnership dissolved between EDWARD HUNT SKILLMAN & SAMUEL HANDY

Died on the 7th, at the house of JOHN FRAZIER, near Ft. Adams, Capt. THOMAS B. DOUGHERTY, 58 yrs of age. Native of Pittsburg

Died the 30th, Mr. WILLIAM L. ELLESBERRY, 22 yrs. of age.

July 17, 1830
Died the 9th, ASA COLVER, near Ft. Adams of bilious remittent fever leaving a beloved mother and relatives. Ill 6 days

Married at Natchez on 6th, by the Rev. GEO POTTS, FIELDING DAVIS, Esqr., Sheriff of this county to Miss LUCENDA NEWMAN, of that city.

Married the 16th by DANIEL BASS, Esqr., Mr. GEORGE POINDEXTER Jr. to Miss HENRIETTA BAILLIE, all of this county.

July 24, 1830
MILO FERRELL, adm'r., of ISAAC M'MGRAW's estate

Died the 22nd at the residence of H. CONNELLY, Esqr., of this County, Mr. ROBERT C. MITCHELL, Jr., late of Alabama.

July 31, 1830

Died on Tuesday last at his residence near this place, Mr. DILLARD COLLINS, door-keeper of Miss. House of Representatives.

Died the 2nd, suddenly at his residence in this county, in the 83 year his age, JOHN D. ASHLEY, a respected citizen, soldier and patriot of the revolution.

Married on Tuesday evening, by Wm. TERRELL LEWIS Esq., Mr. LAZARUS DRAKE to Mrs. MARTHA SPEARS, all of this county.

Died at her residence, on the 16th, Mrs. HARRIETT BROWDER, consort of FREDERICK A. BROWDER, Esqr., of this county.

August 7, 1830

Judge of the County Court names commissioners to divide the tract of land (600 acres) which was purchased by DUNCAN BAILEY, JAMES BAILEY, and ARTHUR RICHARDSON. Same land on which JAMES BAILEY died. JESSE BROWN, guardian of DAVID BAILEY's infant son.

August 14, 1830

Doctors THOMAS LYNE and JAMES LYNE, have associated themselves in the practice of medicine.

ROBERT WHITE, Jr., adm'r., of the will of ROBERT WHITE Sr., applies for forfeited land stock purchased Mar. 7, 1811 by White Sr., and claimed under act of Congress May 23, 1823.

Land of R. B. HAMMETT claimed under same act by WILLIAM HAMMETT. JOHN G. BROWN had purchased this tract from R. B. HAMMETT on February 4, 1818. Credit was extended.

Married Wednesday 11th, at the residence of Mr. JESSE BROWN by the Rev. F. R. CHEATHAM, Mr. JOHN H. SIMS to Miss MARY M. BROWN, all of this county.

WM. F. PAQUINETT, adm'r., of JOSEPH WHETSTONE's estate

NOTICE: In pursuance of an order of the County

Court of Wilkinson County, the undersigned Commissioners will offer at Public Sale for Cash, on the premises, on Tuesday, the 31st day of August, the OLD COURT HOUSE in the town of Woodville. The purchaser will be allowed until the first day of October next, to remove it from the Public Square. Comm'rs: JOHN CONNELL & L. R. MARSHALL. August 5,1830

General assortment of domestic and other articles suitable for planters and country merchants. WM S. LEWIS. "Auctioneer".

August 21, 1830

Died, on the morning of the 19th, Mr. JOHN GORDON who fell into a well while drawing water. He was 28 years of age and a native of Ireland. We understand that he had relatives in New Orleans.

Rev. JOHN C. PORTER will perform divine service in the Episcopal Church on tomorrow morning at 11 o'clock.

Died in the Parish of Concordia, La., on the 13th, Mr. JOHN A. SHIELDS, formerly of this county.

Died the 15th, Mrs. DORINDA BROOKS, consort of Mr. BLUFORD BROOKS, in the 23rd year of her age.

Died the 8th at the residence of the late GERARD BRANDON, Colonel JAMES SMITH, a native of South Carolina, but for many years a citizen of this county. (Originally from the NATCHEZ NEWS)

August 28, 1830

The Hon. ISAAC PARKER, Chief Justice of the Supreme Court of Massachusetts, died lately at his residence in Boston in the 63rd year of his age.

W. TIGNER, adm'r., of ASA COLVER's estate

L. D. BROWN, adm'r., of JOHN W. BRUCE's estate

FREDERICK W. YEIZER, adm'r., of JOHN YEISER's estate

Married on Tuesday evening, Mr. WILEY W. RICHARDSON to Miss MARGARET REID, both of this county.

Died in this County on the 23rd, CORNELIA, daughter of Mr. THOS S. HERBERT.

September 4, 1830
J. PHILBRICK, adm'r., of NATHANIAL L. FULLER's estate

<u>Death of the King of England</u>. George the 4th departed this life on the 26th of June, last. His brother, William Henry, Duke of Clarence, has been crowned his successor and has assumed the title of WILLIAM THE FOURTH.

September 11, 1830
EMANUAL SELLIER's store was robbed.

Runaway! 6 cents reward! Apprentice to the Wagon & Carriage Making business, WILLIAM ILER, 19 yrs. 5', 6" height, dark complexion, slender male.
    Signed by L. DRAKE

Married on Wednesday last by DANIEL BASS, Esqr., Rev. ANDREW ADAMS to Mrs. BAILLEY. (Published Wilkinson Marriage Records states her name as CLARA BAILY)

Died at his residence in this county near Fort Adams on the 27th, Mr. EDMOND GINN, a respectable planter, leaving a disconsolate widow.

Died lately at Natchez, JULIUS C. M'CONNELL, Esqr., formerly of this place.

September 18, 1830
Died at the residence of CALVIN SMITH, Esqr., (Second Creek) on Saturday, August 28, MARTHA A. SMITH, aged 17 yrs., wife of Mr. C. S. SMITH, and daughter of the late Mr. KARY of La. She died of measles which settled in her lungs.

Died in this county on the 13th, Mr. MOSES GORDON.

Died on the 9th of congestive fever, our friend, WM. CROSS.

Died the 15th, in the 5th year of her age, CAROLINE, daughter of the late N. H. BRYANT.

Died on the 15th, in the 3rd year of her age, JANE, daughter of ROBERT NORWOOD.

Died at Princton, on the 29th, Mr. PHILIP A. GILBERT, Representative elect to the State Legislature from Washington Co.

Died lately in Washington City, GEO. GRAHAM, Commissioner of the General Land Office.

Died near Woodville on the 16th, Mr. ASA KIMBALL.

Married Thursday the 16th by JOHN MAYES, Esqr., Mr. RANSOM GRAHAM to Mrs. BIDDY PICKENS, daughter of LITTLEBERRY THOMSON, near Fort Adams.

Married the same evening, Mr. EDWARD DUFF to Miss DELILA THOMSON daughter of LITTLEBERRY THOMSON.

September 25, 1830

WM BROWN, Surveyor of Wilkinson County will resurvey land at the request of ZACHARIAH SMITH and take deposition of PETER SMITH and others, if necessary, to prove lines.

Application to the court by GEORGE W. CARTER and MARY B. CARTER who claims an undivided, 1/3 part of 1/7 of the moiety of the tract of land (2,000 acres) granted to ROBERT STARK by the Spanish Government. Bounded at the time of the original survey by vacant lands, but now on the west by THEODORE STARK, north by REBECCA WILLIRSON, on the east by ZACHARIAH WALKER, and on the south by _____HOPE. Commissioners appointed by court: DICK H. EGGLESTON, SAMUEL LEATHERMAN and GEORGE MORRIS. August 25, 1830

ROBERT H. ADAMS vs. JAS. DUKE   Land to be sold

JOHN R. BROWN vs. JOHN W. GILDART   Land and lot to be sold

Married by DANIEL BASS, Esq., Mr. CHRISTOPHER BARTLETT to Mrs. MARGARET PARKER.

October 2, 1830

VINSON CARTER vs. ROBERT FARR   Land next to BENJAMIN SWAYZEY & THOMAS OWENS, dec'd., and others.

Died the 21st, near Whitestown, THOMAS SCOTT, aged 63, leaving children and friends.

Died Saturday evening last in the 66th year of age, the Honorable ROBERT STARK, Secretary of State. Buried at the family burying ground. His father, Col. ROBERT STARK was confined for 12 months while his son ,then the eldest of the family, was engaged in the service of his country.

The present Mrs. SOPHIA GILDART, was about 11 years of age and left in charge of her younger brothers and sisters, when the Tories plundered them of everything and left this little family destitute. (Revolution War)

Died the 25th, in this county, Mr. EASIAS KAIGLER; Planter.

Died the 12th at the residence of JASH. MURRAY, Esqr., in this town, DABNEY CARR COSBY, Esqr., Counselor at Law. (Originally from the PORT GIBSON CORRESPONDENT)

ANN KIMBALL, admr'x., of ASA KIMBALL's estate

SARAH SHIELDS, admr'x., of JNO A. SHIELDS's estate

Copartnership dissolved between FRANCIS BUCKNER & ZACK A. CANFIELD

October 9, 1830
Application to be made on land purchased Jan. 1, 1809 by JESSE TICKELL now claimed by heirs. CLAIBORNE TICKELL for himself and as guardian for SUSAN TICKELL, SARAH TICKELL, STEPHEN TICKELL and ROBERT TICKELL. WILLIS HUNTER for himself.

ELIZA ANN GINN, admr'x., of EDMUND GINN's estate

Died at his residence in Simpson County, 67 years of age, MOSES BRIDGES, formerly of Pike Co. For 25 yrs, a Baptist.

October 16, 1830
Died Sept 30th at the hotel of WILLIAM P. GADBERRY Esq., JOHN H. FARNANDIS, Esqr., A. M. L. D. in the 32d year of age.

DAN'L McGAHEY & EDM'D JENKINS' land to be sold, formerly known as "Dixon's Old Mills" 6 mi. from Mt. Pleasant.

October 23, 1830
The Rev. DAVIS COLLINS will preach in the Baptist Church in Woodville, tomorrow at the usual hour.

J. O. WILLIAMS will return to New Orleans in consequence of the death of Mr. THOMAS LEE of the firm of T. & G. M. Lee.

Died the 21st, at the residence of Maj. J. L.

TRASK in this county, the Rev. JOHN C. PORTER, Rector of Trinity Church in Natchez. He was 24 yrs. of age and a native of Albany, NY.

Died at the residence of her father near Manchester, S. C., on the 14th Sept., Mrs. MARY REBECCA McDUFFIE, consort of the Hon. GEORGE McDUFFIE, and daughter of RICHARD SINGLETON, Esquire.

Died in New Orleans the 15th, Mr. THOS. LEE, a merchant there.

Died in Vicksburg, the 12th, Mr. HENRY SIMONTON, aged 30 yrs.

Died at his plantaton in Jefferson County, the 10th, ROBERT McCRAY, aged 65 years.

Died in Claiborne County, the 10th, Dr. DAVID D. DOWNING, an emminent physician and valued member of the community.

October 30, 1830

Owner can claim "A Red Morrocco Reticule" found by A. ILER.

Died lately in Pike County, Maj. HENRY QUINN, a respectable citizen of that county.

DANIEL ALTER, adm'r.,. of JOSHUA TIDWELL's estate

November 6, 1830

FRANCIS A EVANS, exec'r., of ELIZABETH METCALF's estate

Note of $100 lost. DAVID FULSON payable to BURREL BENDER

Estate of ROBT. H. ADAMS, deceased, to be sold

ROBT. LAYSON wishes to sell all his property

November 13, 1830

R. CONNELL & K. HOLLIMAN admr's., of MICHAEL HOLLIMAN's estate

Mr. ASA SAPP, a highly valued citizen of this county was thrown from a horse during a race and expired in a few minutes. He has left a disconsolate wife and a large family.

Married in Adams County, the 21st, Mr. DAVID

McALES, Jrn. to Miss FLORIDA A. DAVIS, eldest daughter of JOSEPH E. DAVIS, Esquire.

Married the 11th, JOHN P. RUNNELLS to Miss SARAH COLEMAN, all of Claiborne County.

Married in West Feliciana, La. on the 4th, Mr. PETER SOUTHERLAND to Mrs. MARY ANN ROBERTS, both of this county.

Died in Claiborne County, the 1st, Miss MARGARET BRISCOE, daughter of WM. BRISCOE, aged 19.

Died in Port Gibson the 1st, Dr. P. B. WILCOX, a native of Ky., aged 28 years.

Died in Claiborne County the 1st, Mr. ABRAM ARNES, aged 46, died on the 30th, Mrs. HANSEY MARBLE, consort of ERRA MARBLE and on the 4th, Mr. REUBEN WHITE, aged 21 years.

Died at his residence, the 15th, Mr. M. LINDSEY, Planter, and leaves a large family.

Died in Monticello, Mississippi.,the 27th, Mr. JAMES COURSEY.

November 20, 1830

Died at the residence of WM ECCLES the 20th, Judge CARRAWAY, aged 69. Presided many years over the County & Probate courts.

Died the 9th, JACOB HYLAND, Esq., one of proprietors of the paper. Leaves a widow and children. (Originally from the VICKSBURG REGISTER)

Mr. PLEASANT H. HUNTER, an old and respectable inhabitant of Rapides Parish,La., died the 2nd. His residence was in Cetile.

Died at Philadelphia, Mrs. ANN BROWN, wife of JAMES BROWN Esq., late Minister of the United States in France. She was the daughter of the late Col. THOMAS HART of Lexington Ky. and the sister of the lady of the Hon. HENRY CLAY.

Married at the (unreadable) city, Tenn. the 13th by the Rev. Mr. Weller of the Episcopal Church, JOHN S. SIMPSON Esqr., of Nashville to Miss EUGANIA CATHERINE SAUNDERS, daughter of WILLIAM SAUNDERS, Esqr., of the former place.

Married at Washington City the 18th, Gen. DANIEL S. DONELSON of Tenn. to Miss MARGARET BRANCH, daughter of the Hon. JOHN BRANCH.

Married the 12th, by C. VANHOUTEN, Esq., Gen. G. DAVIS to Miss JULIA BURR, all of Amite County.

November 27, 1830

Commissioners were appointed in July for the NATHANIEL JONES' estate.

Married Thursday by the Rev J. C. BURRUS, Mr. GEORGE JOOR to LAURA SINGLETON, daughter of HIRAM SINGLETON, all of this co.

Married the 16th, by Judge Guion, Mr. JOHN TARBE, merchant of Natchez to Miss ANN BOUIS of the parish of Concordia, La., niece of Mr. JOHN P. ARNAUD.

Died in West Feliciana on the 20th, Mr. ANTHONY H. McDERMOTT.

Final settlement of THOS. R. DOWNING's estate will be given at the next January term by JAMES JONES, administrator.

WILLIS THORNTON & JAMES HORTON, admr's., of the DEMARQUIS THORNTON estate

CHARLES B. HAYNES, adm'r., of DAVID SIX's estate

December 4, 1830

W. C. S. VENTRESS & HARRY CAGE, ex'rs., of MOSES GORDON's estate

WM. P. PERKINS vs. ROBT. M. BOWDEN $120.47.

Harris & Marsh vs. THOMAS FOSTER $133.25.

Wm. Tufts & Co. vs. LEWIS S. TULANE (TULAVE)

DAVID WOOD vs. JOSEPH RORCK $100

JOHN S. BRUCE vs. PATRICK MURPHEY and AARON A. JAMES $300

JESSE BROWN, guardian of minor heirs of BENJAMIN THERRELL to sell "Percy Creek Tract".

SARAH J. JEWELL of Pointe Coupee, cautions anyone in trading for a draft on P. DUBERTRAND of New

Orleans. Draft payable to JOSIAH H. BARRY of Woodville, Mississippi.

JOHN OGDEN & CYNTHIA SAPP, admr's., of ASA SAPP's estate

A. TESTARD and family intends to move to Natchez.

Died the 19th at his residence near Natchez, Doct. SEABORN JONES NOBLE, a native of Georgia.

December 11, 1830

C. P. SMITH & P. W. FARRAR forms copartnership in law

Married the 26th, by GEORGE B. CRUTCHER, Esqr., Mr. WILLIAM A. HARDWICK, of Clinton to Mrs. AMELIA WALKER of Hinds County.

BENJAMIN KILGORE, adm.'r.,of WM. ANDERSON's estate

MARTHA DRAKE, adm'rx., of RICHARD H. SPEARS's estate, was formerly MARTHA SPEARS.

THOMAS HUGHES, Jr. states to the Public not to trade for several notes. Names SAMUEL MOORE, WILLIAM STEWART and WILLIE SIMMONS

Married the 1st, by JOHN ROBERTSON, Esqr., ZACHARIAH COX to Miss ELIZA RANDELL, daughter of the Rev. JOEL RANDELL, all of this county.

JESSE BROWN, adm'r., of THOMAS CREWS'estate to sell land located in Pike County.

JAMES A. GIRAULT to sell his plantation and property

December 25, 1830

(Refer to the December 31st issue for explanation of duplicate dates).

Married Thursday, by the Hon. THOMAS H. PROSSER, BENNETT H. BARROW, Esq., of West Feliciana to Miss EMILY JOOR, daughter of Maj. Genl. JOHN JOOR, of this county.

W. TIGNER has four acres of sugar cane for sale.

December 23, 1830

Franklin County: S. J. BROADWAY, adm'r., of dec'd STEPHEN VANKENREN's estate

POLASKI CAGE, President of board of Marion Academy.

Final settlement of DAVID SIX's estate

December 25, 1830

Married the 23d by J. H. MAURY, Mr. JOSIAH J. WILLIAMS, to Miss RACHEL ROUSE, both of this place. (Originally from the PORT GIBSON CORRESPONDANCE)

Married in Hinds Co. on 16th, by PERRY KING, Esq., Mr. BENJAMIN POTTER (print faint) to Miss MARY DAVIS, all of that county.

Married in Wayne Co. on the 11th, JAMES McDUGAL to Mrs. MARGARET WILLIAMS. On the 18th, WILLIAM COVINGTON to Miss MARY CATOE. On the 1st, Doct. JOHN P. McINTOSH to Miss ELIZA S. POWE.

Died in Port Gibson on the 19th ,Mr. WALTER CARPENTER, at the residence of his brother.

Died at Lake Providence in the Parish of Ouachita, State of La., Nov. 14th, Mrs. ELIZABETH E. FUQUA, consort of JOSEPH FUQUA, Esqr. after a painful and lingering illiness.

LAZARUS DRAKE and MARTHA DRAKE (late Martha Spears & wife of RICHARD H. SPEARS, deceased) claim as her dower, a certain lot of land in Liberty.

PHILIP NOLAND claims certificate of forfeited Land Stock purchased by WILLIAM NOLAND of Wilkinson County.

December 28, 1830

ELISABETH QUINN, RICHARD QUINN, & PETER QUINN, Executors of the dec'd, HENRY QUINN's estate in Pike County.

December 31, 1830

The present number closes the 7th volume of the WOODVILLE REPUBLICAN---Owing to unusual press of business from printing oftener than once a week, we were not enabled to get out our two last papers until after the time of their date.Our next will as we promised, be commenced under a new name; and we hope in a week or two to be regulated, and afterwords to proceed regularly.

Married the 26th by Rev. THOS C. BROWN, Mr. JOHN F. AILES of Monroe, La., to Miss ELIZABETH H. SMITH, daughter of Mr. THOMAS SMITH, of this county.

Married on Thursday, by JOSEPH PATTERSON, Esqr., Mr. DUNCAN C. HENDERSON to Miss MARY ANN OGDEN, daughter of Mr. JOHN OGDEN, all of this county.

Died the 30th, Mr. JOSEPH P. HENLEY, a native of Virginia.

Died Jan. 1st, ELEANOR EUGENIA YERBY, youngest daughter of Wm. W. YERBY, Esquire.

MISSISSIPPI DEMOCRATE
Editor: G. D. BOYD

1831

"Beginning a new name and format for paper and is entirely on new type. "

Final settlement of Wm. BROOKS's estate

January 15, 1831

JOHN E. PALMER, exec'r., of HENRY NICHOLSON's estate

THOMAS DAWSON, Sen.'s plantation for sale, located 9 miles from Fort Adams, and about the same distance from the landing on the Mississippi River, at the mouth of Bayou Tanica. Apply to ROBERT DAWSON, or to JOSEPH DAWSON.   November 1, 1830

ROBERT SMITH, adm'r., of JOHN NESMITH's estate

Married the 29th in Rapides Parish, Mr. ROBERT G. LOCKIE to Mrs. MARGARET MATHEWS.

January 22, 1831

Mr. GEO A. LONG, 24 yrs. of age, was drowned while attempting to cross Bayou Tunica on horseback.

Died the 18th, in this county, Capt. ADAM HOPE.

January 29, 1831

Commissioners appointed for J. W. EDWARDS estate: GEORGE H. GORDON, A. DANIEL, & L. R. MARSHALL

February 5, 1831

Dr. GEO. C. McWHORTER, Medical notice

J. W. GILDART & J. J. EVELETH, Counsellors & Attorneys At Law

CHAUNCEY S. KELLOGG & H. D. KELLOGG, Attorneys At Law

<u>THE MISSISSIPPI DEMOCRAT</u> Printed and published every Saturday by WM. A. A. CHISHOLM, Editor, G. D. BOYD

Died at Wish-ton-rish, the residence of the Rev. JNO. C. BURNS on the 27th, Mr. EDMUND B. CORLEY, a native of Va., aged 34.

W. HAILE wishes to sell his interest in the Ashly Estate.

ELIZABETH A. HENLEY, appointed adm'rx., of the JOSEPH P. HENLEY's estate

SARAH LINDSEY, admr'x., & JOSHUA L. LINDSEY, admr., of WILLIAM M. LINDSEY's estate.

ELIZABETH CHAMBERS, appointed adm'rx., of deceased JACOB CHAMBERS's estate appoints WESTLY CHAMBERS as her agent. (February term 1830)

JER'H NOLAND, adm'r., to sell property whereon HENRY W. LEWIS lately resided, located in Wilkinsburg, commonly called Fort Adams.

<u>February 12, 1831</u>
Col. ANDREW MARSCHALK has taken charge of the "Natchez Gazette" and has relinquished the editorship of the "Cadet" to Mr. J. R. INGRAHAM.

F. S. MAYES & JAS. MAYES wish to sell the plantation on which they live, 4 miles from Ft. Adams, on the Natchez road.

Died at his residence on Buffaloe, on Monday last, Mr. WILLIAM CARSON, about 40 years of age.

Died suddenly Wednesday at his residence, Mr. DAVID F. COON.

Horse stolen from JOSEPH PORCHE. Awards offered: $5 for horse and $30 for thief

HIRAM A. BERRY, guardian of PAMELIA BERRY will sell a 20 acre tract of land, bounded on north by DAVID ARMSTRONG, south by GEORGE B. COLLIER, west by heirs of Wm. BELL, and east by ABRAM QUINE.

Land and property of EDMUND GINN to be sold by Trustee, L. R. MARSHALL. The Deed of Trust was executed March 19, 1830.

R. L. BONER wishes to sell or exchange his situation in Woodville, for a place in the country.

February 19, 1831

THOS. C. ADAMS' land to be sold for taxes. Located near Fort Adams, known as a part of the old Ogden tract, on which the brick house stands. Taxes due, $26.77 on 175 acres

Additional lands sold for taxes: Estate of STEPHEN AMBROSE, Miss ELIZA BATROW, Heirs of JOSEPH BARNARD, ELIHU HALL BAY, RICHARD G. ELLIS, R. E. FLEASON, PATRICK FOLEY's estate, A. B. HAMMETT, WM. HAMMETT, WM. W. IVES, JOHN LOMBARD, WM. F. PARKER's estate, TURNMANN heirs, REBECCA WILSON, HUGH WALLACE WORMLEY, ISRAEL WELLS, WM. RANDOLPH, FRANCIS GILDART's heirs, and JAS N. BOON estate.

February 26, 1831

WM. P. PERKINS vs. ROBT. M. BOWDEN

Editor (G. D. BOYD) remarks. . "Deaths and marriages and other remarkable events belong to the history of a country, and ought to be recorded in the public journals within their vicinity..."

Married in Woodville, Thursday last, by the Rev. J. C. BURRUS, Mr. EZRA WOODS of West Feliciana to Miss CAROLINE AMANDA SMITH.

Married Feb. 17th by DUNCAN STEWART, Esqr., Mr. WM. RUTZELL to Miss RACHEL KING, both of Louisiana.

Married the 3rd by the Rev. Mr. RANALDSON, MATTHEW N. BRANDON Esqr., of Wilkinson county, Ms. to Miss LOUISA S. AUSTIN of West Feliciana. (Originally from the FLORIDA GAZETTE)

March 5, 1831

Election to be held to elect a Major to command the 2nd Battalion of the 5th Regiment, M. M. to fill the vacancy occasioned by the resignation of Major FRANCIS S. MAYES. Captains named: Mt. Pleasant - BENJ. KILGORE; Upper Homochitto - SAM'L McMURTRY; Lower Humochitto - E. GOWER; Percy's

Creek - THO'S J. HART; Fort Adams - WM. S. BUSH; and Pinckneyville - J. W. LEATHERMAN. By order of Brig. Gen. DAVID DAVIS , GEORGE H. GORDON, Col. Commanding 5th Reg. M. M. and R. H. CAMPBELL, Adj..

Died the 18th at his residence, Mr. WM DAWSON about 57 yrs, and citizen of this county for 33 years. He was a member of the Methodist Episcopal Church for 27 years.

Died in this county on Jan. 16 last, Mrs. MARY OGDEN, consort of EDWARD OGDEN. She had been member of the Methodist Episcopal Church for the last 20 years of her life.

Final settlement of CHAPMAN WHITE's estate

THOMAS HUGHES, Jr., appointed adm'r., of ARCHIBALD McMANUS' estate

JAMES POINDEXTER vs. JOSEPH I. SCOTT

March 12, 1831

Died at the "Forest of Bandy" on Tuesday last, in this county, Mrs. C. C. D. PHILBRICK, consort of Captain J. PHILBRICK.

THOMAS HUGHS,Jr. lost a "Red Morocco Pocket Book" containing a note to Mr. HARRELL and one to THOMAS SMITH, of Amite Co.

N. BOWREN, adm'r., of RAFORD PRICE's estate

March 19, 1831

Married the 18th, by Wm. G. MARTIN, Esqr., Mr. JAMES R. GOFF, son of the Hon. JOHN K. GOFF, of Washington Parish, La., to Miss MARTHA COOK, daughter of THOS. COOK, Esqr., of Pike Co. Ms.

Married the 10th, by Wm. G. MARTIN, Esqr., Mr. WILFORD GARNER of Amite Co. to Miss MARTHA PEARSON, of Pike Co. Ms.

Died the 13th, Miss RACHEL GLASS, 16 yrs. of age, daughter of JOEL GLASS of this county.

Died at his residence in this county on the 14th, Mr. ROBERT JAMES, a respectable and worthy citizen.

Died March 2d, Major TULLY ROBINSON (Originally

from the FLORIDA GAZETTE)

A horse was taken up by WILLIAM NETTERVILLE as an estray.

Horse of JAMES E. PHELPS stolen. Rewards offered; $25 for horse, and $50 for thief

March 26, 1831

Property of RICHARD SEAGARS to be sold by Sheriff

JOHN BROWN vs. JOHN L. BRUCE. 375 Acres

The Cotton Gin of Mr. CHARLES NETTERVILLE, 3 miles from this place, caught fire as is supposed by friction, on Wenesday last, and was burnt down, together with about twenty-five bales of loose cotton. The gin was not insured.

MARY S. OGDEN vs. MARY FOSTER

Married on Sunday last, by DAN'L BASS, Esqr., Mr. ALEXANDER HUGHES of Amite County, to Mrs. NANCY BRADY, of this county.

April 2, 1831

Married March 31, by DANIEL BASS, Esqr., Mr. WILLIAM C. GREEN to Miss JANE CLAMPITT, all of this county.

WESTLEY CHAMBERS, adm'r., of ADAM HOPE's estate

THOMAS R. CHEATHAM & A. ROBINSON, ex'rs., of MOSES ROBINSON's estate

ELIZABETH M. JAMES, adm'r., of ROBERT JAMES's estate

WM. R. TAYLOR & JESSE JONES, exec'rs of JOHN JONES' estate

April 9, 1831

SUSAN S. BOYD vs. WILLIAM J. BOYD

Died in Woodville on Tuesday evening last, Captain MATTHEW TOOL, formerly of Amite Couty, and for six or seven years past, a citizen of this county.

JOHN SMITH vs. JONES H. SMITH, et el.

JAMES POINDEXTER vs. JOSEPH I. SCOTT & others

STEPHEN JOHNSON wishes to sell his land on Percys Creek.

JOHN C. WHITE, trustee for THOMAS GILHAM, sells land to clear debt to JAMES WILSON

April 16, 1831
JOHN PHILBRICK, adm'r., for CHARLOTTE C. PHILBRICK's estate. Land in Adams County known as "Hope Farm" and land in the state of Louisiana.

Partnership dissolved between WM. WOODSIDES & MATTH'S OVERMAN

April 23, 1831
April 30, 1831
Mr. HENRY S. FOOTE, has given up his charge as Editor of the MISSISSIPPI ADVOCATE. That paper is to be conducted in the future, by the proprietor, JAMES R. MARSH, Esquire.

May 7, 1831
B. LOVELACE to sell plantation. Apply to L. LOVELACE.

RICHARD HURST vs. EDMUND JENKINS

May 14, 1831
EDMUND JENKINS vs. SAML J. REYNOLDS. Circuit Court

Dr. R. W. HARRIS has located at Laurel Hill, La.

J. C. PATRICK, M. D. will practice in Pinckneyville.

Married the 7th by DUNCAN STEWART, Esqr., Mr. HIRAM ASHLY to Miss MARTHA B. SAUNDERS, all of this county.

The Rev. H. B. BASCOMB will preach in the Methodist Episcopal Church. The organization of a society, Auxilliary to the American Colonization Society, will follow.

May 21, 1831
Meeting held for the purpose of constructing a rail road between St. Francisville, La. to Woodville. A punctual and general attendance is earnestly requested. Mr. JAS BRADFORD, a commissioner of the Louisiana Rail Road Company will be at attendance. Stock will be available.

The final settlement of JOHN P. HAMPTON's estate is to be presented at the July term.

May 28, 1831

Died in Marion County in the 63 year of her age, Mrs. SARAH NORTON, relict of GEORGE H. NORTON, of Marion County.

Died on the 5th at his residence in Belmont, Wayne county, after an illness of six hours, Gen. JAMES PATTON, ex-Lieut. Governor of this state. (Originally from the MONTICELLO GAZETTE)

ARTHUR DANIEL, adm'r., of CALVIN PORTER's estate files an application in the Orphans' Court to show why property should not be sold.

June 4, 1831

JOHN TEMON will not pay debts of his wife MATILDA TEMON since she left his bed and board. Fort Adams, May 30, 1831

JNO. F. CARMICHEL, adm'r., of MOSES HOOKE & HARRIET BROWDER, dec'd., formerly HARRIET HOOKE, gives authorization to JUSTIN W. FOOTE, Esqr., for settlements of accounts.

JAMES THOMPSON authorizes nephew, ROBERT THOMPSON to to handle his business accounts while he is out of town.

ELIZABETH M. JAMES, admr'x., of PETER DRESLER, Jr., appoints JAMES BUFORD, Esqr., to handle affairs.

June 11, 1831

THOS. S. HERBERT, adm'r., of JOHN P. HAMPTON's estate

Final settlement of ANDREW B. McCARTNEY's estate

SPENCER M. WOOD, adm'r., of FREDERICK A. BROWDER's estate

June 18, 1831

WILLIAM W. LOWRY's, appointment as exec'r., of WILLIAM LOWRY, Sr.'s estate was granted in Liberty, Amite County.

WM. S. LEWIS plans to spend the winter and spring in New Orleans. He leaves DAN'L BASS to handle his unsettled business.

Married at Jackson (Ms) the 14th by the Rev. THOS. BRYAN, Col. T. B. J. HADLEY, Auditor of Public Accounts to Miss PIETY LUCRETIA SMITH, all of Hinds County.

Married, Jackson,La., on Thursday by the Rev. Mr. Ranaldson, Mr. HUGH DAVIS, of West Feliciana, to Miss MARGARET A. SCOTT, daughter of Mr. JAMES SCOTT, Jr., of the former place.

Died from falling off a steamboat on the Ohio River, Dr. ROBT. H. CAMPBELL, of this place.

Died the 6th, at his residence in Pike County, VINCENT GARNER, late representative in the legislature.

M. K. L. COOK lost a pocket book containing notes and papers belonging to EPHRAIM THOMPSON.

THOMAS BROWN has taken up a horse with black mane & tail.

June 25, 1831
Married the 26th, by G. D. BOYD, Esqr., Mr. JOHN T. H. ROBINSON to Miss SARAH ANN SIDEBOTTOM, all of this county.

Married last evening at Pilgrimage, near Washinton in this county, Mr. WILLIAM P. MELLEN, publisher of the Natchez, to Miss SARAH C. LEWIS, daughter of ARCHIBALD LEWIS, Esqr.,deceased. (Originally from the SOUTHERN CLARION)

Final settlement of JAMES PHIPPS's estate

Final settlement of MARTHA PHIPPS's estate

WM. STAMPS wishes to be released as administrator of THOMAS M. GILDART's estate.

Final settlement of HENRY MILLER,Senr.,'s estate

July 2, 1831
SARAH McCARSTLE, admr'x., of ZALMON McCARSTLE, claims certificate of forfeited land stock in right of heirs: NILE NELSON, ERASMUA DARWIN, and ARGUS & CULLEN McCARSTLE.

July 9, 1831
Married at the residence of Judge Rhea, on Monday evening the 27th by the Rev. Mr. RANALDSON,_____

HARDSEY, Esq., of Clinton to Miss ELIZA RHEA, of this Parish.

Died at Bayou Sarah Landing on Monday, Mr. JOHN M'VEA, leaving a wife and two children. (Originally from the F. GAZETTE)

July 16, 1831

BENNETT BARROW purchased a number of notes and accounts due JAMES WYSE. Payments to be made to THOS TURNER

SPENCER WOOD, adm'r., of FREDERICK A. BROWDER's estate

Died in Putnam County, Georgia, on the 28th of April, WILLIAM HATHORN, aged one hundred and ten years. He was a native of Ireland, a precipitant in the revolution and he served under Braddock.

Married the 16th, at the residence of JOHN H. SIMS in this county, by G. D. BOYD, Esqr., Mr. VICTOR LABAUVE to Miss ARTIMETIA DUGAS, daughter of ELOI DAGAS, all of the Parish of St. Martin, La. (Published Wilkinson County Marriage Records state the spelling of this couple as, VICTOR LABONE & ARTIMETIA DUGAN)

July 23, 1831

Married on the 19th, by DANIEL BASS, Esqr., Mr. JOSEPH A. LILLY to Miss MINERVA DELOACH, all of this county.

Married at the residence of Maj. WM. L. BRANDON, the 19th, by the Rev'd J. A. RANALDSON, Mr. ROBERT D. PERCY, of Louisana to Miss ELLEN H. DAVIS, of Wilkinson County.

Died the 16th, near Natchez, HARRIETT MATTHEWS, only daughter of L. R. MARSHALL, Esqr., formerly of this place.

July 30, 1831

Died, July 4th, at the residence of his son-in-law, SAMUEL GOVERNEUR, Esqr., ex-president JAMES MONROE of Virginia.

Died the 24th, ELIZABERTH DANIEL, infant daughter of Mr. ARTHUR DANIEL of this place. (7 months)

ROBERT WHITE, adm'r., of JOHN WHITE's estate

August 6, 1831
Married the 5th by DAN'L BASS, Esqr., Mr. SAML. PETERSON to Miss ELIZABETH BOHANON.

Married the 5th by DAN'L BASS, Esqr., Mr. JAMES PETERSON to Miss MARY BOHANON, all of Louisiana.

Married in Liberty the 28th, by RANDALL JONES, Esqr., Mr. MARK HAYES, of this county, to Miss LOUISA HICKS, of Liberty.

Died in Amite county the 25th of July, Mrs. JANE C. DUNN, wife of JOHN A. DUNN, Esqr., 25 years.

Died in Pinckneyville on the 1st, Mr. ABEL W. FARWELL, 21 yrs, formerly of Fitchburg, Massachusetts, and merchant here.

Died the 27th JOHN LEWIS BROWN, infant son of LORONZO D. and SARAH D. BROWN of this county.

August 13, 1831
Married on Thursday, by the Rev. J. C. BURRUSS, Mr. JACOB KELLER to Miss SUSAN A. TOOL.

August 20, 1831
REUBEN SMITH & JESSE KNEHTEN, exec'rs., of LITTLTON CAPELL's estate

Final settlement of WILLIAM CALLIHAM's estate

A. DANIEL, adm'r., of CALVIN PORTER's estate sells a tract of land.

JOHN SIMS petitions for renewel of land certificate for 540 acres.

ROBERT WHITE, adm'r., of JOHN WHITE's estate

DAVID DAVIS, adm'r., of JOHN NEWSHAM's estate

Died the 11th, Mrs. ANN C. BRANDON, consort of Major Wm. L. Brandon.

Died in this town this morning, Mrs. VIRGINIA LEWIS, consort of Col. Wm. T. LEWIS.

Died on the 17th, Mr. JOSIAH H. BERRY of this town.

Died the 17th, at the residence of her son, JOHN

I. BRUCE, and in the 94th year of her age, Mrs. ELIZABETH H. BRUCE. She was the mother of 12 children and left one son and two daughters.

August 27, 1831

Mrs. DON CLAUDIO TARQUIS asks that those who purchased books at the late sale of her husband's property, to allow her to redeem them at the sale price. These books were her private property given to her by friends as presents.

ROBERT D. PIETY, adm'r., of ELIAS WOOD's estate in Amite Co.

JOHN M. EVANS, adm'r., of the deceased, WILLIAM F. I. NICHOLSON's estate

CHARITY WILLIS, admr'x., of WILSON WILLIS' estate

WESTLEY CHAMBERS, adm'r., of ADAM HOPE to sell property

Final settlement by JAMES L. TRASK, exec'r., of WILLIAM P. TRASK's estate

PRISCILLA CLAMPIT, admr'x., of SAMUEL CLAMPIT's estate will present the final settlement.

September 3, 1831

Commissioners granted 3 additional months to examine claims against the estate of NATHANIEL JONES.

JOHN H. REID, adm'r., of WIlIAM CALLIHAM's estate, presents final settlement.

H. C. HILLS, who resides at Society Hill, near St. Francisville will continue delivering goods with his team formerly driven by Mr. HOLMES.

Married Thursday evening last, at the residence of JESSE PELL, Esqr., by the Rev. COOMAN C. BROWN, Mr. Wm. C. DAVIS to Miss ELIZA McGRAW, daughter of the late Mr. PETER McGRAW.

September 10, 1831

MARY L. GULLEDGE, admr'x., of THO. GULLEDGE, Jr.'s estate

G. D. BOYD, adm'r., of JOSIAH H. BERRY's estate

SARAH DIXON, adm'x., of EPHRM DIXON intends to

file for her Dower lands located in Amite County.
WILLIAM E. MEDKIFF vs. CLAUDIO TARQUIS

Sheriff sale of JOSHUA WINTERS' "Steam Saw Mill" in Ft. Adams

September 17, 1831
Married the 8th by Rev. THOS. C. BROWN, Mr. STEPHEN COBB, of Laurel Hill, Louisiana, to Miss MARY ELIZA CARTER, daughter of GEO W. CARTER of this county.

Died the 13th, SARAH CALPHURNIA BRANDON, infant daughter of Major Wm. L. BRANDON.

THOMAS TURNER, adm'r., of DAVID B. LAND's estate

Sheriff sale. JOHN Y. CALLIHAM's 100 acres of land

September 24, 1831
Married on Thursday evening, by G. D. BOYD, Esqr., Mr. JAMES C. WOODS, of the Parish of West Feliciana, La. to Miss EMELINE SHANNON, daughter of the late _____SHANNON of this county.

Married in Claiborne County the 5th, ALEXANDER MONTGOMERY, Esqr., by the Rev. Z. BUTLER, Maj. BENJ. F. STOCKTON, Editor of the "Port Gibson Correspondent", to Miss ELIZABETH W. GILBERT, all of that co.

Died at Pinckneyville, on the 11th, GEORGE B. RANDOLPH, infant son of WM. RANDOLPH.

JOHN GUNLY, adm'r., of RANDAL GOOLSLY's estate, will apply for permisson to sell land.

October 1, 1831
C. PETTIBONE's land known as the "Richland" plantation, is to be sold by the Sheriff.

BROWN ROSS's ex'rs. vs. HENRY HUNTER'S adm'rs. Adams Circuit Court in November Term, 1831. Land to be sold.

JOSEPH BROWN vs. HUGH W. WORMLY, Names listed: MARY WORMLY, dec'd., and her father, ROBERT STARK. Land on waters of Bayou Sarah. Also, ROBERT STARK, Senr., JOHN C. WORMLY, WILLIAM BROEN, and MARY B. CARTER.

WM. N. MERCER, adm'r., of BENJAMIN FARRAR, dec'd,

vs. THEORDORE STARK. Mentions that Theodore was son of ROBERT STARK

Died the 21st in Amite Co., THOMAS TORANCE, Esqr., Leaving a family, and a father.

Died 25th August, Mrs. MADISON in her 80th yr. She was the last surviving sister of PATRICK HENRY. (Originally from BOWLING GREEN KY. ADV.)

Died Saturday last, at the residence of his father in this county, Mr. STEPHEN NOLAND, 22 yrs., son of Mr. PHILIP NOLAND.

Died in Baltimore on the 2nd, Mr. ROBERT DUER NILES, 22 yrs of age, son of HEZEKJAH NILES, editor of "Niles Register".

Died in Natchez the 27th, Mr. R. COX, a highly respectable physician and resident of that place.

Died the 18th Aug., at her residence in this Parish, Mrs. SARAH HAILE, widow of the late BENJAMIN HAILE, Esqr., of Columbia, South Carolina. (Originally from the FLORIDA GAZETTE)

MARTHA DRAKE, adm'x., of RICHARD H. SPEARS has intermarried with LAZARUS DRAKE & who is now the adm'r., of the estate.

C. S. KELLOGG, exec'r., of JAMES S. WAIDE's estate

October 8, 1831
The Rev. JAS. A. RANALDSON will preach at the Baptist Church.

Died the 6th, Mr. JONAS ILER after a short illness, leaving a wife and child.

Died on the 7th, SARAH JANE DOWTY, daughter of Mr. Wm. DOWTY.

October 15, 1831
Married in Columbia, Marion County, Mi. on the 29th, by the Rev. DAVIS COLLINS, Mr. JOSIAH RATLIFF to Miss ANGELINE STOVALL; daughter of CHARLES STOVALL, Esq'r, deceased, all of Marion county.

Died on Monday last, at Cabin Hall, Miss EMILY YERBY, 15 yrs, youngest daughter of the late Col. Wm. YERBY, of this county.

October 22, 1831

Mr. JAMES K. COOK, formerly the editor of the "Ariel" and the "Natchez", is now the editor of "The Emporium" a newspaper published in New Orleans by A. T. PENNIMA,Jr.

Married in this county on Wednesday, by the Hon. HARRY CAGE, Doctor EDWARD T. FARISH, to Miss CAROLINE C. HAMILTON, daughter of the late Col. HAMILTON of the parish of West Feliciana.

Married Wednesday by G. D. BOYD, Esqr., Mr. JOSEPH W. FENNER to Miss ELIZABETH ANN IVES, all of this county.

Married Thursday, by the Hon. HARRY CAGE, Mr. GEORGE MACMURDO of New Orleans, to Miss ELIZA ROSANA STARK, daughter of the late Col. HORATIO STARK, of this county.

Married Thursday, by the same, Mr. JAMES M. WOOD to Miss SARAH SMITH, daughter of Mr. ALEX. SMITH, all of this place.

Died the 17th, GEORGE WASHINGTON ARDREY, 18 mo., 23 days, infant son of Mr. ALEXANDER ARDREY.

Died in Raymond on the 14th, GEORGE HENRY GILBERT, infant son of Mr. JNO. P. GILBERT, formerly of this county.

October 29, 1831

The Town Constable, BENJAMIN TURBEVILLE cautions all owners or overseers not to allow any slaves to come to town without written permission specifying their business.

Died the 18th, of hooping cough, ZACHARIAH JAMES DOWTY, infant son of Mr. Wm. DOWTY, about 17 months.

Died in this county on Saturday last, Mrs. ELIZABETH DIXON aged upwards of forty.

Died at the residence of Mr. JOHN L. BRUCE, near Woodville, on the 26th, Mr. JOHN W. THOMPSON of this place, aged 24 yrs.

Married in Woodville on Thursday, by the Hon. HARRY CAGE, Mr. JOSEPH R. THOMAS to Miss SARAH ANN HAWTHORN.

LYDIA H. NEWELL, exec'x., of GEORGE B. NEWELL's estate

November 5, 1831

T. MOLLEMAN will sell the house in which JOHN LENNOX now resides but generally known as the W. ELLINGTONS residence.

ABR. LANEHART, adm'r., final settlement of JESSE ENLOW's estate

Final settlement of NOEL WADDILL's estate

Final settlement of ENOS BURRIS' estate

S. B. SIMMONS, adm'r., of THOMAS LARD's estate

N. NORWOOD and also ROBERT NORWOOD wish to sell their plantations and etc. Their plantations are 6 miles from Ft. Adams, and both join each other.

Died the 10th, Miss ELIZABETH E. YERBY, 15 years of age.

Married on Tuesday, by Bishop WILLIAM E. MATHEWS, BYTHELL HAYNES, Esqr., of Wilkinson to Miss AMANDA MALVINA GERALD of Amite County.

Died on the 4th, Mr. DOUGAL B. THOMPSON, of this place.

C. S. KELLOG, adm'r., of JAMES S. WAIDE's estate

Final settlement of STEWART COLE's estate by DANIEL SLACK

Wm. T. LEWIS will apply for renewal of Land Certificate which was originally purchased by JOHN DICKSON.

L. D. BROWN, Tax Collector, will sell land assessed to Mrs. Fleeson's 250 acres as her Dower, which was formerly entered by SAMUEL NICHOLSON, and afterwards bought at the Sheriff's sale by R. E. FLEESON. Also, 1500 acres of land of ELIHU HALL BAY will be sold.

November 12, 1831

WM PEBBLES wishes to sell his plantation and etc.

JOHN DUNBAR, adm'r., of R. H. CAMPBELL's estate

S. B. SIMMONS & JAS. BURRIS, ex'rs., of ENOS

BURRIS'estate

Final settlement of NOEL WADDILL estate by GEO. W. KELLER & ABEL WADDILL

November 19, 1831
For sale or rent. Plantation of JOHN SMITH lying on Buffaloe Creek, 12 miles from Ft. Adams. JAMES BUFORD, agent

November 26, 1831
Married the 15th at Belle Grove near New Orleans, by the Rev. JAMES F. JULL, Doctor WILLIAM R. TAYLOR, of this county, to Miss MARIA ANN DAVIS, daughter of Madam HOLLIDAY of the former place.

Died the 23rd, Mr. JOHN CONNELL, late sheriff of this county.

Died on the 24th instant, Mrs. POLLY DELOACH, aged about 47 years--after an illness of nine months. She has left a tender husband and four daughters and five sons to mourn her loss. (JESSE DELOACH)

HENRY CONRAD offers a reward for a horse strayed or stolen

Notice: ELIZABETH DOUGHERTY will file a petition for her Dower of one half of the lands and tenements of her late husband, THOMAS DOUGHERTY. Attorney, D. D. BOYD

Guardians of ALVINA LOUISA & SARAH D. P. CASSELLS, wish to sell land. LEMUEL & ANNE C. REAMS, guardians.

December 3, 1831
Married the 22nd at Sligo in this county by the Rev. THOMAS C. BROWN, Rev. Wm V. DOUGLASS to Mrs. MARTHA E. H. SCOTT, daughter of Capt. JNO. SIMS of this county.

Married the 27th by the Rev. T. C. BROWN, Mr. JNO. McNEELY to Miss MARY ANN McCRANEY, daughter of Squire McCRANEY, all of this county.

Died at his residence on Smith's Creek on the 28th, Mr. ZACHARIAH SMITH, 62, a resident in this county for 44 yrs.

D. S. KELLOG, adm'r., of DOUGALD B. THOMPSON's estate

SPENCER WOOD, adm'r., of F. A. BROWDER's estate

Final settlement of ALFRED M. WILSON's estate

December 10, 1831
JOHN P. SMITH, adm'r., of ELIZBETH DIXON's estate

MARY SHANNON offers $30 reward for return of horse.

J. C. PATRICK, adm.'r., of A. W. FAREWELL's estate

December 17, 1831
From the MISSISSIPPI PATRIOT.. "The 'Mississippi Democrat' published at Woodville, has passed into the hands of ALFRED BYNUM, Esq., The editorial displays a chast and manly style and evinces much reflection,and a thorough knowledge of the science of government."

Married on Thursday at Ashley place, by the Rev. Mr. BURRVSS, Maj. ROBT. M. YERBY to the amiable and accomplished Miss JANE BAILEY, all of this county.

MARTHA ANN ILER, adm'x., of JONAS ILER's estate

HENRY JONES vs. WILLIAM EVERETT

JON. L. BRUCE, adm'r., will sell the personal estate of ELIZABETH BRUCE on Monday the 23d of January.

JAMES LEECH wishes to sell his plantation located 2 miles west of Woodville.

December 22, 1831
Died at his residence on Big Bayou Sarah on the 6th, after an illness of four days, SAMUEL TUELL, aged sixty-one years and two days. A native of Newport, Rhode Island, member of the Methodist Episcopal Church and was a cotton planter.

Married on Sunday by Bishop WILLIAM E. MATHEWS, Mr. JAMES MEEK, of Wilkinson to Mrs. ELIZABETH WAIT of Amite Co.

THOS I. NERSON, adm'r., of ELLEN CARR's estate

Mrs. LELIZA ANN GINN will petition for dower of one half of the property that her late husband, EDMUND GINN possessed.

December 27, 1831

Mr. ALLEN A. ROBERTS, the overseer of Col. JNO. S. LEWIS, was murdered on Friday last by Anthony, one of the slaves on the plantation, the property of Maj. L. D. BROWN.

THE YEAR 1832 COULD NOT BE FOUND

WOODVILLE REPUBLICIAN

1833

January 5, 1833

Married Sunday evening last, by JOSEPH GREEN, Esq., Mr. Wm. DODD, to Miss ANN COTTER, all of this Town.

Final settlement of DAVID KAIGLER's estate by JOHN KAIGLER

R. MUMFORD & JOHN LONG has entered into a partnership at the Bayou Sarah Landing. December 1, 1832

JNO. HOLMES & JOS. PIRAM has entered into a Co-partnership.

Final settlement of CHAS. A. COON's estate by JOHN McNEELY, executor

Final settlement of ASA COLVER's estate by Wm. TIGNER, administrator

Final settlement of JAMES BAILEY's estate by JESSE BROWN, administrator

Final settlement of WM. MELTON's estate by PETER W. SMITH, administrator

Final settlement of ISAAC E. OGDEN's estate by JOHN M. FANNER, administrator

Attorneys with offices in Woodville: A. S. RANDOLPH, PRESTON W. FARRAR, A. M. DUNN, J. W. GILDART & J. J. EVELETH, and THOMAS C. WEST.

CALEB SWAYZE, adm'r., of DAVID SWAYZE's estate

BENJ. KILLGORE resigns as administrator to the estate of WILLIAM ANDERSON, deceased.

NANCY BENTLEY, admr'x., of THOMAS BENTLEY's estate

JOHN JINKS & JAS. QUINE warns public not to trade for note obtained by WM. CONNER.

January 12, 1833

ALFRED BYNUM will practice Law in the Courts.

SUSANNA HAMPTON, adm'r., of HENRY HAMPTON's estate

Land belonging to the PATRICK FOLEY's estate is to be sold.

Land belonging to heirs of BENJAMIN THERRELL is to be sold by JESSE BROWN, guardian of ALBERT P. & JOSEPH E. THERRELL.

JOSEPH SMITH & L. D. BROWN, admr's., of J. J. STOCKETT's estate, will sell personal estate in January, 1832.

Wm. W. PEARSON, exec'r., of NANCY RAIFORD's estate in Pike Co.

Land to be sold by heirs of JAMES O. COSBY.

CHARITY SMITH & MOSES GINN, adm'rs., of ABNER SMITH's estate

WILLIAM L. BAIRD, adm'r., of MICHAEL MURPHY's estate

T. E. SHANNON, exec'r of MARY SHANNON's estate

H. CONNELL, the appointed adm'r., of JOHN CONNELL's estate, will sell land next to land of Judge McGHEE and ELIZA CONNELL's dower land.

Married Thursday evening last, by the Rev. Mr. Bertron, Doctor SAMUEL LESSLEY to Miss MARY KAIGLER, daughter of Mr. WILLIAM KAIGLER, all of this county.

Married Thursday the 27th December, by Bishop Wm. E. MATHEWS, Mr. JOHN A. BECKEM to Miss JANE B. COLEMAN, all of this co.

SARAH NEWSON vs. ARMOND M. BOURGH

ALVIN B. MAGOUN vs. ARMAND M. BOURGH

Final settlement of JACOB HOLLIMAN's estate

Sale of the estate of THOMAS FOSTER, has been

postponed by exectors, WM. K. COLLINS, WM. BARNARD and DANL. McMILLAN.

January 19, 1833
JONES H. SMITH vs. WILLIAM HANEY

Married in this town, Jan. 2nd, by the Rev. Mr. WELLER, Mr. LEWIS CHARLES LEVIN, of Mississippi, to Miss ANN HAYS, daughter of ANDREW HAYS, Esqr. (Originally from the NASHVILLE BANNER)

Died at the residence of her uncle, JUDGE JOHNSON, the 16th, RACHEL NEAL DILLAHUNTY, 9 Yrs of age, daughter of WM. DILLAHUNTY.

Final settlement of ISAAC E. OGDEN's estate

January 26, 1833
JAMES CAIN intends to apply for forfeited Land Stock purchased May 4, 1811, by PETER GLOVER.

F. R. RICHARDSON appointes HIRAM SINGLETON his lawful agent.

BENJAMIN KILLGORE, adm'r., of WILLIAM ANDERSON's estate will sell sundry property belonging to the estate.

Married at the residence of J. P. Gilbert, Esqr., in Raymond, the 17th of January, by the Rev. Mr. Comfort of Clinton, MEREDITH S. BRECKENRIDGE, Esqr., formerly of Staunton, Vs. one of the firm of Wallace & Breckenridge, merchants of the former place, to Miss ELIZA ANN DAWSON, daughter of the late Judge DAWSON, of Wilkinson County.

February 2, 1833
A Country School Teacher wanted--apply to H. D. KELLOG, Esqr.

S. & S. TILLOTSON vs. WILLIAM TARVER. Amite co. Commissioners appointed for estate of THOS J. ROBINSON: R. A. NEELEY, WM. A. KNOX, and E.M. DAVIS.

Commissioners appointed for estate of WILLS DRAKE: CATO C. WEST, DAVID ARMSTRONG, and Wm. A.A. CHISHOLM.

ELENDER STEPHENSON, admr'x., of the WILLIAM STEPHENSON estate

February 9, 1833

Died at Holmesville, Pike County, Miss., on the 17th, Mr. JAMES L. REED, a citizen of that place.

LOUISA HAYES, admr'x., of MARK HAYES's estate

February 16, 1833

Died in this town on Saturday last, Mr. EDWARD FELTUS, Clerk of the Probate Court of Wilkinson County and member of the Masonic Polar Star Lodge.

Married in this town the 15th, by C. C. WEST, Esq, EDWARD MORTON, member of the American Theatre, New Orleans, to Miss CATHERINE JANE CASSEALES, of the same city.

February 23, 1833

Died the 12th, THOMAS, infant son of Mr. L. LOVELACE, 22 Mos.

WM. BROOKS vs. NANCY POOL and others. Mentions BLUFORD BROOKS

March 2, 1833

Final settlement of CHARLES A. COON's estate

Married the 20th by WILLIAM STEWART, Esqr., Doct. SOLOMON WEATHERSBY to Miss JULIA ANN BENNET, all of Amite County.

Died the 26th, JAMES REID after an illness of twenty days.

NELSON P. BURTON, adm'r., of WILLIAM PERDUE's estate

Mrs. E. S. EGGLESTON's boarding house recently occupied by Mr. ALEX SMITH, is situated a few rods south of the Court House.

Final settlement by JESSE BELL, guardian of JANE McGRAW

March 9, 1833

ALEXANDER HUGHES has taken up a bay horse.

ELIZABETH COON, adm'rx., of LEWIS W. COON's estate

H. LARD, exec'r., of THOMAS LARD's estate

March 16, 1833

MARY NETTERVILLE, guardian and late admr'x., of JEREMIAH NETTERVILLE's estate, will sell all the estate.

March 23, 1833
Died in this town on the 21st, Mrs. ANNE TOOLE.

Reward of 1 cent offered by THOMAS J. SMITH for an indentured apprentice to the Wagon making business, GEORGE W. HALL.

NELSON B. BURTON, adm'r., of Wm. W. PERDUE's estate

Copartnership of D. C. HENDERSON & L. C. GLASS has been dissolved.

GEO. HOWELL's adm'r. vs. ISAAC BUSH's adm'r. & J. L. BRUCE

March 31, 1833
DUNCAN STEWART will apply for forfeited land stock entered in 1811 by NATHANIEL BARR, and forfeited in 1817.

Wm STEWART appointed exec'r., of CLEMENT TOWNSEND's estate

Married the 24th by Rev. J. C. BURRUSS, at the residence of Governor A. M. SCOTT, near Woodville, PRESTON W. FARRAR, Esqr., to Miss ELIZA J. SCOTT, only daughter of Governor Scott.

Married at Natchez the 25th, by Rev. GEO. POTTS, Doct. CHARLES H. STONE, of Woodville, to Miss MARY G. NEWMAN, of Natchez.

Married the 28th, by BYTHALL HAYNES, Esqr., Mr. DAVID BOLAND to Miss DRUSILLA McGRAW, daughter of DARLING McGRAW, all of this county.

Commissioners appointed for the JOSEPH P. HENLEY estate in Nov. 1832: DAVID ARMSTRONG, T. C. BROWN, and A. DANIEL.

Commissioners appointed in March 1833, for the ORAIN HICKS's estate: M. M. WHITNEY, R. M. NELSON, and JOHN WALKER.

GEORGE P. TOOLE, adm'r., for ANNE TOOLE's estate

April 6, 1833
ROBERT HANNAH vs. WM. THOMPSON HANNAH. Also states that RICHARD DREAR AND JANE DREAR as not residents

in Miss.

Died at Whitestown, on the 4th, Mr. HENRY FERGUSON, Age 30 yrs.

Died in this city on Monday, Mr. NELSON WOOSTER, 23 years of age.

April 13, 1833

ABRAM ILER gave Deed of Trust to MICHAEL WOODS. ILER owed BENJAMIN LEWIS $2,200.25. Iler's property must be sold to settle debt.

S. D. PLATNER, adm'r., of GEORGE A. FOSTER's estate

LEWIS M. GARRETT, adm'r., of HIRAM SINGLETON's estate

April 20, 1833

CHARLES C. MAYSON, Esqr., has issued proposals for publishing a newspaper at Jackson to be entitled the, STATE RIGHTS BANNER.

JOHN W. LEATHERMAN, is a candidate for the Board of County Police, DAVID McNEELY, candidate for Tax Collecton, FELIX E. STEPHENS & WM BROWN, candidates for County Surveyor, and JOHN I. GUION of Warren Co., a candidate for Attorney General.

April 27, 1833

Died Tuesday evening, Mr. BENJ. S. COLLIER, an aged and respectable citizen of this county was thrown off his horse and under a passing wagon and died an hour later.

Died the 23rd, in the 78 year of his age, Mr. BYTHELL HAYES. He was a soldier in the revolution and for the last 25 years, a citizen of this county.

Married the 18th, by the Hon. JOHN B. DAWSON, General WILLIAM L. BRANDON, of this county to Miss ANN ELIZA RATLIFF, of West Feliciana.

Married the 18th by BYTHELL HAYNES, Esq., Mr. WILLIAM C. IRWIN of Yazoo County, to Miss MARGARET A. ANDERSON, daughter of Mr. DANIEL ANDERSON, of Wilkinson.

Commissioners appointed for the ELIZABETH DIXON estate: MOSES PHARES, Wm. W. USHER, and JOHN

SCOTT.   April 1833 term

WM. T. JONES, adm'r., of RICHARD JONES's estate

BYTHELL HAYNES, Jr. & BALDWIN HAYNES, ex'rs., of the BYTHELL HAYNES's estate   April 1833 term

May 4, 1833

ANNA McCOMAS petitions to have her dower set off. Two lots and houses in Natchez conveyed by JAMES C. WILKINS and wife to her dec'd., husband, JOSIAS H. McCOMAS.

Married April 23rd, by JOSEPH PATTERSON, Esqr. Mr. NOLAND M. LUCKETT, of Jefferson County Kentucky, to Miss ANN C. TIGNER daughter of Capt. Wm. TIGNER, of this county.

Died near Whitesville, in this county last Saturday, Mr. THOMAS W. WEST.

THOS. I. LIPSCOMB lost a Pocket Book containing a note on BENJ. SELLERS of Amite Co., payable to SAML. GOODRICH. Also one school account on THOS. W. WEST.

ELIZABETH BRYANT, admr'x., of ANDREW BRYANT 's estate

PRECILLA CAWSEY, widow & admr'x., of JOHN H. CAWSEY of Amite County, petitions for her dower.

WM. REID, ex'r., of JAMES REID's estate

May 11, 1833

Died at his residence in this County, 1 mile West of Woodville, the 5th, Mr. DAVID CALLIHAM, 67 yrs. He had resided in this county for many years.

SAML. W. LEWIS to sell his property in Fort Adams now occupied by JOHN TIMON. Apply to DANL. C. LEWIS or self.

NANCY FORD, adm'x., & WM. HASLIP, adm'r., of ROBERT FORD's estate. March Term 1833

JOHN C. SIMS, guardian of SARAH BAILEY will sell property

May 18, 1833

Married the 7th, by the Rev. JAMES A. RANALDON, Mr. THOMAS SHANNON of this county to Miss PAMELIA

WOODS, daughter of Mr. ISHAM WOODS, of the Parish of West Feliciana, La.

DAVID ARMSTRONG, adm'r., of ROBERT LYTLE's estate

Deed of Trust issued July 8, 1831 by A. W. ALLEN to Wm. T. LEWIS, to secure to CLEMENT TOWNSEND a certain sum. Sale will take place May 21.

May 25, 1833
JOHANA WOODS, admx., & GERARD C. BRANDON, admr., for SAMUEL WOODS's estate

Married at the residence of JOHN A. GRIMBALL, Secretary of the State, by the Rev. Mr. BRYANT, Dr. DAVID McRAE, of Green City, to Miss ELIZA A. GRIMBALL, of Hinds.

June 1, 1833
Married by the Hon. JOSEPH FORD, Maj. S. M. CATCHING, of Pike, to Miss EADY S. DRAKE, of Marion County, Mississippi.

THOMAS WOODSIDE, admr., of Wm. WOODSIDE's estate

Final settlement of the ARCHIBALD KNOX's estate by Wm. A. KNOX, adm'r., at the June Term, 1833.

CAROLINE M. GUINN, admr'x., for JESSE GUINN's estate

JOHN HENDERSON, trustee for JOHN STEVENS.

June 8, 1833
Married on Thursday evening last by the Hon. A. S. RANDOLPH, Mr. LEWIS DAVIS to Miss MARTHA OCTAVIA WEST, daughter of the late THOMAS W. WEST., all of this county.

Dr. A. L. KEAGY, dentist, has returned to Woodville to make it his permanant residence as well as to practice.

June 15, 1833
Letter to the editor from JAMES G. BIRNEY, Gen'l. Agent of the American Colored Society.

Died in Roanoke, the Hon. JOHN RANDOLPH, in the 60th year of his age. (Originally from the NASHVILLE BANNER)

Married Tuesday by DANIEL BASS, Esq., Mr. RICHARD

T. CHRISTMAS to Miss MARY M. SIMS, daughter of Capt. JOHN SIMS, all of this co.

Married the 9th by the Rev. T. C. BROWN, Mr. HUGH McCRANE to Mrs. ELIZABETH COON, all of this county.

June 22, 1833

A flea bitten grey horse was taken up by Mrs. MARY WOODWARD.

Commissioners appointed for the dec'd., ADAM HOPE's estate meet the 1st Tues of each month: WALTHALL BURTON, SAMUEL LEATHERMAN, and THOS. S. HERBERT.

G. D. BOYD is holding notes and accounts of E. THOMPSON.

Deed of Trust held by C. P. SMITH & A. M. DUNN, will sell items held by WILLIAM DODD; the same lot conveyed to Dodd by JAMES M. WOOD and wife, and JOHN H. COATS, Sept. 1832. Also JAMES MURCH and wife are mentioned in connection to another lot.

June 29, 1833

Commissioners appointed for the dec'd., JOHN L. BRUCE's estate: C. C. WEST, J. J. EVELETH, and JESSE SAUNDERS.

Died at Cherry-Field in this county, the 15th, Mrs. SUSAN HAMPTON, aged 72 years, consort of the late Col. HENRY HAMPTON.

Died at Natchez the 19th, Mr. CHARLES WOOSTER, Publisher of the "Mississippi Journal".

ELIZABETH CHANDLER, admx., & JAMES M. NORWOOD, adm'r., of the JAMES CHANDLER's estate in Amite County.

STEPHEN TILDON surrenders his adm'r., on JAMES M. CROPPER 's estate. September Term, 1833

Last will of ELIJAH THERRELL, Sr. said to sell property, DANIEL LEATHERMAN, & JOHN B. THERRELL

July 6, 1833

Letters of WM STEWART, exec'r., of CLEMENT TOWNSEND's estate, will be surrendered at the next July term for final settlement.

Died at his residence on Buffaloe in this county, on Saturday, in the 68th year of his age, Mr. JOHN BROWN who has been a resident in this county for the last 28 years.

Died at Clinton the 26th, R. P. CATLETT, Esqr., editor of the "Mississippian".

MARGARET ANN ODUM, adm'rx., of the SHADRACH ODUM's estate

ROBERT POOLE, admr., of NAZARA POOLE's estate.

July 13, 1833

Fatal occurrence: Mr. BENJAMIN MITCHELL and his son, STEPHEN T. MITCHELL, were fighting with Mr. Wm. T. ROBINSON, at the store house of GEORGE FINUCANE, in this place. Mr. WILLIAM UNDERWOOD attempted to seperate the individuals and was stabbed in the heart and died within five minutes.

The Rev. JOHN McCLLOCH will preach in the Baptist Church.

Died the 3rd, Mrs. MARY H. WEBB, 20 yrs., wife of Dr. NOAH WEBB, leaving an infant child, an afflicted husband and relatives.

Died July 8th at his residence near Woodville, Col. CHARLES STEWART, 24 yrs. of age, the only unmarried child of Mr. CHARLES STEWART, with whom he lived.

July 20, 1833

A. M. DUNN & H. M. FARISH have a law office in Woodville upstairs in Wm. H. WHITE's new building on Commercial row. May 23, 1833.

JOHN HUTCHINS, a native of Mississippi, born and raised in Adams County, publishes his "Remarks on Cholera".

Married on the 11th, by JOHN DUNCKLEY, Esqr., Mr. WILLIAM A. BROWN to Miss MARGARET B. TURBEVILLE, 3rd daughter of Mr. SAMUEL TURBEVILLE, all of this county.

Died on the 15th, at Arrundale, the residence of FRANCIS A. EVANS, MARY R. FOLEY, 8 yrs. of age, and daughter of Mrs. M. R. FOLEY.

Died July 3rd, COMMODORE BROOKS, age 5 years,

11 months, & 27 days.

JAMES CALLIHAN, exec'r., of DAVID CALLIHAM's estate

July 27, 1833

Died Wednesday after a short illness, Mrs. MARY CALLIHAM, consort of the late DAVID CALLIHAM.

THOS. J. BROWN, exec'r., of JOHN BROWN's estate

JOHN BUTLER of Amite Co., on the 27th, who killed his nephew-in-law JOHN KNOX, fled to Texas, but has been taken, and on Monday last was lodged in the jail in this county. The reward will fall to Mr. MOSES SEALE & Mr. WILLIAM MONTGOMERY of Amite. (Originally from the NATCHEZ COURIER)

Col. AARON BURR who is now in his 80th year, has been united in matrimony to a Mrs. ELIZA JUMEL of New York.

August 10, 1833

Died at Whitesville, the 23rd, WILLIAM LEWIS PECK, aged three years, the son of Mrs. LOUISA H. PECK.

Died at Natchez the 28th, Mrs. MARIA MARSHALL, wife of L. R. MARSHALL, Esqr., formerly of this town.

It is with feelings of pain and regret, that we announce the death of Mr. PETER ISLER, for many years known as Printer of this State. By his children who were motherless, this loss will be long felt. (Originally from the STATES RIGHTS' BANNER, Jackson, Ms.)

JESSE BELL vs. HENRY R. NERSON

THOMAS I. NERSON vs. JOHN F. SAPP

STEPHEN H. STRONG vs. JOHN JAMES

THOMAS TURNER vs. WILLIAM W. YERBY

JOHN BELL vs. WILLIAM W. YERBY

WILLIAM STRICKLAND, adm'r., for HENRY DICKERSON's estate

August 17, 1833

Adm'r., states that possessions of EDWARD WATKINS

is not sufficient to pay debts of said estate. Need to sell same

JAMES MEED, adm'r., in right of wife of JOHN WAIT, dec'd, will sell land in both Laurence and Amite Counties.

Died the 13th, age 50, Mrs. NANCY LEWIS, wife of Col. JOHN S. LEWIS, of this town and a member of the Methodist Church.

Died the 16th at Fort Adams, CHRISTOPHER E. HALL MILLER, age 7 months, only son of WILLIAM MILLER.

Died at Port Gibson, Dr. JAMES S. CARRAWAY, formerly of this town.

Died of Cholera, at Belleville, Illinois, July 20th, NINIAN EDWARDS, late Governor of that state.

N. S. WEBB will dispose of his house in Pickenyville.

August 24, 1833
A bright sorrel horse was taken up by A. HOLMES.

Taken up as a stray by A. GETTER (ARGULAS GETER\ JETER), a bay horse, valued at $60.

August 31, 1833
Final settlement of ZACHARIAH SMITH's estate

Final settlement of BENJAMIN SMITH's estate

Final settlement of JOSEPH P. HENLEY's estate

JAMES JONES appointed D. C. HENDERSON as agent while absent

Died the 26th, WILLIAM W. OGDEN, 27 yrs, son of GEORGE OGDEN. He left a wife and infant son, friends and relatives.

Died the 26th, DUNCAN STEWART, Esqr., 28 yrs. Left a devoted father, a kind and loving wife, and a sweet little son.

A. H. CHAMBERS, adm'r., of EDWARD WATKINS's estate will sell land purchased from ADAM HOPE's adm'r., who had purchased land from JOHN B. POSEY and wife.

September 7, 1833

SAM'L S. BOYD has left his unsettled affairs in the hands of Col. GEO. H. GORDON who has authority to act for Boyd.

ROBERT J. DAVIS & JOHN E. PALMER, guardians, will sell land that belong to heirs of DAVIS, NICHOLSON and others.

Property of WRIGHT ELLINGTON, dec'd., will be sold by the administrator.

Died the 1st, at his residence on Ford's Creek, JOHN DUNCKLEY, Esqr., 55 yrs, of congestive fever.

Died the 2nd, Mrs. LEONORA (LENORA) GORDON, 18 yrs., consort of Col. GEORGE H. GORDON.

Died the 3rd, of malignant fever, 27 yrs, Mr. SAMUEL BROWN. A native of Newburyport, Massachusetts, and for some times past, a resident of this village.

JOHN S. LEWIS vs. DANL. WOODWARD.

LYDIA DOWELL vs. DANL. WOODWARD.

DR. YOUNG BURKE, Surgeon Dentist, has his office in the Woodville Hotel.

TABITHA HARLEP, adm'rx., of ADAM HARLEP's estate

T. J. SPURLOCK, adm'r., of JOSIAH SPURLOCK's estate

K. DUNBAR has erected a large building on the corner next below Mr. J. C. MORRIS'.

Married in Bolton, Mass, July 31st by the Rev. J. W. CHICKERING, Mr. GUSTAVUS U. RICHARDS, of New York, to Miss ELECTRA B. WILDER, daughter of S. V. S. WILDER, Esqr., of Bolton. (Originally from the MASSACHUSETTS YEOMAN)

September 14, 1833

MARY GRIFFIN & JOHN GRIFFIN, ex'rs., of FURNY GRIFFIN's estate in Amite county

W. W. WHITEHEAD gives authority to JOHN HENDERSON to handle his affairs for the next five or six weeks.

For sale: GEORGE OGDEN's plantation seven miles from Ft. Adams, 140 acres, good dwelling house, negro cabins and a stock of hogs and cattle. See D. C. HENDERSON or self.

FRENCH GOLD WATCH on ribbon chain lost near the courthouse by WILLIAM BROWN. Liberal reward offered.

Stolen out of the house of DAVIS & BELL, a small black morocco pocket book containing a note to D. DURANT & a note to PETER STARNS. JAS. M. DAVIS

A. G. FOSTER & CO. vs. DANL. WOODARD

Poem written in memory of Mrs. LEONORA W. GORDON aged 18.

JOHN CAMPBELL, one of the ex'rs., of the JOHN CAMPBELL estate will sell land in Amite Co., Ms.

Died the 6th, 5 yrs. of age, SARAH ELEANOR BURTON, eldest dau. of WALLTHALL BURTON, of this county.

Died the 30th, THOMAS D. McNULTY, infant son of Mr. JOHN McNULTY.

Died the 18th, JULIETT WALKER and on the 2nd, WILLIAM WALKER only children of Mr. JOHN WALKER, of Amite Co.

Died at New Orleans Sept. 1, SOLON HILL, Esqr., formerly a citizen of this county.

September 21, 1833

Died on the 11th, of the prevailing fever of the county, WILLIAM DILLAHUNTY, youngest son of JOHN and ELIZA DILLAHUNTY, aged 18 months and 20 days.

Died on the 11th, near Ft. Adams, JAMES HAYES, 49 yrs of age, a native and worthy citizen of this county.

Died on the 19th, CHARLES HENRY WHITE and on the following day, SUSANNAH VIRGINIA WHITE, children of JAMES & HARRIET B. WHITE, of this town.

Died near Clinton, Louisiana on the 11th, of the prevailing fever of the country, LAWRENCE B. DAVIS, of Baltimore, Maryland, Assistant Engineer on the Rail Road.

WILLIAM W. YERBY will sell interest in Cabin Hall Plantation near Pinckneyville, Ms.

Copartnership dissolved between RICHARD COTTER & JOHN LENNOX. Debts owed to THOMAS C.WEST.

FRANCIS MAYES took up a sorrel horse.

Commissioners for dec'd., THOMAS J.ROBINSON's estate will meet in Liberty, on the 4th Tuesday of each month.

Stolen from J. H. WHEELER's trunk, two pocket books which contain notes to Wm. H. WHITE and JAMES WHITE.

D. B. THOMPSON vs. JOSEPH PORCHE

JAMES L. TRASK vs. JOSEPH PORCHE

B. MARSHALL vs. JOHN STEVENS

JOHN DEAL vs. DANL. WOODARD

M. CARSON HOWIE vs. DANL. WOODARD

A. G. FOSTER vs. DANL. WOODARD

September 28, 1833
Died the 15th in this town, JOHN JOOR, 5 yrs. old, the eldest son of WILLIAM T. and EMILY MAYES.

Died, Mr. JAMES MAYES, formerly of this county.

Died the 15th, Mrs. SUSAN T. GILDART, consort of JOHN W. GILDART, Esquire.

October 5, 1833
Died in this county on Saturday morn, Sept. 21st, CATHARINE STEWART, aged 4 yrs, 5 mo, 5 da. and on the 30th of the same month, McDOUGAL STEWART aged 10 mo and 15 da., both children of JOHN J. & MARY COLLINS.

Died in this town, Oct 1st, Mr. DANIEL RICE.

Married the 24, Mr. THOMAS C. REED to Miss NANCY BENTLEY, all of this town. (Published Wilkinson County Marriage Records state her name as NANCY BENTHAL)

Married Sept 26th, by the Hon. A. S. RANDOLPH,

JAMES MUSE, Esqr., of La., to Miss JULIA EDWARDS, daughter of Mr. CHARLES EDWARDS of this county.

Married on Sept 27th, by Bishop Wm. E. MATHEWS, Mr. JOHN BRIGGS to Miss MARY ADALINE CASTON.

October 12, 1833

EZEKIEL BOATNER, adm'r., of dec'd., QUIN MASSY's estate in Amite Co. September Term, 1833

D. C. HENDERSON, adm'r., for ROBERT McCREARY's estate, makes final settlement.

October 19, 1833

ALONZO PHELPS who murdered OWEN RHODES was captured in Holmes County. Captured by JAMES NEVILL at THOMAS NEVILL's house. Evidence as to murder is entirely circumstantial. (Originally from the VICKSBURG REGISTER)

Died the 7th, Doc. EDWARD T. FARISH, in the Choctaw Nation.

Died in this town on Thursday, Doct. A. L. KEAGY.

Married in Woodville the 17th, by Rev. THOMAS C. BROWN, Doct. YOUNG BURKE to Miss SARAH MATILDA SMITH, daughter of the late Capt. PRESTWOOD SMITH.

October 26, 1833

HIRAM RALPH has taken up a grey mare mule.

Died the 21st, Mrs. PATSEY CONNELL, consort of HUGH CONNELL, Esquire.

Died the 24th, Mr. Wm. NEWELL

Died the 16th, Mr. DANIEL MURPHREY, 23 years of age and leaves a wife.

Died at his residence in East Feliciana on the 19th, Capt. W. J. BOATNER, in the 44th year of his life, and leaves a wife.

Died the 7th, at the house of R. M. WILLIAMS, Esqr., N. G. HOWARD, Esqr., late Representative from Rankin Co., in the State Legislature. (Oiginally from the STATE RIGHTS BANNER)

Died the 10th at Clinton, Miss., Major THOMAS W. GWIN of Washington Co. Miss., late of Sumner County, Tenn. (Originally from the STATE RIGHTS

BANNER)

Died in Yazoo County, last week, Dr. FLOYD, a physician, and former Representative in the State Legislature.

Final settlement of LUCRETIA STUART's estate

<u>November 2, 1833</u>
STEPHEN JOHNSON, adm'r., of DANIEL RICE's estate

<u>November 9, 1833</u>
The gin house of A. DUNBAR burned. Loss of $5,000

Died the 31st, WILLIAM NETTERVILLE, aged 69.

Died the 30th, Mr. WILLIAM B. CONNER

Died lately in this county, Mr. ROBERT E. LOVE

Died the 31st, Mr. GEORGE W. CARTER

M. E. OGDEN, adm'r., of WILLIAM W. OGDEN's estate

JOHN L. WALL & ALEX E. WALL, ex'rs., of the deceased DANIEL WILLIAMS' estate.

JOHN L. WALL, was appointed the adm'r., of both EDMUND GINN and ELIZA A. GINN's estate.

JOHN B. FORD has taken up a stray.

STEPHEN JOHNSON, adm'r., of DANIEL RICE's estate

D. C. HENDERSON, adm'r., of ROBERT McCLEARY's estate, will present the final settlement.

T. J. SPURLOCK, the adm'r., of JOSIAH SPURLOCK's estate will sell land.

School land offered for lease by J. W. LEATHERMAN, President. (T1, R3, W.)

School land offered for lease by F. R. RICHARDSON, President. (T1, R1. W.)

900 Acres for sale by FRANCIS R. RICHARDSON who ownes one half in his own right and the other half belongs to heirs of H. SINGLETON.

JAS BRADFORD of La.,wishes to sell his place on the Mississippi River, in the Parish of West

Feliciana, adjoining the town of St. Francisville. Contains 1500-2000 acres of land.

November 16, 1833

JOHN HENDERSON, exec'r., of ABRAM M. SCOTT's estate

ALEX M. DUNN, adm'r., of SARAH A. DUNN's estate

LYDIA H. NEWELL & E. H. WAILES, guardians of the heirs of GEORGE B. NEWELL, will sell a tract of land (287 acres) known as the "Hammet Tract".

EZEKIEL BOATNER, adm'r., of GREEN MASSY's estate

JAMES BUFORD, exec'r., of JOHN Y. CALLIHAM's estate

Attorneys practicing in Woodville: SAM'L S. BOYD, A. M. DUNN, H. M. FARISH, GEORGE H. GORDON, SAM'L. S. BOYD, A. S. RANDOLPH, WM. S. GRIFFIN, PRESTON W. FARRAR, J. W. GILDART, J. J. EVELETH, and CHAUNCEY S. and H. D. KELLOGG., August 17th, 1833.

PHILIP NOLAND, adm'r.,of STEPHEN M. NOLAND, will present his final account and settlement.

JOSEPH J. EVELETH, adm'r., of ADAM L. KEAGY's estate

M. E. OGDEN, admr'x., of WM. W. OGDEN's estate will sell at the house of MARGARET COLE, all the perishable property of the estate.

ALEX E. WALL, adm'r., of SARAH WALL's estate

F. R. RICHARDSON, guardian of RICHARD, FRANCIS and AMANDA SINGLETON, minor heirs of HIRAM SINGLETON, will sell 148 acres known as the "Johnson Tract".

WILLIAM STAMPS & HAZLEWOOD M. FARISH,adm'rs., of EDWARDS T. FARISH's estate

GEO. FRAZIER wishes to sell 10 or 12 good horses.

Married on Sunday last, by the Rev. Mr. Burtron, Doct. J. C. PATRICK to Mrs. ELIZA CONNELL, all of this county.

JOHN RICHMOND, adm'r., of JAMES RICHMOND's

estate, plans to sell land.

DAVID DAVIS, adm'r., of NARSWORTHY HUNTER's, estate

JOHN L. WALL & JEHU CARLILE, appointed ex'rs., of JOHN H. DURANT's estate

GEORGE OGDEN will sell plantation on which he resides, seven miles from Fort Adams, containing 140 acres. Apply to D. C. HENDERSON at Woodville.

November 23, 1833

Commissioners appointed for the estate of the dec'd., EDWARD WATKINS, will hold their meetings at the store of A. G. FOSTER & Co. in Woodville.

JANE ANDERSON, admr'x., of HARRIS ANDERSON's estate

NATHAN SWAYZE, adm'r., of LYDIA CORY's estate

JAMES VARNELL & MELISSA MURPHREY, ex'r., & exr'x., of DANIEL MURPHREY's estate

ANDREW ADAMS, exec'r., of LUCRETIA STUART, will present his final accounts.

Jewelry and watches left with A. W. ALLEN amd not redeemed, will be sold.

JAMES BUFORD, ex'r., of JOHN Y. CALLIHAM's estate

November 30, 1833

TABITHA HARLESS, admr'x., of ADAM HARLESS's estate

Final settlement of THOS. SCOTT estate, by JOHN F. SCOTT, administrator.

STEPHEN JOHNSON, adm'r., of DANIEL RICE's estate

Married the 27th by the Rev. Wm. Winans, JOHN S. WALTON, Esqr., Merchant of New Orleans, to Miss CYNTHIA ANN, eldest daughter of the Hon. EDWARD McGEHEE, of this county.

Married the 21st by JAMES JENKINS, Esqr., Mr. WILLIAM HAYNES, of Wilkinson to Miss ELIZABETH, daughter of PETER FAUST, of Amite.

JOHN T. SEMPLE was born the 4th November,

1804, and departed this life on the 24th of the same month, aged 29 years and 20 days.

JAMES HAYGOOD, adm'r., of JOHN HAYGOOD's estate in Amite County.

JAMES DUNCKLEY, adm'r of JOHN DUNCKLEY's estate

NANCY BARKLEY & M. E. SAUNDERS, admr'x., & adm'r., of GLASS C. BARKLEY's estate

N. N. McCARSTLE, adm'r., of E. D. McCARSTLE's estate

JESSE BROWN, adm'r., of LUCINDA BAILEY's estate and also guardian of MARY BAILEY

GEORGE H. SWIGART, adm'r., of ELIZA HEADY's estate

Taken up by JOHN M. DELOACH, a dark bay mare

THOMAS B. NETTERVILLE, Administrator debonis non of JESSE NETTERVILLE, dec'd., will sell at his residence about three miles of Woodville, the personal estate of said deceased. November 27, 1833

L. D. BROWN surrenders his Letters of Executorship on the estate of JOHN L. BRUCE, deceased.

L. D. BROWN, guardian of Miss ELIZA BRUCE will present his accounts for final settlement.

F. A. EVANS, exec'r., of the estate of ELIZABETH METCALF will present his accounts for final settlement.

December 7, 1833
NANN, a female slave, the property of Mr. GEORGE MOSS, was tried and found guilty at the last term of the Wilkinson Circuit Court of poisoning her master's family (two of whom died) was in pursuance of the sentence of the court, hung in the vicinity of this town on Friday.

January 4, 1834
Died, at his residence in this county, on the 25th December last, Mr. JESSE BROWN.
Died, in this place on Thursday night, SOLOMON, aged about 68 years. He had been a faithful and honest slave for 54 years, when at the death of

his owner in 1819, he was released from bondage, and at her particular request, remained free till the period of his death.

E. P. KING desires to sell 640 acres of land located on the Louisiana side of the river.

JOHN G. POINDEXTER & LEWIS MORRIS have dissolved their partnership.

Petition of JAMES LYNE, guardian of THOMAS VAUGHAN and THOMAS B. REID, in right of his Wife, and THOMAS B. NETTERVILLE in his own right, wishes to sell a certain tract of land as it cannot be divided equally.

JESSE JONES & W. F. TAYLOR, ex'rs., of the JOHN JONES's estate, will present the estate's final settlement.

"SAMUEL DELOACH & THOMAS S. NEWMAN have entered into a Copartnership, DELOACH & NEWMAN which will conduct a general Grocery and Produce, blended with the Commission and Fowarding, business. It will be located in the house formerly occupied by Mr. Z. CANFIELD, near the Steam Boat Landing at Bayou Sarah." December 28th, 1833

SAMUEL DELOACH plantation for sale, containing 160 Acres, 60 acres cleared land, spring and necessary buildings. It is known by Edwards' place, bounded by JOHN OGDEN, JAMES LEECH, and the Ragged Hill place.

SAML. V. MITCHELL will resume his "School" on Monday.

Final settlement of JOHN JONES' estate. JESSE JONES & W. F. TAYLOR, executors.

All property, real, personal and slaves, belonging to the succession of WILLIAM OGDEN, to be sold.

Post Office at Whitesville is discontinued. All mail is to be picked up in Woodville. PARKER SMITH, Post Master.

Final settlement of SAMUEL PICKENS' estate

January 11, 1834

JAMES F. CONNER, adm'r., of Wm. B. CONNER's

estate

A certain tract of land that is to be sold for court cost, involves JOHN CONNER and HIRAM FOULER.

THOMAS I. NERSON vs. JOHN F. SAPP   500 acres of land is to be sold to cover court cost.

STEVENS & PILLETT vs. DAN'L WOODWARD   30 acres of land on Percy's Creek, the late residence of HIRAM A. BERRY, is to be sold to cover court cost.

REBECCA T. COLEMAN, admr'x ., of LINSAY COLEMAN's estate on December 17, 1833.

ROBERT C. SHEPARD vs. JOHN STEVENS   A certain lot of ground upon which stands the two story house, known as "The Woodville Hotel" and now used as a tavern, by the "Woodville Hotel Company", and located on the south side of the public square, is to be sold.

BENJAMIN F. YOUNG, was appointed adm'r., of JOHN T. SEMPLE's estate on December 30, 1833.

HUGH CONNELL was appointed adm'r., of dec'd KINCHEN HOLLIMAN's estate on December 27, 1833.

Wm T. MAYES, guardian of ROBERT & LEVI CARSON, infant children of WILHAM and LEVICY CARSON dec'd., and PHILIP NOLAND, guardian of MARY L. NOLAND, infant heir of CATHARINE NOLAND, dec'd., & WILLIAM COLEMAN, in his own right, will sell a tract of land (400 arpents). Bounded by lands of ROBERT NORWOOD, FRANCIS S. MAYES, and WILLIAM HUNTER. Land is the same purchased by LEVICY COLEMAN of PETER PRESSLER, Senr., deceased. December 23, 1833

MARY JONES, THOS. J. SPURLOCK, and WM. JONES, were appointed adm'rs., of the dec'd., HENRY JONES's estate on December 10, 1833. They intend to sell several lots of land.

DELANEY TRAVIS was appointed admr'x., to the dec'd., WILSON TRAVIS's estate at the October Term of the Orphans Court in Amite County.

PRECILLA CAWSEY, was appointed adm'x., of JOHN H. CAWSEY's estate. December 20, 1833

LAVICA MIXON, widow of O. MIXON, in pursuance of a petition in the Probate Court of Amite, I will apply for a writ to have my dower set off...

The copartnership of GORDON & BOYD has been dissolved. GEORGE H. GORDON will practice alone.

JOHN HENDERSON & SAML S. BOYD have formed a law partnership.

Lost, a note of hand drawn by JAMES LYNE and payable to OSCAR PILLETT. Signed by STEPHEN JOHNSON

WILLIAM W. PEARSON, executor of BENJAMIN BAGLEY's estate.

E. P. KING, has 640 acres of land to be sold.

Final settlement of JAMES S. WAIDE's estate

Final settlement of DUGALE B. THOMPSON's estate

January 18, 1834

WILLIAM DODD has taken up a white mare.

JAMES LEE has taken up a brown horse.

JOHN FRAZER has taken up a dun mare.

PHILLIP HUFF has lost a bay horse. Reward offered

All persons are cautioned against trading for a note drawn by me last December, in favor of STEPHEN JOHNSON. Signed by CHARLES HESTER

G. D. BOYD has all notes and accounts of EPHRAIM THOMPSON in hand, with positive instructions to sue all who owe Thompson.

Died at his residence in this Parish on Sunday, the 26th, LUTHER L. SMITH, Esqr., an old and respectable citizen leaving a wife and several children. (Originally from the ST.FRANCISVILLE PHOENIX)

R. H. HAILE, living on the road from Woodville to St. Francisville, 2 1/2 miles below Sligo, has lost, or has been stolen, a very high spirited black horse, and offers a liberal reward.

B. BOWREN offers two tracts of land lying in

Wilkinson County for sale. November 27, 1833

B. LOVELACE offers a tract of land, house, gin, mill, as well as the stock and corn. Apply to J. L. WALL at Fort Adams or the subscriber on the premises.

<u>January 25, 1834</u>

JESSE BELL, guardian of HENRY H. BELL, MARTHA JANE CURTIS, formerly MARTHA JANE BELL, and administrator of RUFFIN McGRAW, will present his accounts for final settlement.

JOHN FOULER vs. JOHN CONNER   80 acres to be sold to satisfy claim and court cost. The document also mentions Wm. B. DICKS.

THOMAS I. NERSON vs. JOHN F. SAPP   555 Acres to be sold to settle case and cost.

PATRICK FANNING vs. ABRAM M. GRAY and Wm. S. LEWIS, ABNER SMITH's adm'r., vs. A. M. GRAY & Wm. S. LEWIS. All claim, of WILLIAM S. LEWIS in a lot in the town of Woodville, presently occupied by LUCY YOUNG, and bounded by the property of WM. JOHNSON, which is now occupied by JOHN HENDERSON, and the house that EDWARD FELTUS occupied in 1832, is to be sold to the highest bidder to satisfy case and court cost.

All claim of JOHN STEVENS in a lot in the town of Woodville is to be sold. Suit mentions JAMES JONES & Wife, E. H. WAILED, DICK H. EGGLESTON, heirs of WILLIAM P. TRASK, and MICHAEL WOODS. Levied to satisfy court cost.

Died at his father's residence in Donegal, on the 7th, KINCHEN HOLLIMAN, son of Mr. Z. WALKER, aged 9 years. By his diligence and good behaviour he gained the esteem and affection of his tutors-- and from the facility with which he received instruction, and his ardent desire to excel in learning and virtue, gave hopes to his parents of future usefulness and distinction; but these fond hopes have been utterly blasted by his untimely death.

Died in Woodville, Wednesday night, at the house of Mr. STEPHEN JOHNSON, Mr. HALLETT POTTER, a native of the state of New Work.,and for several years past, a worthy citizen of this county.

Married the 23rd, by DANIEL BASS, Esqr., Mr. ADAM H. CHAMBERS to Miss SARAH N. SIMS.

Married the 16th, by Rev. Mr. BERTRON, Mr. ROBERT TURNER to Mrs. FRANCES ANN SHEPHERD.

Married the 12th, by BYTHELL HAYNES, Esqr., Mr. STEPHEN POYNER of Franklin, Tennessee to Miss ANN RATCLIFF.

JOHN PEEBLES was appointed adm'r., of C. W. PEEBLES' estate in the May term.

February 1, 1834

Died, on Friday morning, 24th January, at the house of his son, at Bayou Sara, of a sudden attack of the pleurisy, Mr. JESSE DELOACH, in the 55th year of his age--and for the last twenty-three years a useful and respectable planter of this state.

The partnership existing between Docts. THOMAS & JAMES LYNE, is dissolved by mutual consent.

February 8, 1834

Married on Friday 7th, at the Woodville Hotel, by DAN'L BASS, Esqr., Mr. CHARLES J. B. F. CASTELL to Miss LOUISA HENRETTA MICOUD, both of New Orleans.

JOHN C. SIMS was appointed adm'r., of JOHN SIMS' estate at the December Term, 1833.

HENRY LARD, adm'r., of THOMAS LARD's estate, will sell a parcel of land in Amite Co.

Final settlement of the SAMUEL C. HEADY estate

Final settlement of the SAMUEL PICKENS estate

Final settlement of the JOHN JONES estate

MICHAEL WOODS wishes to sell his house & lot located in the town of Woodville.

February 15, 1834

FRANCIS S. MAYES, adm'r., of JAMES MAYES' estate

CHARLES NETTERVILLE, Jr., adm'r., of WILLIAM NETTERVILLE's estate

WILEY DELOACH was appointed adm'r., of dec'd., JESSE DELOACH's estate. (His father)

MOSES GINN, surrenders his Letters of Testamentary on the estate of ABNER SMITH, desceased.

Final settlement of the SAMUEL BUSH estate

Died the 26th, at Washington, Mrs. REBBECA LEWIS, of Woodville, aged 46. (Originally from the NATCHEZ COURIER)

GEORGE B. COLLIER, adm'r., of HALLET POTTER's estate

WILLIAM L. BAIRD & NELLY LAW, were appointed admr's., of dec'd., HENRY LAW's estate.

JOHN C. SIMS, adm'r., of LUCINDA BAILEY's estate

JAMES F. CONNER, adm'r., of WILLIAM B. CONNER's estate will sell all personal estate of Conner. Sale will be held at the home of DANIEL LEATHERMAN.

DAVID LEATHERMAN was appointed adm'r., of EPHRAIM FLESHMAN's estate.

DAVID LEATHERMAN was appointed adm'r., of JULIA FLESHMAN's estate. (JULIA LEATHERMAN)

BOARD OF POLICE: Managers of the Military Election: At Woodville, G. D. BOYD, JOS. A. FOSTER, and JOHN S. LEWIS; at Mount Pleasant, JESSE JONES, LEWIS CASON, and Wm. C. S. VENTRESS; at Whitesville, JOHN F. SCOTT, LORENZO D. BROWN, and PARKER SMITH; at Upper Homochitto, A. P. SLOCUMB, BYTHELL HAYNES, and SAMUEL McMUTRY; at Percy's Creek, H. H. BELL, BENJ. MAYES, and JAS. B. BULLOCK; Lower Homochitto, BENJ. KILLGORE, WILLIAM N. HELM, and J. W. MILLER; at Fort Adams FRANCIS S. MAYES, J. L. WALL, and SAMUEL W. LEWIS; at Pinckneyville, JOHN FELLS, SAMUEL ROBINSON, and ROBERT SEMPLE.
        By JOHN NETTERVILLE, Clerk

Final settlement of WILLIAM MELTON's estate

Final settlement of DRUCILLA CLARKSON's estate

SAM'L. P. MITCHELL is leaving Woodville and has left his accounts in the hands of N. SCUDDER,

Esquire.

JOHN NETTERVILLE, trustee, will sell three lots of land in the town of Woodville. Power delegated by a deed of trust, executed 26th day of June 1833, by WILLIAM DODD and ANN DODD, his wife, JOHN NETTERVILLE and CHARLES NETTERVILLE, Jr., and JAMES M. WOOD and JOHN H. COURTS.

MICHAEL WOODS wishes to sell his house and lot in Woodville, and also his 1/2 interest in the lot which contains a grocery, on the west side of the Public Square, near the "Royal Oak".

JOEL GLASS, exec'r., of the BURTON LANDRUM estate, has left all notes in the hands of Dr. J. SAUNDERS.

JESSE BELL vs. HENRY R. NERSON   All rights and claims of HENRY R.NERSON in 555 acres will be sold.

ESALAS KAIGLER's ex'rs., vs. JOHN L.MONKS & W. T. MAYES   Monks rights to a lot and house is to be sold.

February 22, 1834

Final settlement of JAMES S. WAIDE's estate

Final settlement of DUGALD B. THOMPSON's estate

C. NETTERVILLE, T. C. W. C. will sell two town lots in Woodville. Property which surrounds these lots are owned by Mrs. MARY LANGLEY, JOHN S. LEWIS, FRANCIS KELER, THOMAS SMITH, NIAL McCARSTLE, and LUCAS BURNETT'S estate.

Candidates for various offices are: A.P.CUNNINGHAM of Pike County, JOHN JOOR, of Wilkinson County, WILLIAM L. BRANDON, Mr. ROBERT LAYSON, Mr. A. FERGUSON, P. M. GARRETT, JAMES VARNELL and GEORGE P. TOOLE.

Commissioners appointed at the April Term will report on claims against the estate of JOHN L. BRUCE.

Married the 13th by the Rev. T. C. BROWN, Mr. SAMUEL DAVIS to Miss EMMA M., daughter of CHARLES EDWARDS, all of this county.

Died on Monday evening, Mr. JOHN R. HOLLIDAY

LEWIS, eldest son of Maj. S. W. LEWIS of Fort Adams.

The copartnership between JOHN A. F. GRAVIS and J. W. CULLEN is dissolved by mutual consent. (Bricklaying and plastering business)

ELIZABETH H. BROWN was appointed as administrator of the dec'd., JESSE BROWN's estate.

Wm. G. RUSSELL has taken up a sorrell horse.

HENY LARD, adm'r., of THOMAS LARD's estate will sell land lying in Amite County, Mississippi.

March 1, 1834
Final settlement of ELIZABETH METCALF's estate

JAMES LYNE, guardian of T. A. W. VAUGHAN, heir of JESSE NETTERVILLE, will sell a tract of land (106 acres) lying in the County of Wilkinson. Properties which bound this tract are owned by THOS. H. PROSSER, JOHN COULTER, JUDGE STEWART, JOHN PATTON, and GEORGE BROWN.

Doctor SAMUEL LESSLEY, will devote his attention entirely, to the practice of Medicine and Surgery. Office in the late residence of L. PREWETT.

W. HAILE and N. SCUDDER have opened a law office.

THO. J. SPURLOCK, will surrender his administraton as one of the adm'rs., of HENRY JONES'estate.

All persons are cautioned not to trade for a note drawn by JOHN A. F. GRAVIS, in favor of JOHN W. CULLIN, for $153.

STEUBAL & SAMUEL TILLOTSON vs. WILLIAM CAMPBELL $75 attachment.   Amite County

WILLIAM H. DILLINGHAM vs. WILLIAM CAMPBELL $155 attachment. Amite County

B. MARSHALL vs. JOHN STEVENS $1,136 attachment

LAVICA MIXON & BENHADAD MIXON, admr's of OBED MIXON estate, wish to sell land in Amite County.

ELIZABETH BROWNE & WILLIAM H. DILLINGHAM were appointed admr's., of CHARLES DAVIS' estate.

Land owners of land to be sold for taxes and also land surrounding same: DAVID McNEELY, B. KILGORE, heirs of STEPHEN AMBROSE, JOHN OGDEN, J. L. TRASK DAN'l LEATHERMAN, J. ROBERTS or D. I. GRAY's estate, J. S. LEWIS, REBECCA LEWIS, JACOB HUFFMANN & JAMES LEECH, HUGH CONNELL, and PRESTWOOD SMITH's estate.

Horse stolen from W. TIGNER's lot at Millbrook, near Fort Adams, on the 16th.

Six hounds, belonging to JAS. A. STEWART, ran off in the direction of Fort ADAMS. Liberal Reward

EPHRAIM THOMPSON will sell a house & lot formerly occupied by the subscriber as a saddle shop but now occupied by T. E. W. JAMES, as a grocery store.

H. M. FARISH, adm'r., of E. T. FARISH's estate, states that all persons indebted on medical accounts to come foward and settle.

JOHN PEEBLES was appointed adm'r., of dec'd., Wm. PEEBLES' estate at the May term.

T. E. W. JAMES, Jailer of Wilkinson County

Married the 27th, by N. SCUDDER, Esqr., Mr. JOHN JENKS to Miss ARIANN JACKSON, all of this county.

March 8, 1834

Married on Thursday evening last, by the Rev. J. A. RANALDSON, Major THOMAS C. WEST to Miss ELIZA CONNELL, eldest daughter of HUGH CONNELL, Esquire

The Reverend Bishop McKENSIE, will preach in the Methodist Church tomorrow.

Result of the Military Election on Saturday, March 1,1834: Major General, JOHN JOOR; Brigadier General, Wm L. BRANDON; Colonel, R. LAYSON; Lieut. Colonel, P.M. GARRETT; and Major, THOMAS C. WEST. All other polls were not open.

JAMES WEEKS, adm'r., in right of his wife, SUSANNA WEEKS, adm'x., of OEL SWEARINGEN's estate of Amite County, will sell real estate.

H. M. FARISH, adm'r., of E. T. FARISH's estate will sell various parcels of land. Land owners mentioned in the document are: JOHN JOOR, E. H.

WAILES, JOHN P. HARRIS, and JOSEPH H. STREET.

GEORGE H. GORDON & JAMES WALKER have formed a partnership to practice law. Their office is on the west side of the square. February 15, 1834

Woodville ordinance passed stating that it is unlawful for anyone to hitch horses, or other animals to the railing on the public square, around the courthouse. Fine of one dollar on demand by the town constable. Signed by N. SCUDDER President and G. D. BOYD, Secretary.

The copartnership existing between JOHN A. F. GRAVIS & J. W. CULLEN is dissolved by mutual consent.

March 15, 1834
Died on the 2nd inst., after a short illness, Mrs. ISABELLA KNIGHT, consort of the late HENRY KNIGHT, aged about 50 years.

On Friday last, passing by the plantaions of A. SKILLMAN and L. L. SMITH, Esqr., $500.00 in bank notes, of one hundred dollars, of the Planters Bank, Miss., were lost. Generous reward offered. A. CALDER

The Copartnership between PARKER SMITH and WILLIAM SMITH is dissolved by mutual consent.

Final settlement of Wm. WOODSIDE 's estate is to be presented by THOMAS WOODSIDE, adm'r.

WHEREAS my wife, LAURETT ANDERSON, without any cause whatever known to me, did in August, 1832, leave and forsake me, and seems still unwilling to return: I therefore take this method of notifying each and every person, that I will not pay any debt which she may contract on my responsibility. WILSON ANDERSON, March 1, 1834

Final settlement of DANIEL OGDEN's estate by MARY S. OGDEN, admr'x

ARMSTRONG & GOOLEY vs. THOMAS C.REED

THEODORE MOLLEMANS vs. THOMAS C.REID

THOMAS WOODSIDE, adm'r., of JANE WOODSIDE's estate, will sell all the Real & Personal estate, consisting of an undivided piece of land (200 acres), furniture and etc.

TAX COLLECTORS SALE: 800 Acres of land assessed as the property of Dr. SAMUEL BROWN will be sold. The land is bounded by WM. BARTON, HENRY QUINE AND THOMAS BELL.

TAX COLLECTORS SALE: 1500 Acres assessed to A. B. McLEOD and bounded by land of T. G. ELLIS and the Mississippi River. Tax due for 1833 = $22.50.
160 Acres assessed to JOHN TULLIS and bounded by JOHN TYSON, and CHARLES EDWARDS. Tax due for 1832 & 1833 = $1.40
500 Acres assessed to JOHN LOMBARD and bounded by the BUFFALOE, T. G. ELLIS, public lands and JOHN LOMBARD. Tax for 1833 = $7.50

March 22, 1834
Died yesterday, in this city, WILLIAM WIRT, Esqr., age about 62 years. (Originally from the NAT. INT., February 19, 1834)

JOHN B. ANDERSON, guardian of JOSEPH C. GAULDEN, WILLIAM E. GUALDEN and THOMAS F. GAULDEN, will present his account for final settlement.

A bay horse has strayed from the "Indian Mount" plantation. A liberal reward is offered by JOS. G. CLENDENIN.

WM. C. MAXWELL, adm'r., of MARGARET McKNIGHT's estate. Amite County.

Land that JOHN L. MONKS had purchased from BARBARA LOVELACE, is to be sold. Also mentiones heirs of ESATAS KAIGLER and Wm. T. MAYES in document.

WILLIAM DANIEL, ESTER RICE, and others vs. MILO FERRELL, et al. ...The lot on which Ferrell now resides will be sold and is bounded by land formerly owned by JAMES C. WEEKLY and sold to LEWIS ENDT, and lands belonging to Miss MURSROUGH, and WALTER STREET.

March 29, 1834
PATRICK FANNING vs. ABRAM M. GRAY & Wm. S. LEWIS; J. & L. BREWSTER vs. Wm. S. LEWIS; ABNER SMITH's admr. vs. A. M. GRAY & Wm. S. LEWIS. Land to be sold. Lewis's claim to a lot now presently occupied by LUCY YOUNG and bounded by land owned by

-119-

B. JOURDAN, and land formerly owned by Wm. JOHNSON.

Sheriff JNO. SLADE, will sell property of JOHN STEVENS to satisfy court claims. Jan. 11, 1834

Final settlement of SAMUEL C. HEADY's estate

Final settlement of SAMUEL PICKENS' estate

THEODORE STARK vs. Heirs of FRANCIS GILDART, Sen'r.   702 Acres known as "Ashley Tract" adjoining land of JAMES L. TRASK, PENELOPE & JAMES A. STEWART, MABRY & GEORGE MORRIS, as is remaining in the possession of ROBERT S. GILDART, JOHN W. GILDART, FRANCIS GILDART, JOHN FOX & SOPHIA FOX his wife, LEMUEL PITCHER & MARY JANE PITCHER his wife, DICK H. EGGLESTON & ELIZABETH EGGLESTON his wife, MOSES LIDDELL, guardian of FRANCIS B. RUFFIN , and the said DICK H. EGGLESTON as adm'r., of the estate of HORATIO W. GILDART.

DAVID ANDERSON has lost a horse. Reward offered

April 5, 1834
DANIEL BASS & D. F. LEWIS have formed a co-partnership in business.

Public auction to be held on the 29th, without reserve, all the old watches and jewelry left with A. W. ALLEN to be repaired. April 15, 1834, T. G. GRAVIS

Various strays taken up by the following: SAMUEL STEPHENSON, JOHN H. RANDOLPH, JOHN C. HICKS, CARNOT POSEY (on the plantation of JNO. B. POSEY), S. W. LEWIS, and RICHARD CLAMPET.

A horse strayed from the residence of T. F. STEWART

FRANCIS KELLER's property is to be sold for taxes. It is bounded by Mrs. MARY LANGLEY and JOHN S. LEWIS and the public square.

By the virtue of a deed of trust from A. W. ALLAN, dated Feb. 28, 1833 to secure JOSEPH JOHNSON, A. S. RANDOLPH, SAM'L S. BOYD, A. M. DUNN, JNO. HENDERSON, & JNO. STEVENS against certain liabilities. A tract, or house & lot to be sold lying on the main St. Francisville Road and bounded by the lot of Mrs. SMITH, and the lots of GEORGE ADAMS, & Wm. H. WHITE.

April 12, 1834

Final settlement of DRUCILLA CLARKSON's estate

Final settlement of SAMUEL BUSH's estate

Final settlement of ELIZABETH METCALF's estate

Final settlement of Wm. WOODSIDE's estate

GEORGE MORRIS was appointed executor of ISABELLA KNIGHT'S estate.

Dr. W. W. MONETT was shot in the left breast by D. H. BAKER, both citizens of this county, and near neighbors to each other. Dr. MONETT instantly expired. (Originally from the VICKSBURG REGISTER)

Natchez, March 28, Sunday evening in Concordia Parish, La., a man by the name of More, was hanging around Dr. THOMAS HUNT's plantation and attempted to kill Dr. Hunt. The Doctor shot More in the heart and was immediately discharged by the civil authorities.

Married the 8th, by N. SCUDDER, Esqr., Mr. WILLIAM McNEELY to Miss MARY A., daughter of JOHN W. SEYMOUR, Esqr., all of this county.

Married the 10th, by N. SCUDDER, Esqr., Mr. MOSES POOL to Miss MARY, daughter of JOSEPH HENDERSON, all of this county.

April 19, 1834

Postponement of the sale of the real estate of EDWARD T. FARISH, deceased, until further notice.

Final settlement of DAVID HARVARD's estate

Final settlement of ROBERT WHITE, Junr.'s estate

Final settlement of WILLIAM ANDERSON's estate

GEORGE H. SCRIPPS vs. THOMAS C. READ

All the furniture, both house & kitchen of Mrs. SUSAN SCOTT will be sold to the highest bidder. Also her servants will be hired for the balance of the year. JESSE MABRY, agent

JANE DAVIS, will present her account as guardian of SARAH MATILKA VAUGHN for final settlement.

April 26, 1834
Final settlement of JAMES SMITH's estate

Final settlement of SAMUEL BUSH's estate

JAMES WEEKS, adm'r., in right of his wife, SUSANNA WEEKS, adm'rx, of JOEL SWEARINGEN's estate, late of Amite county, will sell land.

E. H. WAILES & HUGH CONNELL, appointed executors of the dec'd., WILLIAM NEWELL's estate at the October term thereof, 1834. (Type error, perhaps 1833 ?)

THOMAS WOODSIDE was appointed adm'r., of JANE WOODSIDE's estate. March 11,1834

Final settlement of DANIEL OGDEN's estate

Dr. BERRY has located at the house of JOHN MAYES, Esqr., on Percy's Creek.

The copartnership between T.W. RADFORD & ROBT. THOMPSON has been dissolved by mutual consent.

May 3, 1834
The copartnership between PARKER SMITH & WILLIAM SMITH was dissolved by mutual consent on Jan. 1, 1834. All notes and accounts are now in the hands of C. S. & H. D. KELLOGG for collection.

Married May 1, by N. SCUDDER, Esq., Mr. JACKSON SIKES to Miss ELIZABETH BAKER, all of this county.

Married on the 20th March last, by Rev. T. C. BROWN, Mr. WILEY DELOACH to Miss BARBARA WALKER, daughter of Mr. Z. WALKER, all of this county.

Died, in this county, at the residence of Mr. CHARLES HESTER, on the 25th, Mr. WILLIAM HUGHEY, aged 39 years, a native of the State of Georgia.

CLEMENT TOWNSEND's exec'r., vs. LAZARUS DRAKE, DANIEL McGAHEY.

CALEB SWAYZE, adm'r., of DAVID SWAYZE's estate will present his final settlement of the estate.

Final settlement of ROBERT WHITE, Senr.'s estate

$500 reward for the delivery of JOHN STEVENS, who absented himself from this place about the 10th of April, 1833. He has swindled several banks in this state, about sixty or seventy thousand dollars. Unspecting men are bankrupt and doomed to poverty. Mrs. S. was formerly the widow of a Mr. Briggs from Raleigh, N. Carolina. The eldest child, ELIZABETH BRIGGS, is 12 yrs. old; WILLIAM BRIGGS is about 6 or 7 years old, and the next child is a daughter, LUCY STEVENS, 3 or 4 years old. Mrs. S. avowed she and the children were to visit her brother in Alabama, at which place she has not arrived. The general opinion is that she is with her husband, JOHN STEVENS. (Synopsis of lengthy advertisement)

May 10, 1834

It is our painful duty to announce the decease of the Honorable LITTLETON P. DENNIS, Representative in Congress, from the state of Maryland. He expired April 4, 1834.
(Originally from the NAT. INT.)

May 17, 1834

Married Tuesday by the Rev. SAML. DAWSON, Mr. JOHN C. HICKS to Mrs. JAMESBY BRYAN, all of this county.

Married Thursday by the Rev. SAML. DAWSON, Mr. JOHN WILEY to Miss SUSAN GROOM, all of this county.

Married the 7th by BYTHELL HAYNES, Esqr., Mr. BALDWIN HAYNES to Mrs. MELISSA MURPHY, all of this county.

Married in Claiborne county on the 8th, by the Rev. Z. BUTLER, Mr. STEPHEN ARCHER, of Wilkinson county to Mrs. CATHARINE BARNES, of Claiborne.

Died the 7th, at the house of Mr. PHILIP NOLAND, in this County, in the 24th year of her age, Mrs. LEVICE NORWOOD, consort of Mr. ROBERT NORWOOD. She left an infant and a disconsolate husband.

PRISCILLA CAWSEY, adm'rx., of JOHN H. CAWSEY'S estate, will sell a tract of Land.

THOS. LEWIS, adm'r., of the deceased, REBECCA

LEWIS' estate.

May 24, 1834
Died at the house of Mr. J. MABRY, in this place on the 23rd, Mr. NEWTON LOVE.

JOHN F. CARMICHAEL ad. TRUSTEES OF SCHOOL LAND

June 7, 1834
Married the 5th by the Hon. A. S. RANDOLPH, WILLIAM S. GRIFFIN, Esqr. to Miss ANN C., daughter of the Hon. MOSES LIDDELL, all of Wilkinson County.

Married the 20th, by N. SCUDDER, Esqr., Mr. LEVI D. DOUGHTY to Miss MATILDA SAPP, all of this county.

A. ILER will offer for sale, to the highest bidder, under the "Royal Oak", on Tuesday the 3rd June next, Phoebe, about 26 years of age.

A. BYNUM informs his friends that he is a "private tutor" and is willing to take charge of five or six scholars.

WESTERN MUSE vs. CASSANDER MUSE   Bill of Divorce

Taken up as a stray by LEWIS BURTON, on the plantation of Maj. TRASK, a mole coloured mule.

BRISBON MARSHALL vs. JOHN STEVENS, and also, ZACH. CANFIELD vs. JOHN STEVENS

JAMES DIXON's adm'r. vs. LUCY SHAFFER, late LUCY SPURLOCK, JAS. SHAFFER & MICHAEL WOODS

JUNE 14, 1834
WALTHALL BURTON forwarns all persons not to trade for a note drawn by him to WILSON P. BURTON for $600.00. This note was given for the benefit of N. A. SPEARS, and BURTON will not now pay.

Point Coupee, May 20th 1834, A murder was committed on Cat Island near the habitation of Mr. A. MOORE. (Originally from the ST. FRANCISVILLE PHOENIX)

THOMAS NETTERVILLE & CO. vs. CHARLES McMORRIES & WILLIAM BAKER

CHARLES CURTIS's heirs vs. LAZARUS DRAKE

Final settlement of Mrs. MARTHA RICHARDSON's estate by F. R. RICHARDSON, executor.

JOHN M. PHILIPS, adm'r., of JESSE BAGGET's estate will sell two tracts of land in Wilkinson County.

MARY SWAYZE was appointed adm'rx., of BENJAMIN SWAYZE's estate at the June Term of 1834.

E. G. ROBERT was appointed adm'r., of the MATILDA VAUGHAN estate at the June Term of 1834.

June 21, 1834
In the August Term, 1834, ALEX. M. DUNN, guardian of JOHN A. DUNN, will offer his final settlemt in Liberty, for the court of Amite County.

June 28, 1834
LOZ. D. BROWN, exec'r., of the JOHN L. BRUCE estate, will offer his final settlement at the August term.

A small silver cup, with EDMOND TRENT EGGLESTON engraved on the outside, was stolen from the residence of E. S. EGGLESTON. Reward of $5.00 offered

July 5, 1834
J. G. POINDEXTER has reopened the Woodville Hotel.

WM. A. A. CHISHOLM, the Proprietor of this Journal, has secured the services of ALFRED BYNUM, Esqr., a gentleman well known in the community.

The Notes due JOEL GLASS, as Executor of the Estate of BURTON LANDRUM, dec'd., are in the hands of N. SCUDDER for collection.

Married on the 29th, by N. SCUDDER, Esqr. Mr. JOHN P. HUMPHRIES to Mrs. ELIZABETH COON, all of this co.

Died at his residence near Woodville on the 4th, Mr. BENJ. H. LEWIS.

Died at his father's residence in this county on the 3rd, of gastic fever, WILLIAM ARTHUR, eldest son of Col. F. R. RICHARDSON, in the 5th year of his age.

Died, on the 2nd July, DUNCAN NOLAN, son of JOHN J. & MARY COLLINS, aged 3 years and 4 months.

Died at the house of Maj. F. MAYES, in this county, on the 23rd, Mr. J. J. MAYES, aged 19 years.

Died 29th June, at Arundale, the residence of FRANCIS EVANS, Esqr., ELLEN KEARY, consort of the Rev. J. C. BURRUSS, aged 19 years and 10 months.

July 12, 1834

Final settlement of JOSEPH J. SOCKETT's estate will be made at the November term, 1834.

Died at the residence of Mrs. MARY S. OGDEN, near Woodville, on the 9th of July, MARY ELIZABETH, the only child of HENRY & ANNA VOSE, aged 1 yr. & 8 mo.

NANCY REED, late NANCY BENTLEY, widow of THOS. BENTLEY, dec'd,, and administratrix of the estate of Thos. Bentley, will petition the court at the August term for her dower of one half of lands belonging to Thos. Bentley. Bounded by lands of Dr. DAVID HOLT and Dr. THOS. LYNE.

July 19, 1834

ARTHUR DANIEL, adm'r., of JOAB WIGLEY's estate.

JOHE C. HICKS, adm'r., of NEADHAM H. BRYAN will present for final settlement, the accounts of his wife, late JAMSEY BYRAN, who was adm'rx., for said estate.

HILL & HENDERSON vs. SIMON P. SHOPE   Amite County

MATHEW M. SMYLIE vs. NEAL L. McNAIR   Amite County

STEPHEN H. STRONG vs. SIMON P. SHOPE   Amite County

ALEXANDER HUGHEY, was appointed adm'r., of WILLIAM HUGHEY's estate at the June term. He also was appointed adm'r., for the estate of JAMES HUGHEY at the June term.

LEMENDER LAND was appointed adm'r., of JAMES LAND's estate at the June term.

GEORGE H. SCRIPPS vs. THOMAS C. READ

A cow and a steer taken up by WILLIAM McNEELY

Property of SAML. McMURTRY is to be sold to cover court cost. LOYAL CASE, SAMUEL McMURTRY, WILLIAM McMURTRY, DAVID ANDERSON, THOMAS HALL, and G. D. BOYD are mentioned.

Sheriff's sale: THOS. J. SMITH vs. A. W. ALLAN. One piano forte, one bureau, one book case, one carpet, one sofa, one sideboard, six chairs, one rocking chair, and one china set; levied on as the property of A. W. ALLAN to satisfy the above stated case and cost. July 9, 1834

McNULTY & WALL, and others vs. JOHN & Wm. H. BELL

July 26, 1834

A "Musical Entertainment" will be given by J. S. JENKINS, on the 29th, in the court house in Woodville. The proceeds are to improve the accomodations at the Sulpher Springs, near Woodville.

Died the 22nd, Mr. SAMUEL GLASS, formerly of Pittsburg, Pennsylvania.

Died at his residence in East Feliciana on the 24th, Col. GREEN B. DAVIS, of congestive fever.

The final settlement of JAMES SMITH's estate will be made by DAVID POOL, adm'r., at the September term, 1834.

August 2, 1834

JOHN GRIFFIN, appointed adm'r., of the JAMES H. WEBB estate. Liberty, Mi., Amite County

WILLIAM McNEELY appointed adm'r., of JOHN W. SEYMOUR's estate at the July term, 1834

FRANCIS S. MAYES appointed adm'r., of JACKSON MAYES' estate at the July term, 1834

640 acres of land, known as the old AMBROSE tract is to be sold for taxes due in 1832 & 1833. Land assessed for $16.00 to heirs of STEPHEN AMBROSE.

CATHERINE ROBINSON & WILLIAM BAKER, Exr's., of JAMES ROBINSON's estate, Liberty, Mi., Amite County

Married the 27th July, by NATHANIEL SCUDDER, Esqr., Mr. ASA ANDERSON to Mrs. MARGARET COATES, all of this county.

Died the 26th of Phthisis Pulmonahs, Mrs. EVELINE R. MAYES, consort of BENJAMIN M. MAYES, of this county, aged 30 years and 7 days. Leaves husband, children and relatives.

August 9, 1834
H. M. FARISH, co-adm'r., of EDWARD T. FARISH's estate will sell all the real estate.

Property of JOHN LOMBARD to be sold for taxes

Property of FRANCIS KELLER to be sold for taxes

Property of MILO FERRELL to be sold to satisfy court cost. WILLIAM DANIEL & ESTER RICE vs. MILO FERRELL, DAVID ARMSTRONG & FIELDING DAVIS, also, STEVENS & PILLETT vs. MILO FERRELL, and HENRY T. BLAKE vs. same.

JOHN GRIFFIN was appointed adm'r., of the JAMES H. WEBB's estate in Amite County, at the March term.

HUGH McCRAINE has taken up a yellow bay horse.

PETER FAUST, was appointed adm'r., of the JAMES FAUST estate at the July term, 1834.

Property of WILLIAM EVANS to be sold for taxes

Commissioners appointed for the dec'd EDWARD WATKINS' estate are: THOMAS S. HERBERT, JOHN B. THERRELL, and WM. A. A. CHISHOLM. July term, 1834

Final settlement of the LEVICA COLEMAN estate

JOHN STEVENS vs. THOS. J. SMITH & JOHN DEAL; MICHAEL WOODS vs. THOS. J. SMITH; STEVENS & PILLETT vs. THOMAS J. SMITH. The property of Smith is to be sold to cover court cost.

GEORGE H. SCRIPPS vs. THOMAS C. READ Read's property is to be sold to satisfy court cost.

C. S. KELLOGG & others vs. NARSWORTHY HUNTER Hunter's property to be sold to cover court cost

Commissioners appointed for Dr. THOMAS COOPER's estate are: NATHANIEL SCUDDER, MICHAEL WOODS, and WM. A. A. CHISHOLM. June 14, 1834

The personal estate of JESSE GUIN, dec'd., has been reported insufficient to his debts.

August 16, 1834

Final settlement of JOHN L. BRUCE's estate

A list of several hundred cases, reprinted from the "State Rights Banner", disposed of at the July term, 1834, of the High Court of Errors and Appeals.

Married August 10th in Woodville by D. BASS, Esqr., CHARLES C. S. FARRAR, Esqr.,to Miss MARY ANN FORT, both of Louisiana.

Died at his residence in this county on the 14th, Mr. LEMUELL P__UETT. (The JOURNAL OF WILKINSON COUNTY HISTORY, VOL.I, 1990, pg. 210, list one LEMANUEL PREWETT b. 1799, d. 8-14-31, and buried in the "Smith 3" cemetery.)

Died on the 13th July, Mrs. SUSANNA NETTERVILLE, consort of Mr. CHARLES NETTERVILLE, in the 56th year of her age.

Commissioners appointed for the dec'd., GREEN MASSY estate are: DAVID PEMBLE, WINSTON GILMORE and W. L. JONES.   Amite County

Final settlement of the TEMPLE STEWART estate

August 23, 1834

EDWARD R. QUARTERMAN has bought out Esqr. Bass in the "Tin" business and intends to carrying it on.

August 30, 1834

Married on the 28th, by N. SCUDDER, Esqr., Mr. WILLIAM PAYNE to Miss SUSAN HUBBARD, all of this county.

Married in Woodville, on the 27th, by DANIEL BASS, Esqr., Captain JOHN PHILBRICK to Mrs. SUSAN SCOTT, all of this county.

Died on the 16th in Liberty, Amite County, Mrs. PENELOPE WHITNEY, aged 32 years, consort of MINOR M. WHITNEY. She leaves a husband and children.

JOHN W. MAYRANT, Attorney At Law's office, is on the east side of the public Square, opposite the court house. August 18, 1834

A. M. DUNN vs. JOHN STEVENS

September 6, 1834
CHARLES RATCLIFF vs. ANDREW D. BATEMEN   Amite County

The Rev. SPENCER WALL will preach in the Episcopal Church tomorrow at the usual time.

The property of HENRY JONES, will be sold by the Administrators, MARY JONES, WM. JONES & THOMAS J. SPURLOCK. Amite county

M. M. WHITNEY vs. H. E. W. JORDAN Amite County

September 13, 1834
Property of A. B. LEOD to be sold for taxes

Wm. H. DILLINGHAM vs. JOHN BUTLER Amite County

Died in this place on Wednesday evening last, of congestive fever, Mr. JOSEPH A. FOSTER, in the 32nd year of his age.

The Rev. JAS. A. RANALDSON will preach in the Baptist Church.

WILFORD GARNER, ex'r., of the JAMES GARNER estate

Final settlement of the WILLIAM BROOKS' estate

Property of JESSE GUNN's estate to be sold subject to the widow's dower, by CAROLINE M. HUNT and HENRY HUNT, adm'rs.   Amite County

Land, adjoining the Fontainbleau plantation, about 1000 acres, being a part of the FREDERICK A. BROWDER estate, will be sold by SPENCER WOOD.

JOSEPH LILLEY, adm'r., of MILES LILLEY's estate

COTESWORTH P. SMITH vs. JOHN STEVENS

ALEXANDER M. DUNN vs. S. P. SHOPE

September 20, 1834
MINOR M. WHITNEY vs. HENRY E. W. JORDAN

Final settlement of the DRUCILLA CLARKSON estate

Property of the estate of JESSE BAGGET, dec'd., to be sold by JOHN M. PHILIPS, administrator

September 27, 1834

The Rev. SPENCER WALL appointed Principal of the "Wilkinson Academy".

At the October Term, 1834, of the Probate Court of Amite county, MARY JONES, widow of DARLING JONES, will apply for a writ to have her dower laid off.

October 4, 1834

$500 reward for the capture of CASEN COOPER, who was engaged with a certain NARSWORTHY HUNTER, (who has now been taken and is in Jail awaiting his trial, and which takes place in Woodville, in October next). Cooper is the uncle of Hunter, who also has a brother, JOSEPH UNTER on which a $50 reward is offered. Sept. 16th 1834

The Rev. M. DRAKE will preach the funeral of Mrs. ELLEN BURRUSS, late widow of Rev. JOHN C. BURRUSS at Pickneyville, on the second Sabbath the 12th.

Died on the 2nd, JOHN M. youngest son of N. HARRIS, of this place, an infant of a few months.

Died the 2nd, ELIZA ANN, daughter of the late (?) and ELIZABETH CLARK of New Orleans and (?) (This issue has unreadable areas.)

October 11, 1834

Property of JOHN KEEN, late of Amite county, to be sold by ALLEN SPURLOCK, administrator.

JNO. BRYANT warns persons not to trade for a note given by Bryant to RICHARD COTTER, for $30.

The Hon. W. H. CRAWFORD died on the 15th in Liberty (?), Georgia, after an attack of twenty-four hours of bilious fever.

LOUISA R. FOSTER & ALBERT G. FOSTER were appointed adm'rs., of JOSEPH A. FOSTER's estate

DIXONS adm'r. vs. JAMES SHAFFER, LUCY SHAFFER, late LUCY SPURLOCK, & MICHAEL WOODS. Property is to be sold to cover court cost.

October 18, 1834

Final settlement of the MOSES GORDON estate

FRANCIS R. RICHARDSON, adm'r., of the JOSEPH CLAY GAULDEN's estate.

JOHN NETTERVILLE, adm'r of SAMUEL GLASS'estate.

HARRIET COTTEN, adm'r., of ABEL COTTEN's estate at the July term. Amite Co.

CELIA PREWETT, adm'r., of LEMUEL PREWETT's estate

A large red speckled steer, belonging to WM. F. PAQUINETT, strayed last winter. Liberal reward

October 25, 1834
First page of this issue is missing

Final settlement of the WILLIAM PURDEW estate by N. B. BURTON, adm'r., will be made at the December term. October 25, 1834

Final settlement of the WILLIAM BROOKS estate

DANIEL PROSSER, adm'r., of REBECCA LEWIS' estate.

JOHN A. QUITMAN, Esqr., has resigned as Chancellor of State. An election will be held for the office.

Property of GEORGE MOSS to be sold to cover court cost of writs of Fi. Fa. with the following: JOHN STERLING, THOMAS NETTERVILLE, ARTHUR DANIEL, & JESSE SAUNDERS.

J. A. LILLEY, adm'r., will sell at Public Auction, at the court house in the town of Woodville, to the highest bidder, on a credit of twelve months, the purchaser giving bond and security, a tract of land, on the waters of Bayou Sara, containing 172 acres, bounded by the lands of JOHN C. SIMS, JOHN W. LEATHERMAN, Z. WALKER, estate of JESSE DELOACH and A. S.RANDOLPH. October 18,1834

DUDLEY RUTLEDGE property to be sold to settle court cost. Suites involve CHARLES NETTERVILLE, JESSE SAUNDERS, STEVEN & PILLETT, and PICO & PEABODY   October 14, 1834

Property of JOHN DEAL to be sold to settle court cost. JAS. JONES vs. JOHN DEAL and JOHN STEVENS vs. JOHN DEAL

November 1, 1834
In October, 1834, JOHN W. GILDART had 18 cases filed against him. Individuals mentioned were:

SOLOMON WEATHERSBY, WM STAMPS, FRANCIS GILDART, SAMUEL JAYNE, LAZARUS DRAKE, WALTHAL BURTON, DICK H. EGGLESTON, CALEB HALL, E. C. BUSHNESS, JAS. THOM, THOS. NETTERVILLE, PALMER SMITH, FRANCIS KELLER, CALEB HOWELL, JAS. HUDSON, JOHN KELLY, JOHN MAYES, OSCAR PILLETT, JOHN STEVENS, WM. F. HYDE, E. B. HYDE, JOHN STARKE, DAVID HOLT, and ROBT. R. STARK. Gildart's property must be sold to cover court cost.

Final settlement of the ANNE TOOLE estate by GEO. P. TOOLE, adm'r.   October 18,1834

A. S. RANDOLPH, Judge of Probate, gives notice that ADAM MORNINGSTAR of Wilkinson county has made an application to claim an undivided half of land in Woodville. Commissioners nominated to divide this lot are: C. WEST, HORACE D. KELLOG, and EDMUND H. WAILES.

Final settlement of the WILLIAM PURDEW estate

Died this morning, Nov. 1st., Mr. JOHN C. HICKS, a respectable citizen of this county.

FRANCIS R. RICHARDSON was appointed adm'r., of the JOSEPH CLAY GAULDEN's estate.

A pumpkin was presented to Maj. S. W. LEWIS, at Fort Adams, in this County, raised by Mr. G. D. D. FOSTER, near that place. The length of which was 3 feet 5 inches, and its circumberence 4 feet,5 inches, and weighing 160 pounds.

C. P. HEARTT, a dentist from New Orleans, will remain in Woodville about one week.

NARSWORTHY BELL forewarns any person or persons, from trading for a note of $300, given to WILLIAM BELL, sometimes in February or March. He refuses to pay it except compelled by law. Sept. 23,1834

DANIEL H.PROSSER was granted adm'r., of the estate of REBECCA LEWIS, dec'd., at the late October term.

NOVEMBER 8, 1834
Final settlement of RICHARD JONES's estate

WILLIAM T. LEWIS will make an application for land stock that DAVID DAVIS forfeited for non-payment.

Married on Thursday, 23rd October, by JOSEPH PATTERSON, Esqr., Mr. PETER LEATHERMAN to Mrs. CHARITY SMITH, all of this county. (Wilkinson County Marriage Book states that on October 11, 1828, a Miss CHARITY THOMPSON married a Mr. ABNER SMITH).

Final settlement of the MARGARET HOLLIMAN estate

G. W. WILSON forewarnes all persons not to trade for two drafts, drawn by hin and made payable to MOSES NORMAN.   St. Francisville, La. Oct. 23, 1834

November 15, 1834

DELOACH & ARDREY, have on hand a complete assortment of groceries and provisions. (SAMUEL DELOACH)

Married on the 10th, by DANIEL BASS, Esqr., JOHN E. PHARES, Esqr., of La. to Mrs. LUCETTA ADELAIDE PENNYMAN of Pinckneyville. (Wilkinson County Marriage Book states that on Nov. 17,1825, a LUCETTA A. ROBINSON married a CHARLES PENNIMAN)

Died on Old River, the 11th, JESSE G. SMITH, of small pox, aged 23 years.

We yesterday received, quoting " The Charleston Mercury" of the 24th instant, the afficting intelligence of the death of the Hon. THOMAS S. GRIMKE, of Cholera, at Columbus, Ohio.

ALEX. HUGHES has taken up a bay horse, as a stray.

YOUNG BURKE cautions all persons from trading for a Note of Hand made payable to HIRAM SPENCER for $200 and fraudulently obtained. Nov. 14,1834

D. P. A. COOK has been appointed exec'r., to the estate of JOHN TURNER, deceased.

November 22, 1834

Married the 12th, by the Rev. SILAS H. HAZARD, ELIJAH M. DAVIS, Esqr., to SARAH ANN W., second daughter of the Hon. WILLIAM LATTIMORE, all of Amite county.

Died the 18th, at her residence in Woodville, Mrs. MARY M. CONRAD, consort of Mr. PETER CONRAD. The deceased was a native of Germany, who together with her husband and family emigrated to this country many years since.

November 29, 1834

WM. STAMPS offers his place, which he now occupies, for sale. The land is located 3 miles east of Woodville and consists of 1500 Acres.

ALLEN SPURLOCK, adm'r., of the JOHN KEEN estate of Amite county, will sell 159 acres.

Property of JOHN STEVENS is to be sold. Persons listed in the sale: J. LEFINEIL, J. P. HARRIS, JESSE SAUNDERS, C. S. KELLOGG, JOHN P. HARRIS, C. C. WEST, E. H. WAILES, and C. S. KELLOGG.

C. N. NETTERVILLE, Jr., adm'r., of WILLIAM NETTERVILLE will sell all perishable and personal property.

EBENEZER WILLIAMS wishes to sell his present residence, containing 222 acres of land.

December 6, 1834

The West Feliciana Rail Road Band, located at this place, went into operation the present week. Col. B. L. C. WAILES, Register of the Land Office at Washington, has been elected Cashier, and JOSEPH JOHNSON, Esqr., President.

Wm. VAN NORMAN of Liberty, answers an inquiry in the previous newspaper.

WILFORD GARNER, of Amite County has been appointed adm'r., of the JAMES GARNER estate and will sell several tracts of land and other personal items.

THOS. TARVER, adm'r., of DAVID WHITE's estate, will sell 159 acres in Amite county.

Deed of Trust executed by MICHAEL WOODS to EDMUND H. WAILES, in trust for, and to secure JOSEPH A. FOSTER, on account of a liability of JOSEPH A. FOSTER, for Woods, to one JAMES COLLES, the said deed of trust has been forfeited, and the land is to be sold.

By virtue of an order of the Probate Court of Wilkinson county, made at the November term thereof, 1834, the undersigned administrator of the Estate of JESSE DELOACH, deceased, will sell at public sale, to the highest bidder, on the first Monday and Tuesday in Jamuary next, all the Personal Estate belonging to said JESSE DELOACH, deceased, consisting of 12 likely Negroes, a good ox wagon & team, about 30 head of cattle, about 40 head of sheep, 5 work horses, 3 Spanish colts, Farming utensils, Household & Kitchen Furniture, & etc., on a credit of six months. Purchasers giving notes with security. WILEY DELOACH, Adm'r.

Final settlement of RAYFORD PRICE's estate

December 13, 1834
SAMUEL DELOACH begs leave to inform the public, that he has opened the "Bayou Sara Hotel" for the accommodation of boarders and persons waiting for the steam boats.   Sept. 5,1834

JAMESY HICKS, adm'r for the dec'd., JOHN C. HICKS' estate on the 28th November, 1834.

J. C. PATRICK will sell the dower land (170 acres) of Mrs. ELIZA PATRICK which contains a dwelling, out-houses, a good well of water, garden and orchard, and has about 60 acres of open land under fence. The balance of land is well timbered, and other-wise of good quality. Being situated upon the line of the contemplated Rail Road, and so near to the town of Woodville, its value and advantages must be apparent to all. The land is known as the "Hadley Tract".

PETER FAUST, adm'r., of the JAMES FAUST's estate, will sell a tract of land.

ALLEN SPURLOCK, adm'r., of the JOHN KEEN's estate of Amite County, will sell a tract of land at Washington, Mississippi.

December 20, 1834
Married in this town by the Rev. SPENCER WALL, Mr. ANAIAS DUNBAR of St. Francisville to Miss HENNIETTA BIGGS, of Jackson, Louisana.

Married the 10th, by the Rev. Wm. WINNS, Mr. JOSEPH C. REILY to Miss SARAH A. JONES, all of this county.

$20 reward for a pocket book lost between this place and Mr. JOHN OGDEN's on the 19th. Among other bills, it contained one receipt for

several bills, left with Mr. JOHN WALKER, Esqr., of Liberty, and an order on me from WILSON GILLILAND for $20.
  SAMUEL T. KING, Woodville,Mi. 1834

December 27, 1834
The steamboat "Freedom" has undergone a thorough repair and will leave Bayou Sara to New Orleans Saturday morning. J. C. WALKER, Master

1835
January 3, 1835
Married the 30th, by Rev. T. C. BROWN, Mr. DAVID A. PALMER, of La., to Miss MARTHA A., daughter of Mr. CHARLES HESTER of this county.

Married by N. SCUDDER, Esqr., the 12th, Mr. WILLIAM PENNY to Mrs. ELIZABETH BROWN, all of this county.

Married the 30th, by N. SCUDDER, Esqr., Mr. MOSES STEWART of Adams county, to Miss ELIZABETH WHITE of this county.

Married on Thursday evening the 1st, by N. SCUDDER, Esqr., Mr. BENJAMIN WALKER to Miss EMELINE DELOACH, all of this county.

Died the 26th of December, Mrs. ANN TUELL, a member of the Methodist Episcopal Church for many years.

Final settlement of JOHN H. DURANT's estate by the exec'rs., JOHN L. WALL, & JOHN CARLISLE.

JOHN S. CARSON, SAMUEL JAYNE, ARTHUR FOX, of the Building Committee, will accept sealed bids for the purpose of building a "Banking House" in the town of Monticello. December 4, 1834.

RICHARD COTTER & JOHN PRESTON have formed a co-partnership in the blacksmithing business.

Final settlement of SAMUEL WOODS' estate by the adm'rs., JOANNA GLASS & GERALD C. BRANDON

JOHN S. WALTON, exec'r. of the dec'd., SOLON HILL's estate, will sell property in Woodville.

January 10, 1835

Property of JAMES LAND's estate to be sold by the the administratrix, LAMINDER LAND.

THOS. TARVER, adm'r,. of the DAVID WHITE estate, wishes to sell 159 acres.

JAMESY HICKS, adm'r,. for the JOHN C. HICKS estate.

Wm. BROWN, County Surveyor of Wilkinson County, will ascertain the dividing line between the lands of WILLIAM L. BRANDON, and the heirs of MOSES HOOK, deceased.

LYDIA H. NEWELL, exec'x., of the GEORGE B. NEWELL's estate, will present her accounts for final settlement at the March term.

JOHN HENDERSON & S. S. BOYD have entered into a partnership in the practice of law.

January 17, 1835

MARTHA ANN ILER, adm'rx., of the JONAS ILER estate, will sell a part of the estate.

A final settlement of the ANDREW McCARTNEY estate will be made by JOSEPH DAOGHERY, adm'r., at the next March term.

JACOB SEEBER, adm'r., of the URIAH McGRAW estate, will sell all the personal property belonging to the estate.

MAYSON E. SAUNDERS was appointed adm'r., of the THOMAS HAYNES' estate.

A final settlement of the TEMPLE STEWART estate will be presented by ROBT. P. STEWART, executor.

Samuel Deloach begs leave to inform the public, that he has opened the "Bayou Sara Hotel" for the accommodation of boarders and persons waiting for the steam boats.   September 5, 1834

January 24, 1835

The Brandon Academy opens with JAS. O. H. VAN VACTER, as principal.   Dec. 29, 1834

SUSAN PHILBRICK offers a reward for the return of Louisa.

JAMES BRADFORD of St. Francisville, because of "continued indisposition" and the necessity of seeking in another climate and restoration of health, desires to sell his entire estate.

DICK H. EGGLESTON has placed all his accounts in the hands of JOSEPH J. EVELETH, Esquire.

E. H. WAILES, an a agent of an insurance company in Woodville, reduces the rate on gins to three percent per annum.

LAMINDER LAND, adm'r., of JAMES LAND's estate, offers all of the lands, tenements and hereditaments belonging to said James Land.

MAYSO E. SAUNDERS, adm'r., of the THOMAS HAYNES' estate

A. KILBOURN, dentist in Woodville, will visit Liberty, in Amite County in February.

A. ADAMS, executor of LUCRETIA STEWART's estate will present his accounts for final settlement.

January 31, 1835
RICHARD COTTER & JOHN PRESTON have formed a co-partnership in blacksmithing.

A. W. BELL, painter & glazier

SAMUEL DAWSON, adm'r., of WILLIAM DAWSON's estate will present his accounts for final settlement.

A note sent by the mail contractor, HIRAM FOWLER, Esq., on Monday last, stated that Mr. JOHN HALL and his daughter, ELIZABETH HALL, were killed and Mrs. HALL and a negro girl were very dangerously injured, when a hurricane passed over the town of Liberty in Amite County on the night of the 14th. Mr. Z. P. BUTLER had a leg broken. Mr. Hall, who is mentioned above as having fallen a victim to the wind, was a highly respectable gentleman and useful citizen. He leaves a large family to lament his untimely fate. (Originally from the NATCHEZ COURIER & JOURNAL)

Died the 16th, at the residence of Dr. S. ROBINSON, JAMES WILLIAM FOLEY, only son of Mr. M. P. FOLEY. His short life was one of protracted suffering and pain.

LEWIS ENDT, vs. JOHN DEAL & THOMAS J. SMITH
Land is to be sold where JOHN LENNOX'S blacksmith shop is located.

GEORGE C. McWHORTER has placed his accounts in

the hands of C. S. & H. D. KELLOG.

B. F. SCOTT HAS 2200 acres of land to be sold.

WM. ST. JOHN ELLIOT, President of the Board of Police.

C. S. KELLOGG & C. C. WEST were appointed commissioners to receive proposals for a plan and building of a jail, in the town of Woodville, to be composed principally of brick & wood, not to exceed fifty feet square in the outside walls.

JOHN H. REED, adm'r., of PETER RABB's estate will present his accounts for final settlement.

Names mentioned in the stated writs concerning JOHN W. GILDART, from the Circuit Court : SAMUEL JAYNE, LAZARUS DRAKE, WALTHAL BURTON, JOHN W. GILDART, D. H. EGGLESTON, CALEB HALL, C. E. BUSHNESS, FRANCIS GILDART, JAMES THORN, THOMAS NETTERVILLE, OSCAR PILLET, MORGAN DAVIS, JOHN KELLEY, FRANCIS S. MAYES, A. M. DUNN, ALBERT G. FOSTER, PALMER SMITH, FRANCIS KELLER, CALEB HOWELL, JAMES HUDSON, JOHN STARK, DAVID HOLT, ROBERT R. STARK, and JOHN STEVENS.

February 7, 1835

JAMES BRADFORD's horse was stolen in St.Francisville on Saturday the 27th.

JNO. PEEBLES, adm'r., of the WM. PEEBLES' estate will sell all the person estate as well as land.

JAS. L. TRASK will sell 1500 acres of land.

EDMOND N. SALE is moving to New Orleans and wishes to sell his plantation. Apply to Rev. S. WALL or to JAMES WHITE, Esquire, in Woodville.

All who are indebted to the estate of JOSEPH A. FOSTER, and to A. G. FOSTER, must pay immediately!

JNO. McNULTY & JNO. L. WALL dissolves their copartnership and have associated themselves in business at Fort Adams with NICHOLAS NORWOOD.

J. A. STEWART has lost a small bay mare.

Married Thursday evening by DANIEL BASS, Esq'r., CHAUNCEY S. KELLOGG, Esq'r., to Miss REBECCA B. C. WALLER, daughter of Mrs. REBECCA F. COLEMAN, all of this county.

Married on Thursday, the 5th, by the Rev. T. C. BROWN, Mr. Wm. ALEXANDER, to Miss ELIZA COMBS, daughter of JONATHAN COMBS, all of this county.

Died at Fort Adams on the 30th of January, Mr. JOHN McNULTY, aged 34 years.

February 14, 1835

THOS. PANNELL of Jackson, La., offers $20 reward for the return of two horses which were stolen.

Married the 12th by the Rev. T. C. BROWN, Mr. WILLIAM TILLER to Miss LAURA ANN RICHARDSON.

The approaching anniversary of Genl. WASHINGTON's birth night, (the 22nd of Feb'y) falling on Sunday, will be celebrated in this town on Monday Evening the 23rd instant, by a splendid Ball at the Rail Road Hotel. Gentleman wishing to participate on the occasion are requested to call on the proprietor, Mr. T. W. RADFORD, and enroll their names.

R. T. CHRISTMAS, adm'r., of the WESLEY CHAMBERS' estate will present his accounts for final settlement.

NATHAN SWAYZE, adm'r., of the LYDIA CORY estate will present his accounts for final settlement.

WILLIAM ILER has enlarged his waggon and coach-making shop. Also, next door is the blacksmithing shop of NICHOLAS MESSENGER.

ROBERT STEWART, adm'r., of the GREGORY FERRELL estate

February 21, 1835

Married the 15th by JOSEPH PATTERSON, Esq'r., Mr. JOHN DOWNS to Miss SARAH TICKELL, all of this county.

CHRISTOPHER BANCKS, Deputy Surveyor for Wilkinson county.

Final settlement of the DANIEL MURPHREY estate by JAMES VARNELL, executor.

MARY NETTERVILLE has lost a large bay horse.

Lengthy notice of ELIZABETH KIRKHAM's petition for her allotment of her dower to the THOMAS KIRKHAM estate. On the 22nd day of February, 1833, the said THOMAS KIRKHAM died, leaving five children.

JOHN S. HOLT has taken up two horses as strays.

February 28, 1835

THOS. BELL, guardian of the WILLIAM BELL estate, will present his final settlement.

Died on the 22nd, after a severe illness of six days, Mrs. MARIA ASHLY, wife of JOHN ASHLEY, Esqr., of this county.

Died in New Orleans on the 20th, Maj. JEREMIAH NOLAND, a highly respectable citizen of this county.

Died in Amite County on the 16th, Mrs. ELIZABETH DUNN, wife of Maj. SYLVESTER DUNN, leaving a large family.

There is in this town a reed from the high Black Mountain in Germany. It is called Black Oak.---The mountain is three hundred and sixty-three miles high. There never was but one man that got to the top of it, and he cut the stick off the top of the Mountain, and made a present of it to a gentleman in Germany, and that gentleman brought it to the United States and presented it to a citizen in Woodville.

The land of CADE HAVARD, deceased, will be divided among the legal heirs.

JANE DUTY, adm'rx., of the BENJAMIN DUTY estate

MARY JONES, the widow of DARLING JONES will petition for her dower rights.

March 7, 1835

H. CONNELL, adm'r., of the KINCHEON HOLLIMAN estate will sell all the personal property.

PETER FAUST, adm'r., of the JAMES FAUST's estate will sell the real estate.

The Post Office at Whitestown, has been re-established, and Maj. L. D. BROWN appointed Post Master.

Died at her residence in this county, on Sunday after a few days illness, Mrs. JAMEST HICKS, consort of the late JOHN C. HICKS.

Died on the 4th at his residence in Columbia, South Carolina, Gen. WADE HAMPTON, in the 81st year of his age.

W. H. WILKINSON, J. B. THERREL, and A. G. FOSTER have bought Mr. J. MABRY's stock of goods, and formed a business together.

THEODORE MOLLEHAN vs. THOS. C. REED

The executors of DANIEL MURPHREY's estate, JAMES VARNELL, and BALDWIN HAYNES, in right of his wife Melissa, formerly MELISSA MURPHY, presents their accounts for final settlement.

March 14, 1835

JOHN A. SCOTT and H. A. MOORE are candidates for the Sheriff of Wilkinson County.

JOSEPH H. & HENRY G. STREET, have formed a partnership and will practice law in the courts.

JOHN W. SCOTT, adm'r., of the URIAH VINING estate

RICHARD COTTER, the adm'r of the DURANT H. HARPER estate will sell all the personal estate.

Tax sale mentions Wm. HAILE, H. B. ESKEU, WILEY M. WOOD, Wm. R. HATTON, JAMES NICHOLSON, and JUSTUS ANDREWS.

Attorney N. G. PERKINS, has located in Woodville.

Citizens who had suits against JOHN DEAL: LEWIS ENDT, A. G. FOSTER, G. D. BOYD, Wm. H. WHITE, Wm. W. SNODDY, GEORGE EVANS, C. C. WEST, MILO FERRELL, THOS J. SMITH, JAS. JONES and A. FERGUSON.

March 21, 1835

A "Deed of Trust" mentions EDMUND G. VINING and wife, and JOHN L. WALL, the surviving partner of McNULTY & WALL.

A list of cases disposed of by the High Court of Errors and Appeals, at the January Term, 1835, originally appeared in the STATE RIGHTS BANNER.

Married the 19th by the Rev. T. C. BROWN, Mr.

JOSEPH B. S. WYATT, of Tennessee, to Miss JOSEPHINE NETTERVILLE, daughter of Mr. THOS NETTERVILLE, of this county.

Suits against J. M. WOOD mentions EDWARD P. FORNEQUET, ALEXANDER SMITH, THOMAS LYNE, THEODORE STARK, ALENANDER SMITH, GEORGE B. COLLIER, LOYAL CASE, and JOHN NETTERVILLE. J. M. WOOD's land must be sold to satisfy court cost.

Notice: I do hereby forewarn all persons from trading for a certain Note, given for $700 by THOMAS NUTT to BENJAMIN F. SCOTT, for a certain negro man, named PETER, dated March 12, 1835, as I am determined not to pay, as security, any part of said Note, as I did not know what the instrument of writing was. Signed PETER CONROD March 13, 1835

T. E. SHANNON offers his plantation for sale

W. E. GREEN, guardian of MARGARET M. LUSK, will sell 315 acres of land lying in Wilkinson County, bounded by the lands of JOSEPH SANDERS, and WILLIAM & BEHULA SWAYSE. (Originally from the NATCHEZ COURIER)

March 28, 1835
ELIZA WILLS and JEPHTHA V. DAY, administrators of the BENJAMIN B. WILLS' estate

ROBERT LONGIMIRE, adm'r., of the JOHN CAPEL estate

JOHN J. LOWRY, adm'r., of the ELIZA BENNET estate

A brown horse was taken up as a stray by THOMAS McDOWELL, in Liberty. M. M. WHITNEY, Ranger, Amite County.

April 4, 1835
WILLIAM T. MAYES is also a candidate for sheriff.

Married the 2nd., by JOSEPH H. SSTREET, Esqr., Mr. THOMAS W. RADFORD to Miss LUCY WOOD, all of this town.

Died in Hancock County on March 15th, in the 62nd year of his age, Judge CHARLES STEWART, of this county.

April 11, 1835
EBENEZER WILLIAMS has lost two horses which

strayed from his residence on Percy's Creek.

ELIZABETH HOPKINS, adm'x., of the SOLOMON HOPKINS' estate

ALGERNON S. RANDOLPH, Judge of Probates appointed CHAUNCY S. KELLOGG, EDWARD McGEHEE and CATO C. WEST as commissioners, to divide a tract of land into two equal shares. THOMAS LYNE claims one half.

Citizens who had suits against JOHN SLADE were: JOHN OGDEN, Wm. H. WHITE , L. D. BROWN, T. E. W. JAMES, E. M. EGGLESTON, ALEX. SMITH, JOHN SLADE ,THOS. J. SMITH, and WILLIAM HUGHEY.

A. H. CHAMBERS, adm'r., of the EDWARD WATKINS' estate

ELIZABETH HOPKINS, adm'x., of the SOLOMON HOPKINS' estate

THOMAS WOODSIDE, adm'r., of the JANE WOODSIDE estate, presents his accounts for final settlement.

BASS & LEWIS vs. LUCY SHAFFER $123.57 due

JAMES M. WOOD vs. FONES McCARTHY $71.11 due

JOHN H. GREADY vs. VINCENT M. LEWIS $57.14 due

JAMES QUINE has purchased the tract of land on Percy's Creek known as the "Hudry Place", being the same where Capt. JOHN HUDRY formerly resided.

Married the 5th by JOHN MAYS, Esqr., Mr. JOHN ILER to Miss AMANDA TURNER, all of this county.

MOSES LIDDELL vs. ALEXANDER ARDRY

Citizens who had suits against JOHN LENOX: JOHN BRYANT, RICHARD COTTER, DICK H. EGGLESTON, THOS. J. SMITH, THEODORE MOLLMAN, P. X. NEWTON, JOHN DEAL, JAMES JONES, JESSE SAUNDERS, JOHN PRESTON, STEPHEN JOHNSON, and Wm. H. WHITE.

April 11, 1835
Married the 9th by the Rev. T. C. BROWN, Mr. RUFUS M. RICHARDSON, to Miss MARY ANN GLOVER, daughter of Mr. GLOVER, all of this county.

Died in Hinds County on the 5th, Mrs. EUGENIA A., wife of Col. JOHN A. GOMBALL of that county.

JAMES WALKER, Esqr., has received the executive appointment of Judge of the 3rd Judicial Dictrict, since the Hon. A. M. KEAGAN, has resigned.

SARAH Y. WALL, adm'rx., of the FRANCIS P. WALL estate

EVELINE D. McNULTY, ex'rx., of the JOHN McNULTY estate

WILLIS HUNTER, adm'r., of the CLAIBORNE TEKEL estate

W. TIGNER, adm'r., of the PIERCE NOLAND estate

A. H. CHAMBERS, adm'r., of the EDWARD WATKINS estate will present accounts for final settlement.

Land of Mrs. ELIZABETH YERBY will be surveyed. This land belongs to the WILLIAM YERBY estate and is bounded by lands belonging to WM. BROOKS, Mrs. ISABEL SEMPLE, and B. F. YOUNG.

April 25, 1835

GERALD C. BRANDON, adm'r., of the JEREMIAH NOLAND estate

PRESTON W. FARRAR, Esqr., is a candidate for the House of Representatives.

H. M. FARISH, Esquire, is a candidate for the office of District Attorney, for the Third Judicial District, to fill the vacancy occasioned by the resignation of JAMES W. WALKER, Esquire.

A note of hand drawn by Mrs. R. T. COLEMAN for $140, payable one day after date, was lost. If found, return to Col. G. H. GORDON of Woodville, or R. A. NEELY in Liberty.

H. R. AUSTIN has purchased the "Mississippi Springs", formerly BANDSTON's Springs, situated in Hinds County, ten miles from Jackson, five miles from Raymond, and six from Clinton.

PRISCILLA CAUSEY, adm'x., of the JOHN H. CAUSEY estate, will sell a tract of land.

JEHU HOLLAND, adm'r., of the JOSEPH WRIGHT estate

will present his accounts for final settlement.

JAMES VARNELL, adm'r., of the DANIEL VARNELL estate will present accounts for final settlement.

S. JOHNSON, adm'r., of the DANIEL RICE's estate

May 2, 1835

WILLIAM BRYANT vs. THE STATE   Bryant was indicted in the Circuit Court of Wilkinson County, for practicing medicine without a license.

JOHN BURNEY vs. Wm. R. BAYETT   Appeal from the Circuit Court of Lawrence County, mentions JOHN BAYETT, & JOHN TUTTLE. (Originally from PORT GIBSON CORRESPONDENT)

A hurricane passed over the lower part of Tennessee, killing eight persons, and wounding many others. Amoung killed were: Mr. FRANCIS G. DEGRAPHENREID, 21 years, Mr. ELIAS LUSK and wife, and several children. (Originally from the BOLIVER FREE PRESS in Tennessee)

May 9, 1835

CHARLES HESTER, adm'r., of the JAMESY HICKS' and also adm'r., of the JOHN C. HICKS' estates.

FIELDING DAVIS, adm'r., of the BENJAMIN LEWIS' estate

Married the 8th by the Rev. T. C. BROWN, Mr. WRIGHT B. ORR to Miss MARTHA N., daughter of Mr. JAMES B. RICHARDSON, all of this county.

JABEZ BUTLER vs. JOHN BUTLER $810.11

WILLIAM EVANS wishes to rent his premises.

PARKER SMITH has lost or mislaid a note given by L. D. BROWN for $400.32.

THOMAS McDOWEL vs. JOHN CONWAY $320.67

EZEKIEL BOATNER & GILLAM A. HUDSON vs. SYLVESTER D. ROBERTS $154.56

JAMES TAYLOR vs. JAMES M. CARR $131.03

May 16, 1835

JOHN HENDERSON, adm'r., of the Dr. WILLIAM C. SMITH's estate will present his accounts for a final settlement.

BRIGADE ORDERS. An election will be held to fill the vacancy of Colonel to command the 1st Battalion of the 5th Regiment, M. M. as Col. ROBERT LAYSON has resigned. Inspectors: Fort Adams - J. L. WALL; Percys Creek - GEO. B. COLLIER, F. S. MAYES & W. R. DAVIS; Pinckneyville - J. O. FELLS, W. JOHNSON, & R. M. YERBY; Lower Homochitto - W. M. HELON, N. E. RAYMOND & JAMES LEE; Woodville-C. C. WEST, A. DANIEL & J. P. HARRIS; Whitestown-L. D. BROWN, J. F. SCOTT & C. S. COSBY; Mount Pleasant - JESSE JONES, LEWIS CASON & DAVID McNEELY.

May 23, 1835

Rev. A. S. SIMMONS will preach at the Methodist Church in Woodville, on the 2nd Sabbath of June.

Married the 14th at Prospect Hill, Adams County, by the Rev. J.C.BURROAS, Mr. HENRY I. BASS of Woodville, to Miss MARGARETTE, daughter of JOHN ROBSON, Esqr., of the former place.

Married on the 19h by the Rev. T. C. BROWN, Mr. JAMES McDONAL, formerly of Macon, Georgia, to Mrs. ELENDER KELLER, daughter of the Rev. NOEL WADDILL, of this county. (Wilkinson County Marriage Book states that ELEANOR WADDELL M. GEO. KELLER, 3-12-1819)

Married the 21st, by the Rev. T. C. BROWN, Mr. CHARLES R. LEWIS to Miss LAURA L. SEWELL, all of this county.

Married the 21st, by the Rev. T. C. BROWN, Mr. BENJAMIN M. MAYES to Miss ELIZABETH SMITH, all of this county.

May 30,1835

Married the 28th by the Rev. Wm. WINANS, the Hon. JAMES WALKER to Miss MARY B. NEWELL, all of this county.

Died on Friday the 22nd, Mr. ABRAM ILER.

Rev. A. S. SIMMONS will preach at the Methodist Church in woodville, on the 2nd Sabbath of June.

A new paper to be established in Natchez entitled "Mississippi Free Trader and Natchez Gazette" and also the revival of the "Southern Galaxy".

THOMAS E. HELM has taken up a mule as a stray.

Two suits against THOS. J. NERSON

June 6, 1835

Married on Tuesday last, by the Rev. WILLIAM WINANS, Mr. DABNEY F. LEWIS to Miss ANN E. MAYES, daughter of Major F. S. MAYES, all of this county.

Married on Thursday last, by the Rev. E. C. BROWN, Mr. RUFUS R. RICHARDSON to Miss HESTER ANN ROGERS, all of this county.

Mr. DANIEL WOODARD was elected Colonel of the 1st Battalion 5th Regiment, M. M., on Saturday last, without opposition.

MARY HARSON, adm'x., of the JOSEPH HARSON estate will present her accounts for final settlement.

Mr. ROGERT NORWOOD's health has declined and must leave the southern country, consequently he has withdrawn his name from our firm. FELLS, SAUNDERS & NORWOOD.

GEORGE H. GORDON and THOMAS C. WEST have formed a partnership in the practice of law.

Catalogue of medicines listed

June 13, 1835

THOS. G. ELLIS, guardian of MARTHA ANN CUMMINS, HARRIET JANE CUMMINS, & THOMAS BERNARD CUMMINGS, infant heirs of JOHN CUMMINGS, deceased, will sell 69 acres of land on the Homochitto river bounded on the north by JOHN R. FORD'S land and on the south by lands of the estate of JAMES PHIPPS.

CADE HAVARD, late adm'r., of the DAVID HAVARD estate, will sell 640 acres of land bounded by lands of the estate of THOMAS FOSTER, and land belonging to JOSEPH HOLMES.

CALVIN MERRILL, adm'r., of the JAMES GAINS estate in Hancock County, will sell the interest that Gains held in a tract of land on Gains' Bluff. This is one half of that occupied by his mother, ANN GAINS, deceased, in right of her dower.

DICK H. EGGLESTON's brother, WILLIAM B. EGGLESTON, and his friend, JOSEPH J. EVELETH, are authorized to act in his behalf while he is absent.

June 20, 1835

Married Sunday morning at the Methodist Church by the Rev. THOS. C. BROWN, Mr. M. A. JENKINS of Benton, Mississippi, to Miss ROSELIE P. CARTER, of this county.

Died Friday morning the 18th after a short illness, CHARLES WEST, infant son of THOS. J. HAMILTON.

JANE MOORE & ERASMUS CASTON, adm'rs., of the GREEN G. CASTON's estate will sell land.

The real estate of JOHN E. WITHERSPOON, dec'd., of Amite County will be sold.

The real estate of ISHAM RANDAL, dec'd., will be sold to pay his debts.

E. R. QUARTERMAN has enlarged his establishment and is now prepared to cast boxes of any composition that may be required for Gin Stands, Steam Engines, or Saw Mills. He also has on hand, large and small Bathing Tubs.

JOHN NETTERVILLE, adm'r., of the DUNCAN STEWART's estate

ALEX. M. DUNN, exec'r., of the estates of both ROGER DUNN and SARAH A. DUNN, will present his accounts for both estates.

June 27, 1835

JOHN KAIGLER, late guardian of ISABELLA KAIGLER, now ISABELLA CONY, will present his accounts with said ward for final settlement.

TRISTRAM S. EASTON, adm'r., of the WILLIAM PHIPPS estate

July 4, 1835
July 11, 1835

E. A. MONKS, adm'r., of the WILLIAM MONKS' estate, will sell all the interest in one half of five lots lying in Fort Adams.

Died this morning after an illness of 8 days, in the 6th year of her age, MARTHA JANE, eldest daughter of Wm. A. A. CHISHOLM, of this town.

The death of our late partner WILLIAM BULLITT, Esqr., in April last, has not affected the business, nor has the death of Mr. SHIPP.

July 18, 1835

The good people of Vicksburg undertook on Monday last, to expell the gamblers from that city. They went to the coffe house kept by ALFRED NORTH and in forcing entrance, Doctor HUGH SHIELL BODLEY was killed. North and four other gamblers were hung.

Doctor B. WALLER TAYLOR has settled in Woodville. At night he can be reached at the residence of his brother, Dr. WILLIAM R. TAYLOR and messages left with Mr. J. P. HARRIS will be attended to.

REBECCA STEPHENS, adm,'rx., of the FELIX E. STEPHENS estate

L. GARNER, adm'r., of the JOHN SPURLOCK's estate in Amite County

Died the 13th in the 17th year of her age, ELEANOR C. CARTER, daughter of G. W. & M. B. CARTER.

July 25, 1835

ROBERT STEWART, adm'r., of the GREGORY TERRELL estate in Amite County will sell land.

PETER FAUSE, adm'r., of the JAMES FAUST estate will sell land in Amite County.

A man named JOSEPH DAMON was executed at Mayville, Chantauque County, New York on the 15th for the murder of his wife & swore he was unjustly accused by false witnesses.

Married the 23rd, by the Rev. T. C. BROWN, Mr. JOHN CONWAY, formerly of Amite County, to Miss REBECCA M., daughter of Mr. JOSIAH GAYLE, of Amite County.

Married the 23rd, by the Rev. T. C. BROWN, Mr. JOHN B. THERREL to Miss JANE A. DUNLAP, all of this county.

THOS. F. GRAVIS is a candidate for coroner.

WM. ILER, adm'r., & PHEREBY ILER, admr'x., of the ABRAM ILER estate

August 1, 1835

If Capt. JOHN W. LEATHERMAN will consent to run as a Candidate for Police Juror, he will obtain the support of many voters.

Died near Woodville, on Sunday 26th of July, ELIZA ANN, daughter of Mr. SAMUEL TILLOTSON, of Liberty Mi., aged nine years, 3 months.

August 8, 1835

JOHN C. BURRUSS has lost a brown horse, formerly owned by Mr. Wm. S. GRIFFIN, of Woodville.

Sheriff H. HUNT, of Liberty, Amite County, has a runaway who is said to belong to JOHN TURNER, who lives near the Petit Gulf, Miss.

ELIZABETH M'CULLOCH's place is for sale. 580 acres

Died on Thursday, July 30th, 1835, at her residence on Buffaloe, in this county, in the 49th year of her age, Mrs. SARAH SMITH, consort of the late PRESTWOOD SMITH.

"The Burlington Sentinel gives the following account of the imprisonment of three Revolution Soldiers. We had an invitation to visit the jail of Chittenden County; where are now confined not for crime, but for debts of $5, $10, and $20, which they cannot pay, three old Soldiers of the Revolution. Upon inquiry, we ascertained the ages of these veterans to be as follows--72, 75, and 85 years.
The above is a fine comment upon the laws which allow incarceration for debts".

Died at the residence of her mother, near Woodville, on the 13th, Miss ELEANOR C. CARTER, aged 16 years, daughter of the late GEO. W. CARTER. Jackson, La. August 15, 1835

R. L. BONER wishes to exchange his place of 3 acres on which he resides in Woodville, for a place in the country.

August 15, 1835

If Wm. M. HELM will become a candidate for the Police of Wilkinson County, he will receive the support of many voters.

Died in Woodville, on Sunday the 9th, Mrs. ELIZABETH A. HENLEY, consort of the late JOSEPH P. HENLEY.

SAML. W. LEWIS vs. Wm. H. HUNTER

JOHNSON & WOOD vs. THOS. J. NERSON

JESSE JONES & WILLIAM HALL, adm'rs., of the ALLEN CAIN estate

August 22, 1835

Death of WM. COBBETT was learned by the arrival of the Roscoe, at New York, from Liverpool, with dates to the 24th June, we are appraised of the death of this celebrated man, on the 18th of June last, in the 75 year of his age.

The Rev. J. A. RANALDSON, of Jackson, La., will preach in the Methodist Churst in Pinckneyville, Mi. on Sunday 30th.

Married the 11th August, by JOHN ASHLEY, Esqr., Mr. THOMAS FLOYD to Miss MARY COLE, all of this county.

EZEKIEL BOATNER, adm'r., of the WILLIAM BACHELOR estate

JAMES W. SMITH, & EZER E. WOODS, adm'rs., of the SARAH SMITH estate

POLASKI CAGE, ex'r., of the JOHN STEWART estate

JAS. J. GRAVES, & GABRIEL CASTON, ex'rs., of the JAMES RAOUL estate

R. A. NEELY & STEPHEN R. DAVIS, ex'rs., of the ROBERT CRAIG estate

JACOB SEEBER, adm'r., of the URIAH M'GRAW estate will present his accounts for final settlement.

August 29, 1835

HENRY CONRAD, who lives seven miles from Woodville, has taken up two strayed bay horses.

DAVID PEMBLE, of Amite County, is a candidate for governor.

NATHAN CHALFANT, adm'r., of the JOHN E. WITHERSPOON estate, will sell land in Amite County.

J. J. LOWRY & SOL. WEATHERSBY, adm'rs., of the HUGH BENNET estate will sell land in Amite County.

JESSE SAUNDERS, vs. FRANCIS ONEAL $289

WILLIAM NETTERVILLE vs. JAMES P. BOSWELL $275

JACOB KELLER vs. JAMES P. BOSWELL $800

JOHN L. WALL vs. ROBERT P. STEWART $346.57

September 5, 1835

$5,000 will be raised by LOTTERY for the purpose of building a Female Seminary. THOS. F. GRAVIS is hereby appointed Agent to superintend the same.

I. T. BROWNING vs. RANSOM GRAHAM   To be sold: The claim of Ranson Graham to one quarter section of land adjoining Clark's creek, and it being the tract lately sold by said Graham to PETER LEATHERMAN; levied on as the property of said Graham, to satisfy the above stated case and cost.

Married the 27th of August, by the Rev. SAMUEL DAWSON, Mr. WESTERN W. MUSE to Miss NANCY COMER, all of this county.

Married the 19th August, at Nashville, Tennessee, by the Rev. Doct. EDGAR, Mr. N. W. BUTLER, of Madisonville, Mi., to Miss ANN P. MARSHALL, of this place.

Married the 3rd, by the Rev. T. C. BROWN, Mr. THOMAS JOHNSTON to Mrs. SARAH D. POURCHE, all of this county. (Wilkinson County Marriage Book states SALLY ARMSTRONG m. JOSEPH POURCHE ,8-16-1827)

Married the 26th by J. H. STREET, Esqr., Mr. ALEXANDER MITCHELL to Mrs. MARGARET LAWRENCE, all of this place.

Married the 3rd, by the Rev. SAMUEL DAWSON, Mr. ELISHA S. SIMS to Miss MARTHA PRESLER, all of this county.

Died, at the residence of Mr. T. S. EASTON, on Thursday evening the 20th August, Miss JULIA K. RAYMOND, the only daughter of Dr. N. E. RAYMOND, aged thirteen years.

JOHN B. THERREL & CO. vs. VINCENT M. LEWIS $61

The Misses CALDER have removed from Mt. Hope, and have moved to the house lately occupied by Mr. L. SHAFFER, near the Baptist Church in Woodville.

J. S. M. COON offers a tract of land for sale.

September 12, 1835

List of citizens who were candidates for various offices: WILLIAM M. HELM, SAMUEL TURSEVILLE, DAVID McNEELY, THOMAS NETTERVILLE and DAVID PEMBLE.

THOMAS TARVER, adm'r., of the DAVID WHITE estate will sell land.

MOSES M. PHARES offers his plantation on which he now resides for sale. It is located three miles west of Laurel Hill, and two miles west of the Rail Road route, leading from Woodville to St. Francisville, containing 400 acres. It contains a good dwelling house, corn house, mill and gin, and all necessary out houses, and a never failing spring of execellent water.

Married the 6th by Rev. T. C. BROWN, Mr. JOHN F. SCOTT to Miss ELIZA, daughter of Mr. SAMUEL GOODRICH, all of this country.

Died on the 8th, at the residence of the Hon. MOSES LIDDELL, WILLIAM S. GRIFFIN, Esquire.

Died the 15th, at the residence of Mr. GEORGE BROWN, after a lingering illness, Mr. WILLIAM BROWN, in the 69th year of his age.

(An extensive article on the outbreak of cholera in Versailles, Ky., listing 59 names of citizens who died and another list of 24 inmates who died in the Tennessee penitentiary, and the county from which they came, is given by JOHN M'INTOSH, agent and keeper of the penitentiary.)

September 19, 1835

JOHN B. THERREL & CO. vs. VINCENT M. LEWIS $61.63

JOHN WATKINS and WILLIAM DODD are candidates for offices.

Died the 10th, HENRY C. CONNELL, eldest son of the late JOHN CONNELL, aged about 7 years.

Died in Woodville the 13th, Mr. J. A. WELLS, aged about 27 years, a native of New York City. The deceased was formerly a member of Brown's Circus.

Died, on the 13th, Mr. H. P. LIPSCOMB.

Died the 15th at his residence near Woodville, Mr.

WILLIAM STEWART.

Died the 7th, Mrs. ELIZA ANN DILLAHUNTY, daughter of the late MARK and ANN KIRKBY, of New York, and wife of JOHN N. DILLAHUNTY, Esqr., of this county. She became ill while caring for her sick children, who survived their mother.

THOS. J. HAMILTON, adm'r., of the WILLIAM S. GRIFFIN estate

A. B. STEELE, adm'r., of the ISHAM RANDALL estate will sell land known as "Randall's Mills".

HALL & JOHNSON vs. JAMES P. BOSWELL $150

JOHNSON & WOOD vs. THOS. J. NERSON

SAML. W. LEWIS vs. Wm. H. HUNTER

September 26, 1835

Married the 10th by NATHAN E. RAYMOND, Esqr., Mr. THOMAS I. LANIER, of North Carolina, to Mrs. ELLEN OLD, of this county.

NANCY ELLSBERRY vs. JAMES P. POSWELL Attachment against the property for $60

ELIZABETH HOLMES, adm'rx., of the estate of AHAB HOLMES

October 3, 1835

EZER E. WOODS' offers his plantation in West Feliciana for sale.

Married the 27th of September, by the Rev. T. C. BROWN, Mr. GEORGE JONTE to Miss MINERVA OGLESBY.

Married the 1st, by the Rev. JOHN C. BURRUSS, Capt. ROBERT SEMPLE to Miss LEONORA, second daughter of HUGH CONNELL, Esqr., all of this county.

Married the 1st, by the Rev. SAMUEL DAWSON, Mr. ALEXANDER S. ISLER to Miss MALISSA TURNER, all of this county.

Died in this county the 31st, Mr. JOSHUS L. PEARCE

October 10, 1835

WILLIS HUNTER, adm'r., of CLAIBORNE TICKELL and guardian of STEPHEN TICKELL & ROBERT TICKELL, infant heirs of SUSANNAH TICKELL, dec'd., will sell 601 acres being the tract purchased by Susannah Tickell from JAMES BUFORD in 1829.

Married September 17, by JOHN MAYES, Esq., Mr. A. P. REID to Miss MARY E. PRESBURY, of Maryland.

G. SLEEPER, guardian of the minor heirs of the estate of TALIFERRO STRIBLING, late of Amite County, will sell 100 acres of land. (Originally from the NATCHEZ COURIER)

ANDREW BARLAND, adm'r., of the WILLIAM BARLAND, Sen., estate, will sell 640 acres ajoining the lands of THOMAS FORD. (Originally from the NATCHEZ COURIER)

October 17, 1835

MATILDA TRENTHAN, adm'r., of the MARTIN TRENTHAM estate in Amite County

JOHN RICHMOND, adm'r., of the JAMES RICHMOND estate in Amite County, will sell land.

PETER FAUST, adm'r., of the JAMES FAUST estate in Amite County, will sell land.

M. W. CALLICOATTE, adm'r., of the estate of THOMAS H. HALL estate

RUFUS M. RICHARDSON wishes to sell 130 acres.

D. C. HENDERSON, adm'r., of the JOSEPH COOPER estate

JOHN SMITH wishes to sell his lands on Buffaloe. Enquire of Fr's S. MAYES, living adjoining, or W. T. MAYES, living in Woodville.

Dr. P. N. NORRIS has removed his office.

Married the 15th by JOSEPH H. STREET, Esqr., Mr. MILES E. LILLEY to Miss VIRGINIA WATERS, all of this county.

Married the 11th, by JOHN McCREA, Esqr., Mr. ELIJAH R. BROWN to Miss MARTHA M. GAULDEN.

NATHAN SWAYZE, adm'r., of the LYDIA CORY estate will sell items belonging to the estate.

ALFRED BYNUM will resume the Woodville Academy, & will extablish a "Seminary of Learning."

October 24, 1835

Died at Jackson, La. on Sunday evening 18th, Mrs. ANN T. OSWALD, consort of Col. T. H. OSWALD, of Wilkinson County, Mississippi, aged 32 years, 1 month, and 18 days.

Married Thursday evening last, by Rev. SAM'L DAWSON, Mr. MATTHEW COMBS to Miss LAVICE L. LAND, all of this county.

Any one having in their possession, Books belonging to me, will confer a favor by returning the vols. Signed by Mrs. PALMER SMITH

October 31, 1835

GEO. H. SWIGART, adm'r., of the ELIZA HEADY estate will present his accounts for final settlement.

A. P. SLOCOMB on the Homochitto river has taken up a stray horse.

Persons friendly to the cause of LIBERTY in Texas, will meet in the Court House in Woodville, on Tuesday next, at 9 o'clock, A. M., to take into consideration the propriety of forming a Company of Volunteers, to aid their brethren in their present glorious struggle for the RIGHTS of MAN.

November 7, 1835

Fire! The Steam Saw Mill and Cotton Gin, on the plantation of Mr. THOS. O. ENOS, 3 miles from this town, was consumed by fire on Saturday night last, with about 200 bales of Cotton in it. We have not learned whether it was by accident or design. The loss must be very considerable.

November 14, 1835

L. SCARBOROUGH will furnish the public supplies at all time from his lumber yard.

Married at Natchez, 5th Nov., by Rev. GEO. POTTS, ALBERT G. FOSTER, of this town, to Miss SARA JANE, daughter of Mr. JOSEPH NEWMAN.

Married on the 12th, by H. STREET, Esqr., Mr. THOMAS M. ILER to Miss MAHALA, youngest daughter of Mr. MABRY MORRIS, of this county.

Drs. SAMUEL & R. T. LESSLEY, respectfully offer their professional services to the public, the former in Woodville, and the latter on Percy's Creek.

November 21, 1835

HEZ FURGUSON has purchased the stock of E. NELSON, and will carry on the Boot and Shoe making.

November 28, 1835

The partnership of McWHORTER & SALE dissolved in September, 1835   Signed HENRY E. SALE

The amount of tickets sold for the "Lottery" was not enough to justify a drawing. Money will be refunded.

December 5, 1835

The Rev. J. N. MAFFIT will preach in the Methodist Church in this town tomorrow at 11 o'clock .

Those who are emigrating to Texas, will prepare themselves with a good gun, brace of pistols and other weapons, or weapons, as they may for a time, be under the necessity of procuring necessary food by hunting wild game, & etc. We, who intend shortly to emigrate to Texas, will leave Woodville on the 15th day of December, 1835.
C. C. McWHORTER, Chairman, JAMES M. DOWNS, Sec'ry

C. P. SMITH, Adm'r., & etc. vs. JOHN SMITH & others --900 acres of land on Buffaloe Creek, and bounded by lands of M. E. SAUNDERS & F. S. MAYES, LEVI CROW, W. T. MAYES, & M. E. SAUNDERS. Also a tract of 160 acres JOHN SMITH purchased of A. M. SCOTT, and SUSAN, HIS WIFE in December, 1832.

December 12, 1835

Died at his residence in Amite County, on Sunday the 15th, Mr. ELIAS BOATNER, about eighty years of age. He has left a disconsolate widow, together with a great number of relations and friends.

THOS. WOODSIDE has 540 acres of land for sale located seven miles west of Woodville.

JNO. B. COURTNEY has lost a pocketbook containing $5 in silver money and two notes, one from J. C. BROWN and the other from THOMAS L. TARKINSON.

December 19, 1835

WILLIAM LEAKE has a "General Agency, Forwarding and Commission Business" at Bayou Sara.

Married on the 10th, by JOS. H. STREET, Esqr., Mr. WILLIAM CIZZEE to Mrs. JANE ANDERSON, all of Wilkinson County.

Died the 25th of November at the residence of his brother, Maj. J. L. TRASK, Col. I. E. TRASK, of springfield, Mass.

Died on the 25th November at his residence near Pinckneyville, Mr. RUFFIN DELOACH, aged about 75 years.

MARY STEWART, exec'x., of the CHARLES STEWART,Sr., estate will apply for her dower. 1200 acres three miles east of Woodville and bounded by lands of M. F. DEGRAFFENREID, CHARLES HESTER, JESSE BROWN estate, THOS. OSWALD, Mr. CARTER, J. S. M. COON and A. ADAMS.

M. OVERMAN is leaving the country and he hopes those who are indebted to him will settle their accounts.

The partnership between ARCHIBALD DUNBAR and THOS. O. ENOS has been dissolved.

THOS. A. G. BATCHELOR, adm'r., of the WALTER STEWART estate

December 26, 1835

Proposals will be received for the constructing the WEST FELICIANA RAIL ROAD COMPANY, in Woodville until Jan. 15th, 1836.   JOSEPH JOHNSON, Prest.

Dr. J. N. HODGEN, recently from Kentucky, informs the public that his office is at Mrs. PENELOPE STEWART.

D. H. PROSSER, adm'r., of the REBECCA LEWIS estate will sell a certain town lot.

ELIZABETH GIBSON, adm'r., of the THOMAS GIBSON estate

JOHN P. HUMPHREYS, adm'r., of the MILAS STOUT estate

JNO. M. DELOACH, exec'r., of the RUFFIN DELOACH estate

COLLINS W. MILLER, adm'r., of the SAMUEL A. FREEMAN estate

"St Catharine House and Race Course" to be sold by the owner, R. T. DUNBAR in Natchez. Inquire with his agent, CHARLES E. WILKINS.

JOHN OGDEN, adm'r., & CYNTHIA SAPP, admr'x., of the ASA SAPP estate

GEORGE H. GORDON & THOMAS C. WEST, formed a partnership to practice law.

1836
January 2, 1836

JOHN KAIGLER, guardian of WILLIAM W. KAIGLER, one of the minor heirs of DAVID KAIGLER, will sell property of the estate.

GEORGE I. JOHNSTONE has no longer power or authority to transact any business relative to the estate of the late PALMER SMITH & Co. Signed by S. C. SMITH.

WM. JONES wishes to sell his 350 acres of land.

COLLINS W. MILLER, adm'r., of the SAMUEL A. FREEMAN estate

January 9, 1836

The Rev. Mr. A. D. WOOLDRIGE, Professor of Ancient Languages in the Louisiana College, will preach the funeral sermon of Mrs. ANN OSWALD, deceased, tomorrow, in the Methodist Church.

The Rev. JESSE YOUNG will have a meeting at Bethel, Bayou Sara, on the last Saturday and Sunday.

NANCY ELSBERRY will sell a tract of land containing 198 acres, situated on Brown's Creek, near the Calidonia road, five miles from Woodville. This tract has 50 ares cleared, a good dwelling house and out buildings. Terms--CASH

Lost some time during the summer of 1835, a note drawn by SAMUEL HOLLIMAN and endorsed by JOHN D. KAIGLER, for one hundred dollars. Any one finding the same, will please to hand it to the drawer, as it has been paid. Signed by JAMES D. BEARDIN

SAMUEL TURBEVILLE will sell his plantation lying on the Natchez road, containing 240 acres. Sale held before the "Royal Oak ."

JAMES QUINE will sell personal property on which JOHN SLADE now resides.

WM. T. LEWIS, ex'r., of the CLEMENT TOWNSEND

estate will sell a tract of land known as the Race Tract Place, 470 acres, and bounded by lands of HUGH CONNELL, JOHN HENDERSON, JOHN CONNELL's heirs, MOSES LIDDELL, MARY OGDEN and JOS. I. SCOTT--one half of which said tract belongs to the heirs of BENJ. H. LEWIS, deceased.

January 16, 1836

L. D. BROWN, guardian of ELIZABETH BRUCE will sell her property.

JOHN OGDEN, adm'r., & CYTHIA SAPP, adm'x., of the ASA SAPP estate will present their accounts for a final settlement.

Plantation for sale by Mrs. C. GUIBERT

D. C. HENDERSON, adm'r., for the THOMAS COOPER estate will present his accounts for final settlement.

All persons who are indebted to the estate of JOHN TURNER, make immediate payment to D. P. A. COOK, administrator.

Married in the parish of East Feliciana, on Tuesday the 5th, Mr. DAVID HESTER, of Wilkinson, to Miss ANNE R. SCOTT, of Louisiana.

F. B. HAYNES, adm'r., of the ARMSTEAD HAYNES' estate

JACOB LANEHART, guardian of SUSAN CURTISS presents his accounts for final settlement.

January 23, 1836

JA'S. SHAFFER wishes to sell his house and lot adjoining the town of Woodville.

W. TIGNER wishes to sell the "Shannon" place, located eight miles from Woodville on the road to Fort Adams, consisting of 250 acres, gin and mill.

D. P. A. COOK, exec'r., of the JOHN TURNER estate will present his accounts for final settlement.

D. C. HENDERSON, adm'r., of the THOMAS COOPER estate will present his accounts for final settlement.

Dr. S. E. POTTS, late of Adams, County, offers his professional services of Wilkinson county. He may be found at all times, when not professionally engaged, at his plantation, 5 miles south of Woodville, on the Sligo road, the former residence of Mr. FIELDING DAVIS.   August 29, 1835

ISAAC H. STANWOOD announces to the citizens of Woodville and vicinity, that he has rented a house on the main street in this Village, immediately under the Office of the "Woodville Republican," where he has recently opened a general assortment of desirable GOODS, selected particularly for this market, and well adapted to the season, which he offers for sale at prices which cannot fail to give satisfaction.   December 19, 1835

The amount of property consumed by the late fire at Natchez, UNDER THE HILL, is said to be, at least $109,600.

Married at the residence of his mother in the Wilkinson County, on the 23rd of December, 1835 by JOS. H. STREET, Esqr., Mr. Wm. D. WHITE to Miss REBECCA ANN ROSS, all of said county.

Married at the residence of Mr. GEO E. FRAZIER, in Wilkinson County, on the 31st December, 1835 by JOS. H. STREET, Esqr., Mr. SAMUEL ESTIS to Miss FRANCES ELIZA FRAZIER, all of said county.

Married at Woodville, in the State of Mississippi, on the 21st November, 1835, by JOSEPH H. STREET, Esqr., Mr. JOSEPH JEWELL, of Point Coupee, La., to the much accomplished Miss JANE ELIZA LEWIS, of New Orleans.

CAROLINE S. FARISH offers the residence of the late Doctor EDWARD T. FARISH, for sale. Persons wishing to purchase, will call on H. M. FARISH who is authorized to sell.

THOS G. PERCY offers a small tract of land for sale. Persons wishing to purchase, will call on THOS. G. ELLIS, Esqr., who is duly empowered to sell the same.

JOHN M'NEELY, adm'r., of the D. H. HARPER estate

JOHN RIST will sell property of 2500 acres lying on Black Creek, five miles from Jackson, La., and one mile from the contemplated Rail Road, from Clinton to Port Gibson.

JNO. L. WALL, adm'r., of the EDMUND GINN estate, will sell 360 acres of land bounded by land of C. E. WALL, and the DANIEL WILLIAMS heirs, known as the "Brick House" place.

REBECCA OGDEN will apply for a certificate of forfeited land stock entered the 30th day of November, 1818, by her and now reclaimed under the act of Congress of the 23rd of May, 1828.

T. C. BROWN has removed from Woodville.

January 30, 1836
SUSAN HART, adm'r., of the JOHN HART estate

GEORGE P. FOSTER, adm'r., of the A. R. FOSTER estate

MASON E. SAUNDERS, adm'r., of the THOMAS HAYNES estate will present his accounts for final settlement.

JOEL GLASS, surviving executor of B. LANDRUM, dec'd., will present his accounts on said estate for final settlement.

B. MARSHALL has sold his business, located at Bayou Sara Landing, to Mr. JOHN HOLMES.

R. MUMFORD has resumed the storage and commission buisness at Bayou Sarah.

We understand that the Contractors for the Rail Road between this place and Bayou Sara have commmenced their work. They say it will be completed in 20 months.

The High Courts of Errors and Appeals have appointed ROBERT HUGHES, Esqr., of Jackson, their Reporter.

We are informed that the Gin House of Mr. AMOS ADAMS, near this place, was burned on Wednesday morning, with 30 bales of cotton.

February 6, 1836
DAVID DAVIS, adm'r., of the N. HUNTER estate will present his accounts for final settlement.

Dr. P. N. NORRIS has moved his office to the building opposite Dr. EGGLESTON's boarding house, formerly occupied as an office by Dr. STONE.

The Rev, JESSE YOUNG will preach at the Baptist church in Woodville, on Monday evening.

Married the 31st of January by J. H. STREET, Esqr., Mr. DAVID CARLIS, to Miss ANN NETTERVILLE, all of this county.

Married at the residence of Mr. WILLIAM GLOVER, in this county on the 5th, by the Rev. SAMUEL DAWSON, Mr. DANIEL MILLER, to Mrs. MARTHA S. HUFF, all of this county.

Our DEVIL has requested us to remind all our marrying friends, that he is entitled to a fee of a good sizeable piece of cake, for every Hymenal notice he inserts; and he says (but delicacy almost forbids us to speak) that he has known editors to receive as many as ____ ____ONE bottle of champaigne, at least, on such occasions, to drink the health of the happy couple.
"Oh! who would be an old bachelor?"

Departed this life on Saturday the 30th of January, Mr. ELISHA HODGES, of this county, of a short illness, leaving a wife and three children.

R. SMITH, ex'r., & J. P. BUFORD, exec'x., of the S. H. BUFORD estate, will sell 340 acres, lying near Whiteville and bounded by lands of DANIEL WILLIAMS, JOSEPH SMITH, and Z. M'CORRLES heirs.

J. O. WILLIAMS' horse has strayed. Reward offered

The well known residence lately occupied by Judge SMITH, situated one and a half miles from Woodville, consisting of 240 acres, dwelling house and out houses, are for sale. Possession can be given January 1, 1837.   BEN. F. SCOTT.

A sorrel mare has strayed from the plantation of Mrs. JANE NOLAND, near Fort Adams. A. P. NOLAND

A. H. CHAMBERS, adm'r., of the ADAM HOPE estate presents his accounts for final settlement.

G. C. BRANDON, adm'r., of the JEREMIAH NOLAND estate will present his accounts for final settlement.

February 13, 1836
JEHU HOLLAND, adm'r., of the JOSEPH WRIGHT estate will present his accounts for final settlement.

$1,000 reward for a negro boy named Sam or Sampson who after committing an atrocious murder on JOHN M. NETTERVILLE on the 12th, & made his escape. Said Negro was bought of REECE HOWELL, of Tennessee, Lincoln County in the year of 1829. He is 21 or 22 years of age and it is possible that he has a white accomplice. Etc.....

ANNA G. OWENS, adm'x., of the THOMAS OWENS estate will sell 544 acres of land known as Fractional Section No.44, T5, R1W, and bounded on the n. by Homochitto river, on the e. by A. B. METCALF's land, on the s. by lands of ANNA G. OWENS, and on the w. by lands of THOMAS BRANNON. Feb. 9, 1836

Married on the 31st of January, by J. H. STREET, Esqr., Mr. DAVID CARTER to Miss ANN NETTERVILLE, all of this county.

February 20, 1836
JACOB LANEHART, guardian of SUSAN CURTISS, will present his accounts for final settlement.

To the Citizens of Wilkinson County. Circumstances altogether unexpected, and of an imperative nature have compelled me to remove from the county, and I therefore resign into your hands the office which it was your pleasure I should fill.
Signed by GEO. C. M'WHORTER

SUSAN HART, admr'x., of JOHN HART's estate, will sell all the personal estate of the deceased.

The negro fellow who killed Mr. JOHN M. NETTERVILLE, of this county, has been tried, and found guilty, and was executed on Wednesday last.

Married the 11th February, 1836, by the Rev. WILLIAM WINANS, HORACE D. KELLOGG, Esqr., to Mrs. MARY ANN STEWART, all of this place.

Married on the ___February, 1836, by the Hon. A. S. RANDOLPH, Mr. WILLIAM REID to Miss JANE RIDDLE. (Wilkinson County Marriage Book states that WILLIAM REED married 2-9-1836 to Miss JANE RIDDLE.)

Married February 17th, 1836, by the Rev. BENJ'N. SHAW, Mr. LEVI BLOUNT to Miss LAVINIA CALDER.

Married the 24th January, 1836, by JOHN ASHLY, Esqr., Mr. JOSEPH J. MOSS to Miss MARTHA COATS.

Married the 19th January, 1836, by V. N. HARRIS, Esqr., Mr. THOMAS WISNER to Miss EMILY RAWLINS.

Died on the 13th February, 1836, after a lingering illness, Mrs. FRANCES DUNCKLEY, in the 60th year.

THOS. J. HAMILTON, adm'r., of the WILLIAM S. GRIFFIN estate. Sept. 19,1835

JAMES CALLIHAM, exec'r., of the DAVID CALLIHAM estate will sell 416 acres, late residence of David Calliham.

WM. T. LEWIS will apply for a certificate of forfeited land stock, entered on the 14th day of July, 1819, by JAMES McCALOP.

We are authorized to announce that Mr. WILLIAM B. DAVIS and Mr. A. B. WILES as candidates for the vacancy in the Board of Police by the resignation of Dr. GEO. C. McWHORTER.

March 5, 1836

GEORGE MORRIS, adm'r., of the ISABELLA KNIGHT estate will present his account for final settlement.

MARY STEWART, exec'x., of the CHARLES STEWART estate

THOS. H. OSWALD warns any person not to cut wood on his tract of land, known as the "Race Tract Plantation."

A. LEFFINGWELL, is the secretary of the Woodville Library society.

A. M. FELTUS offers his plantation, six miles from Woodville, for sale.

Mr. CESAR FRAISSE would inform the inhabitants of Woodville and its vicinity, that as he is desirous to introduce in this town, the fashion of WALTZING as they practice it in the Northern cities, Washington, Philadelphia, Baltimore, New-York and all over Europe. He will teach Ladies in private, if required.

THEODORE MOLLEMAN had several personal items stolen from him. Reward offered

L. DRAKE, adm'r., of the WILLS DRAKE estate will present his accounts for final settlement.

March 12, 1836

WM. L. BAIRD, adm'r., of the MICHAEL MURPHY estate will present his accounts for final settlement.

Additional candidates for offices: THOMAS ELLIS, WILLIAM B. DAVIS, A. B. WILES, S. S. BOYD, Esqr., JOHN I. GUION, Esqr., and ALFRED T. MOORE.

Died at his residence near Woodville, on the 5th, Mr. JAMES LEECH.

Died in Woodville on the 8th, Mr. JOEL LANDRUM.

Commissioners of the Sinking Fund vs. JOHN SLADE, JAMES QUINE, et al. Additional names mentioned: JOS. P. HENLEY's heirs, and CHARLES H. STONE.

March 19, 1836

Wm. B. DAVIS was elected to fill the vacancy caused by Dr. GEO. C. McWORTER's resignation.

BENAJA LAND has lost a small bay horse.

JEREMIAH D. BROWN, ex'r., of the JOHN GERMANY, Sen.'s, estate

WM. A. AUSTIN has lost a brown bay mare.

JOHN A. SCOTT will sell at public auction on Tuesday the 11th, to the highest bidder for cash, the large Brick House, lately owned by Doct. THOMAS LYNE. March 18, 1836

FRANCIS COOLEY, exec'r., of the JAMES LEECH estate will sell all the real estate belonging to the estate.

THEODORE STARK vs. JOHN W. GILDART, JOHN B. FOX & SOPHIE his wife, LEMUEL PITCHER & MARY JANE his wife, DICK H. EGGLESTON & ELIZABETH his wife, MOSES LIDDELL, guardian of FRANCIS G. RUFFIN, and DICK H. EGGLESTON, adm'r., of HORATIO N. GILDART, deceased, and Goods & Chattels, Lands & Tenements of which FRANCIS GILDART died, seized & possessed. The 700 acre tract known as the "Ashley Tract" to be sold. Land bounded by lands of JAMES L. TRASK and MABRY MORRIS and others.

MAUNSEL WHITE vs. JOHN BELL 1/11 pt. in 450 acres of land belonging to the heirs of JOHN BELL, deceased, adjoining the lands of RUFFIN DELOACH and others.

April 2, 1836

PLANTERS BANK STATE OF MISSISSIPPI vs. ALANSON FERGUSON. Property of Ferguson to be sold.

AUGUSTUS WELCH has taken up a brown bay horse.

Attorneys in Woodville: JOS. H. & H. G. STREET, JOHN C. WATROUS & JOHN B. JONES, A. M. DUNN, H. M. FARISH, C. C. CAGE, N. SCUDDER. JOHN NETERVILLE, CHAUNCEY S. & K. D. KELLOGG, GEORGE H. GORDON & THOMAS C. WEST, PRESTON W. FARRAR, and N. G. PERKINS.

B. F. YOUNG, adm'r., of the JOHN T. SEMPLE estate will present his accounts for final settlement.

Married by the Rev. J. WOOLDRIDGE, near Jackson, La., on the 23rd March, Col JOHN S. LEWIS, of Woodville, Miss. to Miss EUNICE W. HIGGINS, of Ellsworth, Me.

Married on the 31st March by V. N. HARRIS, Esqr., Mr. MATTHIAS OVERMAN to Miss ELLEN ROACHE, both of this county.

Rev. Mr. Barlow will preach at Woodville, the funeral sermon of Messrs. JOEL and BARTON LANDRUM.

WM. T. LEWIS vs. WM. STAMPS   1500 acres to be sold bounded by lands of E. McGEHEE, M. F. DEGRAFFENREID, HUGH CONNELL and WM. STEWART.

MARY S. OGDEN, guardian of GEORGE P. OGDEN will sell 1/4 interest in a 53 acre tract of land.

April 9, 1836

JAS. DUNCKLEY, adm'r., of the JOHN DUNCKLEY estate & guardian of GEO DUNCKLEY, will sell all the estate of the said deceased.

T. J. HAMILTON, adm'r., of the WILLIAM S. GRIFFIN estate.

MICHAEL WOODS executed a deed of trust to EDMUND H. WAILES, for and to secure JOSEPH A. FOSTER, to one JAMES COLLES, and now has been forfeited. Land in Woodville must now be sold to pay cost.

FELIX HUSTON, of Natchez is raising troops for the Texian service. Mr. Huston has been for some years, an eminent and successful lawyer of Mississippi.

April 16, 1836
AURELIA DAVIS and others vs. JAMES SHAFFER

SPENCER WOOD, adm'r., of the F. A. BROWDER estate will present his accounts for final settlement.

A. H. CHAMBERS, adm'r., of the ADAM HOPE estate will present his accounts for final settlement.

FR'S. COOLEY, ex'r., of the JAMES LEECH estate

JOHN HOPE, guardian of GEORGE T. OGDEN, MARGARET A. OGDEN, REBECCA OGDEN, and MILISSA OGDEN, minor heirs of ISAAC E. OGDEN, deceased, will sell all right to one undivided tenth, a part of 66 2/3 acres of a tract of land of 200 acres formerly belonging to JAMES OGDEN, and which was laid off and set apart to ELIZABETH OGDEN, the widow of said JAMES OGDEN, as her dower.

DAVID POOL, adm'r., of the ROBERT ANDERSON estate will sell 162 & 21/100 acres of land.

JOHN A. GIBSON, & MASON E. SAUNDERS, adm'rs., of the GILFORD D. D. FOSTER, estate

JOHN F. SCOTT, adm'r., of the ROGERT JAMES estate will present his account for final settlement.

April 23, 1836
SPENCER WOOD, adm'r., of the F. A. BROWDER estate will present his account for final settlement.

BYTHELL HAYNES AND BALDWIN HAYNES, ex'rs., of the BYTHELL HAYNES, Sr., estate will prsent the accounts for final settlement.

JAMES BURNS vs. WILLIAM EVERETT's estate $110
Unless WILLIAM EVERETT shall appear, give special bail, and plead, on or before the Second Monday in September next, judgment will be entered in this case, and the Estate sold. R. WILLOUGHBY, Clerk of Marion County, State of Mississippi.

HENRY N. MARTIN vs. HENRY E. SALE $132,00,

FR'S. COOLEY, ex'r., of the JAMES LEECH estate

We learn from accounts brought to this place by two gentlemen that there have been no engagement between Houston and Santa Anna, when they left Texas. The citizens of Vicksburg have contributed

$3,500 in aid of Texas.

Married in this place by V. N. HARRIS, Esqr., Mr. THOS. BILLS to Miss MARY B. BILLS, both of Baton Rouge.

The notes due JOSEPH A. FOSTER have been placed in out hands. CAGE & SCUDDER, Att'ys.

Dr. SAMUEL BROWN's land known as the "Brown Tract" of 1100 acres, is for sale.

JAMES S. MOOR, guardian of JOHN WIGLEY, JACOB WIGLEY, ROBERT WIGLEY, and FRANCIS WIGLEY, will sell all the personal property belonging to the wards, at the residence of JACOB ELLSBERRY.

D. W. HAXALL, owner of the race horse, "Hugo".

April 30, 1836

A letter dated April 21, 1836, Mobile, Ala., from JAMES A. MILLER, Jr. to Mrs. MARY C. MARSHALL. His nephew, ALFRED BYNAM, was in Goliad, Texas and in his letter to his uncle, he described the conditions in Texas and the fighting with the Santa Anna forces. He wished Mrs. Marshall to know that her son was well but remarked that Dr. C. P. HEARTT of Woodville had been slain together with Col. Grant and 10 or 12 more men who had ventured into the province of "Tamanlipas to gather horses". In a footnote, Mr. Miller wrote to Mrs. Marshall that he feared the death of his nephew since disastrous accounts had arrived from Texas.

A. P. SLOCUMB, adm'r., of the C. C. SLOCUMB estate will sell 536 acres of land bounded by the lands of A. P. SLOCUMB and the lands of JOS. HOLMES.

May 7, 1836

ROBERT S. MORRIS, guardian of HENRY I. KNIGHT, will sell personal property of the ward.

Married on Thursday the 5th, by V. N. HARRIS, Esqr., Mr. J. M. MILLER to Miss FRANCIS ANN SMITH, all of this place.

Dr. W. BYRD POWELL, Professor of Chemistry in the Medical College of Louisiana, proposes to give twelve lectures on the Science of PHRENOLOGY, to the citizens of Woodville, provided thirty subscribers be obtained at $10 each.

JOHN WADDILL forwarns all persons against trading for a note of hand given by him on the second day of April, to M. P. HATFIELD.

May 14, 1836

CADE HAVARD, adm'r., of the REBECCA HAVARD estate will present his accounts for final settlement.

A. M. DUNN, guardian of JOHN A. DUNN will present his accounts for final settlement.

Married on the 11th by the Rev. B. SHAW, Mr. JOHN P. HARRIS, Merchant of Woodville, to Miss ELIZA S. COSBY.

HUGH McCRAINE, guardian in right of his wife, of CHARLES A. M. COON, AMANDA COON, and ADALINE COON, minor heirs of CHARLES A. COON, deceased, will present his accounts for final settlement.

May 21, 1836

It has become our painful task to announce the death of Gen. JOHN JOOR, of this county. He was accidentally killed by a fall from his horse on Sunday evening last, while coming into Woodville.

Married the 12th, by the Hon. A. S. RANDOLPH, Mr. MASON E. SAUNDERS to Mrs. JANE NOLAND, all of this county.

Married the 12th by the Hon. C. P. SMITH, Mr. ROBERT NORWOOD to Miss E. E. C. LEWIS, all of this county.

MARRIED the 16th by the Rev. SAMUEL DAWSON, Mr. WILLIAM B. WOODS to Miss SOPHRONIA COURTNEY, all of this county.

Died the 19th, after a few hours sickness, JAMES BAILEY, infant son of Doct. J. SAUNDERS of this place.

THOMAS H. OSWALD will be absent from the state for a few months and has appointed Maj. JOS. JOHNSON, JOHN OGDEN and JESSE SAUNDERS, his agents.

May 28, 1836

WM. H. SCOTT has just returned from the north with an entirely new stock of goods. He is established in the brick building recently occupied by A. LEFFINGWELL, as a jewelry establishment.

F. COOLEY, exec'r., of the JAMES LEECH estate will sell all the personal property belonging to the estate.

JOHN O. RUTLEDGE has taken up a bay horse as an estray.

June 4, 1836

JOHN TIMON intends to leave Fort Adams and wishes to sell his house and lot.

JOHN HUBBARD & others vs. ROBT. MILLER & THEO. MOLLEMANS.

MOSES LIDDELL, ANN CALDER, and sundry others vs. FRANCIS GILDART & others, and JNO W. GILDART

MORRISON & PARKER, and others vs. WM. STAMPS & others, & LUCAS & STAMPS

June 11, 1836

JNO. NETTERVILLE lost or mislaid, a note drawn by JOHN NETTERVILLE in favor of CHARLES NETTERVILLE, and endorsed by him, THOS. S. HERBERT and WM. H. SCOTT.

Seldom has a more painful and melancholy duty devolved upon us than the annunciation of the death of our friend and townsman, JOHN P. GILBERT, Esqr. He was killed by HARDY B. HERRING, who had left this place about 14 months since under circumstances not creditable to himself. Herring stabbed Gilbert with a Dirk or Bowie knife of which he instantly died. We also learn that Herring received severe wounds in the conflict, of which it is expected he will certainly die. (Originally from the STATE RIGHTS BANNER)

N. S. WEBB wishes to sell his residence and four lots in the town of Pinckneyville. Apply to R.M. YERBY to see the property.

JOHN A. SCOTT has property to sell. Apply to Wm.H. SCOTT, or CHAS. L. HYATT, agents.

P. W. FARRAR will be absent for a few months. His attorney is CHARLES L. HYATT and his professional business will be attended by J. B. JONES, Esquire.

June 18, 1836

ISAAC N. HODGEN has just received a good assortment of genuine Thomsotian Botanic Medicines from the north. He still resides at Mrs. P. STEWART's, 3 miles south of Mount Pleasant, Wilkinson,County.

June 25, 1836
P. & W. SMITH vs. FRANCIS O'NEAL   158 acres

WM. C. MXWELL, FRANCIS WREN, & E. M. DAVIS, adm'rs., of the STEPHEN H. STRONG estate will sell land.

July 4th celebration will be held at the White Sulphur Springs, near this place. WM. T. MAYES, F. T. GRAYSON, Esqr., and Dr. E. W. MOISE will deliver an oration while Wm. H. WEST will read the Declaration of Independence.

WILLIAM EVANS vs. HENRY BURROUGHS $542.50

HENRY N. MARTIN vs. HENRY E. SALE $132.00

DANIEL WOODARD wishes to sell his plantation.

Married in Cincinnati, Ohio, Col. GEO H. GORDON, of this place, to Miss ELLEN WHITE, of the former place.

Married on Thursday 16th, by V. N. HARRIS, Esqr., Mr. JACKSON CARROLL WHETSTONE to Miss ELEANOR C. RAWLINS, of this county.

Married Monday 20th, by the same, Mr. JOS. N. WALKER to Miss LAVINA DODD, of La.

There will be a preaching at Old Bethel Church, the third Sunday in July, by J.N. HODGEN & B. L. D. SPAIN.

July 2, 1836
Wm. T. MAYES, adm'r., of the JAMES LAND estate will present his accounts for final settlement.

July 9, 1836
Wm. HAILE has resumed his practice in Woodville.

July 23, 1836
We will have completed, by next week a pamphlet on the subject of Slavery, by the Rev. JAS SMYLIE, of Amite County.

WM. F. PAQUINETT wishes to sell his plantation in Louisiana containing 400 arponts, being the same place formerly owned by EZER E. WOODS. Apply to the undersigned or to WM. M. CRESP, on the place.

McMORRIES's adm'r. vs. KIRKHAM & BERRY

Married the 14th by BYTHELL HAYNES, Esqr., Mr. WILLIAM TILLERY, of Amite County, to Miss MARTHA L. KING, of this county.

Married the 17th, by V. N. HARRIS, Esq'r., Mr. WILLIAM E. L. BAUM to Miss SARAH DANCER, all of this county.

The law partnership between JOHN HENDERSON & S.S. BOYD has been dissolved. Mr. Henderson has removed to the Bay of Lt. Louis.

JAMES LEE has procured two new stages to run between Natchez and St. Francesville.

To copartnership between SAMUEL BUDLONG & JOHN L. MONKS has been dissolved.

CADE HAVORD, adm'r., of the REBECCA HAVARD estate will prsent his accounts for final settlement.

The copartnership between DANIEL BASS & HENRY I. BASS has been dissolved. H. I. BASS has formed a connexion with JOHN ROBSON at the same store.

July 30, 1836

A. P. SLOCUMB, adm'r., of the C. C. SLOCUMB estate will sell 493 acres.

FRANCIS COOLEY has a good second hand copper pump for sale.

Married, on Thursday, 21st of July, 1836, by V. N. HARRIS, Esqr., Mr. JOHN H. BUTT to Miss MARY A. HUNGERFORD.

FELLS & SAUNDERS vs. HEZEKIAH BURNETT $120.28

August 6, 1836

THOMAS SHORT has purchased the property formerly occupied by Mr. THOS. RHODES, at East Pascagoula and has been fitted up in the most extensive and commodious manner for a Public House. (Advertisement for a summer retreat)

Married the 28th, by the Rev. JAMES SMYLIE, HENRY G. STREET, Esqr., of Meadville, to Mrs. VICTORIE CAROLINE BUCKHOLTS, of this county. (Originally from the LIBERTY ADVOCATE)

August 13, 1836

SAMUEL MOORE's land in Amite County is to be sold.

HENRY VOSE's Southwestern Directory for 1837 is for sale.

A. M. DUNN, guardian of JOHN A. DUNN will present his accounts for final settlement.

August 20, 1836

Married the 7th, at the Episcopal Church, by the Rev. SPENCER WALL, Mr. TUMAN POWELL, to Mrs. SARAH W. FELTUS, all of this county.

Married on the 11th, by Rev. Wm. WINANS, Mr. HIRAM FRAYARD to Mrs. ADALINE NEWELL, all of this county.

Died at Ft. Adams on the _____ July, Mr. DUDLEY RUTLEDGE, an old and respectable citizen of this county.

WILLIAM BEARD vs. THOMAS CONKLIN

August 27, 1836

Departed this life on the 13th at the residence of his uncle, Maj. J. L. TRASK's, Mr. I. T. BROWNING. The deceased has left an aged father and mother in Massachusetts to deplore his loss.

20 rattle-smakes were killed on Doctor HOLMES plantation near this place---all in a gang.

DANL. McGAHEY has taken up two strays.

RHOMAS B. PERCY has lost a mare and colt.

F. COOLEY, ex'r., of the JAMES LEECH estate will sell the remaining unsold personal property.

September 3, 1836

Married the 31st of August, by J. B. JONES, Esqr., Mr. JAMES CRAIG BELL to Miss MARY TOOL, all of this county.

Married the 1st of Sept., by the Rev. SAMUEL DAWSON, Mr. GEORGE HELMER to Miss MARY ANN SILVEY, all of the county.

J. & W. B. DUNCKLEY wish to sell 370 acres on

Fords Creek.

JAMES M. MILLER will sell at auction held under the Royal Oak, two lots in Woodville.

September 10, 1836

THOS. A. G. BATCHELOR, adm'r., of the WALTER STEWART estate will present his accounts for final settlement.

Died the 19th of August, Mr. HUGH M'CRANE, with congestive fever. He has left a wife and five children to lament his death.

Gen. JAMES C. WATSON of Columbus Ga., has withdrawn his name from the Van Buren Electorial Ticket of Georgia.

JOHN N. DILLAHUNTY will sell his two places.

FRANCIS GILDART cautions all persons against cutting down and taking away any timber, or trespassing on the land commonly called the Ashly plantation, decreed inn 1816 to THOMAS M., ROBERT S., JOHN W., FRANCIS, and HORATIO L. GILDART, and FRANCES ANN, SOPHIA, MARY J., and ELIZABETH GILDART.

C. W. BANCKS forewarns all persons from trading for a note drawn by him in favor of Dr. M. W. SATTERWHITE, for four hundred dollars.

Dr. RICHARD ANGELL at Whitestown, wishes to sell 255 acres of land formerly known as McGAHEY's Mill seat, being the property of SAMUEL KING.

Stolen from JAS. SHAFFER's pocket book, a receipt drawn by H. M. FARISH for two promissory notes, one on A. MORNINGSTAR and JOHN NETTERVILLE, and the other on T. MOLLEMANS.

September 17 1836

WILLIAM EVANS and MARY M. EVANS, his wife, conveyed to C. S. KELLOGG, a certain lot in the town of Woodville, to secure HIRAM H. RALPH's payment of a promissory note.

JAMES J. GRAVES & GABL CASTON, adm'rs., of the JAMES RAOUL estate will present their accounts for final settlement.

CHARLES NETTERVILLE, Jr., adm'r., of the WILLIAM

NETTERVILLE estate will present his accounts for final settlement.

HIRAM ENLOW, guardian of BETSEY C. ENLOW, will sell the undivided 1/8 part of 300 acres of which JESSE ENLOW, did possess at the time of his death.

JONES H. SMITH vs. YOUNG BURKE $136

JOHN B. THERRELL & Co. vs. THOMAS CONKLIN $143.75

FOSTER & THERRELL vs. JOHN A. F. GRAVIS $433.33

September 24, 1836
A. DANIEL, adm'r., of the WILLIAM UHLMAN estate will sell personal property of the deceased.

GEORGE BROWN, adm'r., of the WILLIAM BROWN estate will sell personal property of the deceased.

JOHN F. SCOTT, adm'r., of the ROBERT JAMES estate will present his accounts for final settlement.

October 1, 1836
The ASHLEY plantation is bounded by the lands of J. L. TRASK, MABRY MORRIS & GEORGE BROWN, JAS. A. STEWART, and T. H. POSSER. (Refer to FRANCIS GILDART of September 10th entry)

October 8, 1836
EMILY JOOR, exec'x., of the JOHN JOOR estate

GERALD C. BRANDON, was appointed adm'r., of the JEREMIAH NOLAND estate, eighteen months ago and now he will apply for final settlement.

J. & A. S. ILER will sell at public auction at the Court House in the town of Woodville, 197 acres of land, with house, kitchen, mill and gin, and other necessary out houses, situated on Percy's Creek.

Property belonging to PRESTWOOD SMITH's estate to be sold.

October 15, 1836
Mrs. G. L. POINDEXTER will commence giving lessons on the Piano Forte and Guitar, at her residence in Woodville. Ladies please make applications soon.

Married the 13th by V. N. HARRIS, Esqr., Mr. HENRY DIXON HOLLAND to Miss RACHAEL HOPE, all of this county.

DAVID HUBBARD, adm'r., of the JOHN HUBBARD estate

T. S. EASTON, adm'r., of the WM H. FAIRCHILD estate

JOHN N. EVANS, adm'r., of the EVANS HALL estate

LEMUEL C. GLASS & WILLIAM O. GLASS, exec'rs., of the JOEL GLASS estate

All who are indebted to JOHN C. ALEXANDER, are requested to make payment.

S. LEATHERMAN forwarns any person against cutting wood on the tract of land bounded as follows: N W by B. SPADE, S W by DAVID HOLT; E by W. ILER, and S BY S. O. CHAMBERS.

WM MORGAN TEW, adm,'r.,in right of his wife Sarah, & SARAH YOUNG TEW, admr'x., of the FRANCIS P. WALL estate, will sell land. One tract known as "Berry Hill" containing 400 arpans, bounded by lands of the estate of GLIZA ANN GINN, the lands of ROBERT NORWOOD, and the lands of THOMAS LOVELACE heirs, land formerly belonged to JOHN WALL, deceased.

JOHN HOPE, guardian of the minor heirs of of ISAAC E. OGDEN, will sell 225 arpans of land, being the same originally granted to WM. VOUSDEN, by the Spanish Government. Land bounded by lands of ROBERT NORWOOD, and WM. TIGNER.

ELIZABETH HOPKINS, admr'x., of the SOLOMON HOPKINS estate will present her accounts for final settlement.

NATHAN SWAYZE, adm'r., of the LYDIA CORY estate will present his accounts for final settlement.

WILLIAM HASLEP, adm'r., of the ROBERT FORD estate will present his accounts for final settlement.

MARY WHITE, admr'x., of the ANDREW WHITE estate will present her accounts for final settlement.

GEO. H. SWIGART, adm'r., of the ELIZA HEADY will present his accounts for final settlement.

CHARLES HESTER, adm'r., of the JOHN C. HICKS estate and also the JAMESY HICKS estate will present his accounts for final settlement.

October 22, 1836

Land of MARTIN TRENTHAM, deceased, to be sold.

We are authorized to announce JOHN A. QUITMAN as a condidate for Congress, to fill the vacancy occasioned by the death of the Hon. DAVID DICKSON.

THOS. S. HERBERT, adm'r., of the HENRY HAMPTON estate will present his accounts for final settlement.

ROBT. SMITH, ex'r., of the SAMUEL H. BUFORD estate will present his accounts for final settlement.

REBECCA JACKSON, adm'rx., of GEORGE JACKSON estate

POLASKI CAGE wishes to sell his plantation 13 miles south-east of Woodville.

JAMES WEEKLY has a house and lot for sale.

Land of WM. H. FAIRCHILD's estate is to be sold by T. S. EASTON, appointed administrator of estate.

JOHN N. EVANS, adm'r., of the C. EVANS HALL estate.

DAVID HUBBARD, adm'r., of the JOHN HUBBARD estate

JESSE EDWARDS has 333 acres of land for sale.

October 29, 1836

JOHN N. DILLAHUNTY will sell his plantation adjoining Maj. FELTUS'.

SPENCER WALL will recommence his Academy in Woodville in a commodious and retired building now being erected on the lot of the Episcopal Church.

WM. ILER has purchased the Carriage shop formerly occupied by Deal & McKee and intends to carrying on the carriage making business.

MOSES M. PHARES wishes to sell his plantation of 560 acres situated on the road leading from Whitesville to St. Francisville, about one quarter of a mile from Whitesville and about seven from Woodville. Apply to self or to JOHN E. PHARES, Jackson, La. Oct. 29, 1836.

Married the 27th October by the Hon. N. SCUDDER, Mr. JOHN KNIGHTEN, of Yazoo County, to Miss JULINA

MEEK, of Wilkinson.

Married the 20th, by J. B. JONES, Esqr., Mr. JOHUSA DORSEY to Miss SARAH GLASS.

Married the 27th by J. B. JONES, Esqr., Mr. MICHAEL HOOTSELL to Miss ELIZA ANN MAYES.

November 5, 1836
Married on Thursday evening, 3r , by the Hon.N. SCUDDER, Mr. JOHN W. FUQUA of Manchester, to Miss MARY Y., youngest daughter of Maj. SAMUEL W. LEWIS, of Fort Adams.

Married in this town, on Thursday the 3d, by J. B. JONES, Esqr., Mr. MICHAEL COTTER to Miss MARY E. SMITH.

Married on Thursday evening the 20th of October by JA. K. COOK, Esqr., WILLIAM ILER of Woodville to Miss DELIA FULLER, the residence of her father, WASHINGTON, Mi.

WILLIAM SWAYZE has 415 acres of land for sale, 3 miles south of Kingston, and 16 miles from Natchez, immediately on the Homochitto in Wilkinson, County.

Dr. ALBERT T. LEFFINGWELL death has just reached us. He emmigrated to Texas last May, as a member of the "Madison Volunteers".

November 12, 1836
J. O. WILLIAMS has a barouche, and a pair of first rate horses for sale.

WM. T. FRASER has sold his business to Mr. E. E. WOODS. Accounts left in the hands of Mr. T. POWELL

November 19, 1836
Will of the late Col. AARON BURR names the following: MATTHEW L. DAVIS, PETER TOWNSEND and HENRY P. EDWARDS, his executors. BRIDGET WILLIAMS, $900, daughters FRANCES ANN BURR, 6 years, residing with Mrs. FRANCES WATSON and her daughter, Mrs. SARAH MINTHRONE TOMPKINS, and ELIZABETH BURR, residing with Mrs. GUAYNETTA CONKLIN, leaves SAMUEL CORP $200, and all private papers to go to MATTHEW L. DAVIS. Kinsman, THEDOSM PREVOST. Witnesses: A. E. HOSACK, M. D. & H. O. TAYLOR, OGEEN E. EDWARDS & H. O. TAYLOR

Died the 10th, Mr. SOUTHARD AITSBURY, of this county, in the 38th year of his age.

Married in Woodville on the 17th Nov., by the Rev. B. SHAW, Mr. ALFRED SWINGLE to Miss LAURA E. TOOLE.

EUNICE VINING forewarns persons from trading for two promissory notes, one given to me by WILLIAM BUSH, and the other to EDMUND VINING by JANES BELL.

D. P. COOK, ex'r., of the WILLIAM M. BARTON estate

FRANCES NELSON, admr'x., of the HUGH NELSON estate will sell 160 acres of land.

WILLIAM H. SCOTT has sold his goods in the Brick House on Commercial row, to Mr. P. G. TIGNER.

THOS. J. BROWN, guardian of JOHN & DAVID BAILEY, and JOHN C. SIMS, guardian of MARY W. & SARAH BAILEY, and A. ADAMS, guardian of JAMES S. BAILEY, minor heirs of JAMES S. BAILEY, will sell land.

LABAN BACOT, ELBERT COOK, MICHAEL COOK, guardians of the minor heirs of THOMAS COOK, deceased, will sell one town lot and one store house in the town of Holmesville and the farm in the county of Pike, on which said Thomas resided.

<u>November 26, 1836</u>
Rev. WILLIAM WINANS will preach in the Mehodist Church in Woodville, on tomorrow at 11 o'clock.

Commissioners appointed to examine claims against the estate of ABLE W. FAIRWELL: JOHN L. WALL, RICHARD PARKER, and SAMUEL W. LEWIS.

D. P. A. CLARK, ex'r., of the WILLIAM M. BARTON, estate

WILLIAM EVANS vs. HENRY BURROUGHS   640 acres

A. T. WELCH, adm'r., of the ISRAEL T. BROWNING estate

JOHN C. SIMS, guardian of MARY W. BAILEY will sell all the stock of cattle belonging to the ward.

THOS. J. BROWN, guardian of JOHN BAILEY will sell

personal property belonging to the ward.

HENRY G. STREET, VICTORIA C. STREET, J. M. BATCHELOR, & FRANCIS WREN, adm'rs., of the A. H. BUCKHOLTS, deceased, will sell 342 acres of land directed to be sold at Washington, Mi., reserving 13 acres, heretofore sold by M. TOOL, to TIMOTHY TERRELL, and afterwards transferred to GAYLAN & TORRANCE.

RENE, LAROCHE & Wife vs. GEORGE POINDEXTER 640 acres of land bounded by lands of GEORGE POINDEXTER, JEREMIAH NOLAND, D. H. EGGLESTON, and the lands now owned and occupied by JESSE DELOACH and the land belonging to the estate of BENJAMIN THERREL, dec'd. Also, 369 acres adjoining the above tract of land, JESSE DELOACH, and adjoining land of MOSES LIDDELL AND GEORGE POINDEXTER. Land to be sold to satisfy balance due of $3020.36.

SPENCER WOOD, adm'r., of the F. A. BROWDER estate will present his accounts for final settlement.

December 3, 1836
ANGUS WILKINSON died at his residence in Amite County, on the 21st, in the 63 year of his age. He was a member of the Convention which framed the old constitution of the state of Mississippi, in 1817, and afterwards a member of the legislature.

Died the 29th JOHN OGDEN, Jr., leaving a wife and one child to lament their loss.

Died at his residence in Donegal, on Friday, Nov. 25, Mr. JOHN H. MACKEY, after twelve days' severe sickness, of pleurisy. He has left a wife and two small children to deplore his loss.

JNO. NETTERVILLE, adm'r., of the DUNCAN STEWART estate will present his accounts for final settlement.

WM. ILER, adm'r., & PHERIBY ILER, adm'rx., of the ABRAM ILER estate will sell the estate, lying about 4 miles west of Woodville, on the road leading to Fort Adams by Percy's Creek, containing 550 acres. Also personal property will be sold.

ROBERT M. YERBY, was appointed Brigade Inspector which carries the rank of Major, by General WILL L. BRANDON.

BENJAMIN KILGORE wishes to sell his plantation on the Homochitto river, adjoing the lands of F. L. CLAIBORNE, containing 1133 acres.

H. P. MORANCY wishes to sell his plantation where he now resides, situated on the Mississippi River in Millikin's Bend, 20 miles south of Vicksburg, containing 1250 acres. Also the well known plantation formerly owned by Maj. JOHN MILIKIN, situated half a mile below, containing 800 acres. Apply to Doctor WOODSON WREN in Natchez, or to the subscriber in Millikin's Bend, parish of Carroll, Louisiana.

C. ARMAT has lost a small Morocco Pocket Book.

JOHN OGDEN, adm'r., & CYNTHIA SAPP, adm'rx., of the ASA SAPP estate, will present their accounts for final settlement.

N. N. McCARSTLE, adm'r., of the E. D. McCARSTLE estate will present his accounts for final settlement.

WM. B. DUNN has lost a sorrel horse.

December 10, 1836
Married on Thursday the 1st, by the Hon'ble N. SCUDDER, Mr. ELBERT MOCK, of Franklin County, to Miss MARY ANN MEEK, of this county.

Married the 4th by the same, Mr. ABRAM DECKER to Mrs. SUSAN WEBB, all of this county.

THOS. S. HERBERT, trustee, will sell personal property in Woodville, bounded by lots belonging by Wm. H. SCOTT, and J. P. HARRIS.

December 17, 1836
Died at the residence of CLEMENT B. PENROSE, Esqr., Mrs. ELIZA ROSANA McMURDO, aged 24 years. (Originally from the N. O. COM. BULLETIN)

A. ADAMS, guardian of ARCHIBALD M. STUART, one of the minor heirs of LUCRETIA STUART, deceased will sell personal estate of the ward.

A. ADAMS, guardian of JAMES BAILEY, one of the minor heirs of JAMES BAILEY, deceased will sell personal estate of the ward.

Real estate of FURNEY GRIFFIN, deceased, to be

sold.

Real estate of GEORGE GAYDEN, deceased, to be sold.

E. H. BROWN, adm'x., of the JESSE BROWN estate will sell personal property.

SUSAN HART, adm'rx., of the JOHN W. HART estate will sell personal property.

MARY HARSON, admr'x., of the JOSEPH HARSON estate will sell an undivided 2/6 of a tract of land containing 92 acres in all.

EZER E. WOODS, adm'r., of the SARAH SMITH estate, will sell under the Royal Oak, personal property of the estate.

Mr. CESAR FRAISSE will expose for sale at his Fancy Grocery Store, all kinds of Christmas Gifts, to suit any person or taste. He is not in New Orleans selecting the articles.

J. KELLER has lost a large bay mare.

THEODORE O. STARK has lost a light bay mare.

December 24, 1836

THOS. S. NEWMAN, adm'r., of the NANCY HUNTER estate will present his accounts for final settlement.

MARGARET NESMITH, guardian of MARY A. NESMITH, will present her accounts for final settlement.

WM. B. DUNN, of Mount Pleasant, Miss. has lost a sorrel horse. Reward!

Died on Nov. the 16th, after two months sickness, Miss SUSANNA LANGFORD, who was a respectable and an exemplary member of the Methodist Church.

WM HAMBERLIN & MARGARET E. HAMBERLIN, formerly MARGARET E. OGDEN, and administratrix of Wm. W. OGDEN, dec'd., will present their accounts for final settlement.

POLASKI CAGE, ex'r., of the JOHN STEWART estate will present his accounts for final settlement.

A light brown cow has ranged for many months with

my cattle and now has a calf. She carries the brand of an "H". The owner is requested to take her away. Signed by JOHN B. POSEY.

December 24, 1836
A man named JOHN HUGHES was shot and killed in self-defense, at the "Feliciana Hotel". (Originally from the FELICIANA REPUBLICAN)

To the patrons of THE WOODVILLE REPUBLICAN:--As there will be a change in the proprietorship of the Republican, in a week or two, we request all those indebted to the establishment to make immediate payment.

SAMUEL DAWSON, agent for the heirs of Wm.DAWSON, will sell under the Royal Oak in Woodville, for cash, 166 acres of land and other personal property.

JAMES GOTTSCHALD vs. HENRY M. A. CASSIDY $119 Circuit Court of Hancock County.

JOHN L. WALL, RICHARD PARKER, SAMUEL W. LEWIS, Commissioners of the estate of ABLE W. FAIRWELL.

1837
January 7,1837
THOMAS TORRANCE's land in Amite County is to be sold.

F. A. EVANS will sell 320 acres, the tract of land on which C. E. HALL last resided on Percy's Creek road, about 3 miles from Fort Adams.

Married on the 1st January, 1837 by the Rev. S. DAWSON, Mr. JESSE ENLOW to Miss EVELINE LUSK, all of this county.

Married the 5th, by V. N. HARRIS, Esqr., Mr. JAS. S. MOON, to Miss MARY ANN FENNER, all of this county.

CURTHY ANN COTTER, admr'x., of the RICHARD CARTER estate

January 14, 1837
WILLIAM A. AUSTIN, agent for MARTIN P. CLARK, will sell land and personal property of Clark.

T.O. STARK offers his land known as the "Tanyard Place", about 1 mile south of Woodville, for sale.

It contains 60 acres, a comfortable dwelling & out houses.

THO. JOHNSTON forwarns all persons from cutting or removing wood from what is known as the "Bentley" tract, or face prosecution.

Married on the 8th January, 1837, by V. N. HARRIS, Esqr., Mr. GEORGE SHROPSHIRE to Miss MARY JANE ANDERSON.

ROBT. McCAUSLAND's horse was stolen along with a double reined bridle, martingale, and a saddle.

JAMES McDONALD, adm'r., & ELEANOR McDONALD, admr'x., of the GEORGE W. KELLER estate, will sell all of the personal estate.

DAVID HUBBARD, adm'r., of the JOHN HUBBARD estate

STEPHEN JOHNSON, JOHN P. HARRIS, & JACOB KELLER, commissioners for the estate of ROBERT LYTLE.

JNO. A. GIBSON & M. E. SAUNDERS, admr's., of the GILFORD D. D. FOSTER estate

January 21, 1837

JOHN HOLMES, commission, receiving & forwarding merchant in Bayou Sara.

FORT ADAMS was the first port of entry that was established in Mississippi.

On the petition of JOHN SLADE and others, it is ordered that DAVID ARMSTRONG, L. B. THOMPSON, JAS. F. THOMPSON, JOHN SMITH and RICHARD PARKER, be appointed commissioners to divide into 5 equal parts, a tract of land lying near Ft. Adams, known as the "Purdy" tract consisting of 300 acres.

Married the 15th January, 1837, by the Hon. N. SCUDDER, Mr. JOHN STEMDRIDGE to Miss MATILDA ANDERSON, all of this county.

Married on the same evening, by V. N. HARRIS, Esqr., Mr. JAMES SMITH to Miss ELIZAABTH COLE, all of this county.

Married the 19th January, 1837, by V. N. HARRIS, Esqr., Mr. THO. E. CORY, of Franklin County, to Miss ESTHER McGRAW, of Wilkinson.

JAMES L. TRASK, adm'r., of the WILLIAM P. TRASK estate will present his accounts for final settlement.

WILLIS HUNTER, guardian of STEPHEN TICKELL and ROBERT TICKELL, will sell about forty head of cattle belonging to the wards.

January 25, 1837

AMOS ADAMS will sell all of his personal property at his residence on Monday, the 6th February.

HENRY VOSE will apply for half of an original Spanish grant of 550 arpents, known as the Fort Adams tract on which Mr. NORWOOD now resides.

Married the 25th January, 1837 by the Hon. N. SCUDDER, FRANCIS A. FAIR to ELIZA HALL, both of West Feliciana, La.

Died the 21st, Mr. JOHN WILEY, a respectable and useful citizen of this county.

February 4, 1837

Land in Amite County belonging to ABEL H. BUCKHOLTS is to be sold.

DAVID HOLT wishes to sell his property.

HENRY C. TURNER has lost a horse which was stolen or strayed from his plantation 12 miles west of Woodville.

JAMES McDONALD, adm'r ., & ELEANOR McDONALD, admr'x., of the GEORGE W. KELLER estate will sell all the personal property of the estate.

A. T. WELCH, adm'r., of the ISRAEL T. BROWNING estate will sell all the personal property belonging to the deceased.

February 11, 1837
February 17, 1837

Married on the 12th Feb., 1837, by J. B. JONES, Esqr., Mr. JOHN C. GLASS to Miss ELIZABETH WOODARD, all of this county.

Died in this town on the 13th, ABRAM SCOTT, infant son of the Hon. PRESTON W. FARRAR.

Died at the residence of Maj. S. F. Mayes, Mr. JOHN FOSTER, on the 26th in the 80th year of his age. He came to this state from South Carolina, where he raised a large family. In the year 1825, he moved to Texas and procured a large quantity of land. At the commencement of the late war, the deceased being very old, came to Mississippi, where he remained until his death, leaving in Texas, four sons.

ELEMDER STEPHENSON, admr'x., of the WILLIAM STEPHENSON estate will sell a tract of land, excluding that which is the portion of the widow's dower, containing 364 acres originally from JAMES CROW and wife.

The personal estate of GILFORD D. D. FOSTER is insufficient to pay the debts of the estate, the land must be sold.

JOHN M. DELOACH will sell personal property of the estate of RUFFIN DELOACH THE 25th day of March.

A. T. WELCH, adm'r., of the ISRAEL T. BROWNING estate

C. NETTERVILLE will sell tracts of lands for taxes. One assessed as land of ROBERT COCHRAN. 400 acres bounded on the east by JOHN WATKINS & THOMAS DAVIS, on the north by the HOMOCHITTO river, on the south by lands of ELISHA DUVALL, on the west by Mrs. SUSAN RABB. Taxes due, $6.26. Also, the Farish place assessed as the property of SAML. A. CARTWRIGHT. Taxes due, $13.87. Lots lying in the town of Fort Adams, assessed as the property of the heirs of LEWIS DUBRILL. Tax due, $5.33.
160 acres on the waters of the Buffalo bounded by lands of W. SHROPSHIRE, T. J. BROWN, and MURDOCH McCRAINE, assessed as the property of heirs of GEORGE McDUFFIE.

February 25, 1837
Land of GEORGE W. KELLER to be sold to satisfy debts of the estate.

Attorneys C. C. CAGE & N. SCUDDER's office is on Commercial Row, two doors west of A. G. & C. J. FOSTER's store.

MISSISSIPPI COLLEGE at CLINTON is about to be opened under auspices more favorable than have recently marked its progress, and such, as they confidently hope, they will secure its permanent success.

CYNTHIA ANN COTTER, who lives in the house of Mr. Stafford, respectfully solicits the ladies of Woodville and its vicinity, in the line of "Mantua Making", or any kind of needle work.

WILLIAM W. KAIGLER, adm'r., of the SAMUEL HOLLEMAN estate will sell all of the personal estate.

March 4, 1837

LABAN BACOT, MICHAEL COOK, and ELBERT COOK, guardians of the minor heirs of THOMAS COOK; NATHAN, WM., MALINTHA, THOMAS, TAYLOR and MILBRY COOK, will sell land on which THOMAS COOK last lived, lying on and extending across Little Taunchepaho, on which there is a saw mill, a grist mill and a cotton machine.

Married the 26th Feb., 1837, by V. N. HARRIS, Esqr., Mr. J. W. SMITH to Miss ELIZA ANN ROBERTS, all of this town.

Married on Feb. 27th, by Wm. M. HELM, Esqr., Mr. FELIX S. HOLMES to Miss SARAH ADELIS HOLMES, all of this county.

Died in this town on the 27th after a short illness, JOHN WEBB, age 19.

Died thursday evening the 9th of February, Mr. JOHN O. WILLIAMS, formerly of New Orleans. He has left a wife and two small children to lament their irreparable loss.

GEO. B. COLLIER, exec'r., of the JOHN JENKS estate

Amite County courts orders that WILLIAM McDOWELL's land in Madison County is to be sold.

Caution.--Whereas my wife MATILDA has left my bed and board without any just cause or provocation,-- this notice is therefore given to caution all persons from crediting her on my account, as I will pay no debts of her contracting.--And all persons are furthermore cautioned against harboring her, as I am determined to punish such offenders to the extent of the law. Signed by JOHN TEMMON, Fort Adams, Feb. 26, 1837.

THOS. BELL, adm'r., of the JOHN BELL estate will present his accounts for final settlement.

Mrs. M. STEWART had a bay hore stolen from her plantation on big Bayou Sara about a week ago.

FIELDING DAVIS, adm'r., of the BENJAMIN H. LEWIS estate will present his accounts for final settlement at the next April term.

JANE W. OGDEN, adm'rx., of the JOHN OGDEN, Jr., estate will sell 82 acres of land and the personal property (except Drape) of the estate.

HANNAH, aged 30 and her 3 children, belonging to the RUFFIN DELOACH estate, will be sold by JOHN M. DELOACH, exec'r., at his residence.
Also, same for Dave.

Lands of GILFORD D. D. FOSTER, deceased, must be sold to pay debts of his estate.

GEORGE P. FOSTER, adm'r., of the JOHN FOSTER estate

JOHN LENNEX has moved to the shop occupied by GEORGE EVANS last year, and is now well prepared to do any kind of blacksmith work.

The wagon "Ben Franklin" will continue to make two trips a week from Woodville to Bayou Sara. Persons wishing hauling to or from either place, can by leaving an order at the store of the subscriber, have it promply attended to. T. WISNER.

The Steam Boat Commerce, Captain MAHE, will make regular trips from Fort Adams to New Orleans every Monday. The Commerce is a new and substantial Boat, (being her first season,) with a comfortable upper cabin.....

March 11, 1837
JAMES QUINE wishes to sell his house and lots in the town of Woodville, formerly JOHN SLADE's.

Land of the deceased, ABEL H. BUCKHOLTS', land in Amite County, to be sold.

JOHN NETTERVILLE, adm'r., of the SAMUEL GLASS estate will present his accounts for final settlement of the estate.

WM. ILER has just employed a first rate Coachmaker, Painter and Trimmer. He will also execute Sign and Fancy Painting.

(A CHRONOLOGICAL HISTORY OF THE UNITED STATES prepared for the Woodville Republican dating from 1493 to 1837 is listed on the front page of this issue).

A list of the 30 newspapers published in the state of MISSISSIPPI in 1837. There was one paper published in the state in 1799, 4 papers in 1810, 7 papers in 1822, and 11 in the year of 1828.

Died in Rankin County, FRANKLIN E. PLUMMER, Esqr., drowned in crossing a small but very much swollen stream. He was a member of the State Legislature for several years. (Originally from the "Raymond Times, Mar. 4, 1837).

800 acres of land belonging to the heirs of Dr. SAML. BROWN to be sold. Bounded by lands of Wm. M. BARTON, HENRY QUINE and THOMAS BELL. Tax due for 1836, $35.48.

N. N. & A. M. McCARSTLE wishes to hire a small boy about 13 or 14, to act as a clerk in a dry good and hardware store at Laurel Hill. They agree to teach him the art of keeping a set of books & etc.

SAML. A. CARTWRIGHT's land known as the Farish (Parish) place is to be sold. Tax due for 1836, $13.87.

ROBERT COCHRAN's 400 acres of land to be sold, bounded by lands of JOHN WATKINS & THOMAS DAVIS, Mrs. SUSAN RABB, and ELIXHA DUVALL. Tax due for 1836, $6.26.

R. MUMFORD has taken Mr. WALTER N. BARRELL into copartnership in storage, forwarding, commission & produce business. Bayou Sara, Feb. 1st, 1837.

March 18, 1937
Census of Woodville states that there are not less than 833 souls, viz: 462 whites, and 371 slaves.

Died on the 12th, in this town, CHA'S L. HYATT.

Died lately at Rodney in Jefferson County, THOMAS J. HAMILTON, a citizen of this town.

Property of ELI M. ROBINSON in Choctaw County, Mis. to be sold. Witness, the Hon. JOHN WALKER, Judge of the Probate Court of Amite County.

75 acres in Amite County belonging to the estate of JARED WHITTINGTON, deceased, is to be sold.

MARY WHITE, adm'rx., of the ANDREW WHITE estate will sell 162 acres of land bounded on the west by lands of THOMAS ELLIS and Wm. PHIPPS, and on the east and north by vacant lands, and on the south by lands of AGELILAUS JEETER.

LEWIS CASON, adm'r., of the SAMUEL WRIGHT estate will present his accounts for final settlement.

JAMES DUNCKLEY, adm'r., of the JOHN DUNCKLEY estate will present his accounts for final settlement at the next May term.

March 25, 1837

EZER E. WOODS & M. OVERMAN have entered in to a copartnership in the clothing business.

Died on the 18th in this town, Mrs. EMILY WISNER, consort of Mr. THO. WISNER.

340 acres of land, belonging to ZACHARIAH GRAVES, deceased, in Louisiana near Dr. CALLFIELDS, 25 miles from Woodville, and also personal property is to be sold.

SUSAN HART, adm'rx., of the JOHN W. HART estate will present her accounts for final settlement.

SUSAN JEETER vs. JAMES WOODS   Attachment for $65.

JAMES SHAFFER, vs. H. T. BLAKE & JOHN DEAL
A lot belonging to Wm.M. BARTON in his lifetime and willed to JOHN DEAL, will be sold to settle court cost.

JOHN B. THERREL & JOSEPH E. THERREL vs. YOUNG BURK

April 1, 1837

CHRISTIAN MILLER vs. RUFUS M. RICHARDSON $75.

A. FLECHEUX will sell 20 arpents of land situated in Point Coupee, about 27 miles above the church.

CHARLES MACKEY, adm'r., of the JOHN H. MACKEY estate

MARY HARSON, adm'x., of the JOSEPH HARSON estate will sell the undivided 2/6 of a tract of land containing 92 acres of land in all (being the interest that MARY & MARGARET HARSON has in the tract formerly owned by Joseph Harson).

April 8, 1837

AURELIA DAVIS, B. JORDAN & others vs. JAMES SHAFFER   Shaffer's lot next to Baptist Church to be sold.

TIMOTHY O'LEARY & JACOB KELLER vs. WOODVILLE HOTEL COMPANY.

BENJAMIN KILGORE will sell his plantation on the Homochitto river, adjoining the lands of F. L. CLAIBORNE, containing 1133 acres. Enquire of Wm. McNEELY or Benjamin Kilgore.

FRANCIS Mc'GEE forwarns all persons against trading for a note for $200, given by ELIZABETH GIBSON to FRANCIS Mc'GEE, who has lost or mislaid the same.

J. P. HUMPHREYS, adm'r., of the LEWIS W. COON estate will present his accounts for final settlement.

READ & McWHORTER vs. B.F. SCOTT
Brick house built by THOS. LYNE and sold to B. F. SCOTT by Lyne, also tract of land about 3 miles west of Woodville, known as the "Oak Grove" place on which JOHN A. SCOTT lately resided and 200, 52/100 acres of land to be sold.

April 15, 1837

ELEANOR McDONALD, adm'rx., & JAMES McDONALD, adm'r., of the GEORGE W. KELLER estate, presents the accounts for final settlement. Also will apply for an order of removal of said estate into the parish of West Feliciana, La., where letters of Curatorship have been granted according to law.

LOUISA R. FOSTER, adm'rx. & A. G. FOSTER, adm'r., of the JOSEPH A. FOSTER estate will present accounts for final settlement.

JOHN F. CARMICHAEL, adm'r., of the HARRIET BROWDER estate will present accounts for final settlement.

J. RIDDLE intends to visit friends in Richmond, Va. and offers all of his stock for sale.

WRIGHT B. ORR, adm'r., of the RUFFIN H. ORR estate

THOS. C. WEST, adm'r., of the THOMAS J. HAMILTON estate

NOLAN STEWART, surviving executor of the will of JOHN STEWART, deceased, will make a final settlement of the estate.

JOHN McNEELEY, A. FERGUSON, & ALFRED BYNUM vs. REUBEN L. BONER & F. COOLEY.

SUSAN PHILBRICK is forced to sell on Tuesday the 25th, under the Royal Oak, in Woodville, for cash, a valuable family. Sarah, a first rate cook, ironer and washer, about 35 years old and her two children, William, 13 and Cesar, 9. "Sarah is well known in Woodville and nothing would induce me to part with her but the want of money, that cannot be had any other way." April 15, 1837.

JESSE ENLOW, guardian of JAS. ENLOW will sell 300 acres of land belonging to the JESSE ENLOW estate.

April 22, 1837
JOHN M. DELOACH, ex'r., of the RUFFIN DELOACH will present his accounts for final settlement.

MOSES LIDDELL, ex'r., of the Wm. H. RUFFIN will present his accounts for final settlement.

Died in this place on 21st, Dr. SAM'L LESLIE, of pulmonary consumption.

Died near this place on the 17th, of small pox, HENRY VOSE, Esqr.,. He was educated at West Point, N. Y. and in 1830, he published "An Almanac for Mississippi and Louisiana".

April 29, 1837
Two horses came to JOHN M. DELOACH's plantation near Pinckneyville.

MARY E. WILLIAMS, adm'rx., of the JOHN O. WILLIAMS estate

Stolen from the house of MATTHEW COMBS, a red morocco pocket book containing a note against HENRY A. TOMS, and a note against JOHN GILDART.

May 6, 1837
WM. WEED has opened a Livery Stable in the town of Woodville.

983 acres of land to be sold, bounded by lands of JOHN F. CARMICHAEL, SAML. W. LEWIS, the heirs of R. DELOACH, and the heirs of JOHN BELL. Suit against DAVID ARMSTRONG, DUNCAN C. HENDERSON, F. COOLEY and W. HUNTER.

May 13, 1837
JOHN C. WATAROUS & JOHN B. JONES, Attorneys at Law., Woodville, Miss.

Land belonging to the heirs of LEWIS DUBRILL to be sold for taxes due for 1836, $5.33.

The Steamer, Ben Sherrod, Capt. CASTLEMAN, took fire about one o'clock yesterday morning and was totally destroyed. Negroes from the plantation of Mr. WILLIAM STAMPS came to rescue as many as they could. There were between 200-300 souls, of whom about only 40 were saved.

Census of Wilkinson County listed 8954 Blacks, and 3274 Whites.

Married by the Hon. N. SCUDDER on the 4th, Mr. WILKINSON M. DOLES, to Miss LYDIA NOLAND, all of this county.

DAVID POOL, adm'r., of the ABRAHAM POOL estate

GEORGE B. COLLIER, executor of the JOHN JENKS estate will sell a chest of carpenter's tools and other articles.

May 20, 1837
J. P. HUMPHREYS, adm'r., of the LEWIS W. COON estate

GEORGE P. FOSTER, adm'r., of the JOHN FOSTER estate

Married the 9th by the Hon. N. SCUDDER, Mr. JEREMIAH D. NOLAND to Miss ELLEN ANN DOWNS, all of this county.

Died on the 15th after a short illness, Mr. JOHN McCREADY, a respectable citizen of this county.

Died at Cold Spring, Malvina, only daughter of M. W. CALLICOATE, aged 15 months.

JAMES M. BRADFORD offers a $5 reward for the return of a bay horse.

May 27, 1837

VALENTINE C. GROOM, ex'r., of the JOHN WILEY estate

WM. M. HELM, ex'r., of the JOSEPH W. MILLER estate

L. D. BROWN & JOS. SMITH, adm'rs., of the J. J. STOCKETT estate will present their accounts for final settlement.

ASA ANDERSON, adm'r., of the BENJAMIN DUTY estate will present accounts for final settlement.

Married the 25th May, by Rev. Mr. MARSHALL, Mr. CHARLES PASCOE to Miss ANN R. THOMAS, all of Woodville.

Married the 23rd May, by JOHN McCREA, Esqr., Mr. DAVID YARBOROUGH to Miss SARAH WALTON, both of East Feliciana, La.

JOHN H. READ & R. H. McDANIEL's partnership has been dissolved. Dr. R. H. McDANIEL continues to practice in Woodville and vicinity.

JOHN H. RANDOLPH has lost a brown work horse. Reward is offered.

B. C. STEWART, adm'r., of the FRANCES STEWART estate

THOS. C. WEST, adm'r., of the THOMAS J. HAMILTON estate

E. H. WAILES, executor of the WILLIAM NEWELL estate

Two horses and a mule came to Greenland Plantation on Buffalo, 8 to 10 days ago.   FRS. S. MAYES.

ISAAC H. STANWOOD intends to spend several months in the Northern Cities--leaving this place the first of the month.

PETER SMITH has lost a gold watch, chain, seal and key. $10 reward.

M. W. CALLICOATTE informs his friends and public that he is prepared to accomodate travellers and boarders at the COLD SPRINGS HOTEL, situated 16 miles north of Woodville, on the Natchez road, and 21 miles below the latter place. There is on the premises a beautiful spring of the purest water, and a convenient bath house and etc...

June 3, 1837
Married 1st of June, by JOHN McCREA, Esqr., Mr. THOMAS M. MAGEE to Miss ANN ELIZA HATFIELD, all of Wilkinson County.

June 10, 1837
Suit in Marion County, Ms. against THOMAS BROWN

Died the 23d of May, at the residence of Mr. STERLING, om the Ouachitta, Mrs. MARY COOK, wife of Mr. D. P. A. COOK, formerly of this county.

WM. ILER lost or mislaid a note drawn by DANIEL WILLIAMS in favor of JOHN N. DILLAHUNTY.

Candidated for the next November elections:
M. F. DeGRAFENREID, P. W. FARRAR, TRUXTON DAVIDSON, STEPHEN JOHNSON, WILLIAM B. DAVIS, B. F. HERBERT, JOHN C. ALEXANDER, ARTHUR DANIEL, WM. T. MAYES, WILLIAM T. LEWIS, MATHEW BRYANT, A. H. CHAMBERS, GEO. L. POINDEXTER, JAS. W. SMITH and ROBERT THOMPSON.

June 17, 1837
Married the 7th, by JOHN McCREA, Esqr., PATTON H. GUTHRIE to SARAH WILLIAMS, both of West Feliciana.

JOHN A. GIBSON & M. E. SAUNDERS, adm'rs., of the GILFORD D. D. FOSTER estate will sell land.

J. C. PATRICK, adm'r., of the A. W. FAREWELL estate will present accounts for final settlement.

J. B. THERREL, adm'r., of the J. S. WHITNEY estate will sell all the personal property of the estate.

MARY A. LESSLEY, exr'x., JAMES LESSLEY & ROBERT T. LESSLEY, executors of the SAMUEL LESSLEY estate

JAMES SHAFFER, adm'r., of the DAID SPURLOCK estate

ANN KELLER, adm'rx., of the FRANCIS KELLER estate

R. SLACK, ex'r., of the JAMES CAIN estate

JOHN A. SCOTT, adm'r., of the WILLIAM HAILE estate

A bay horse came to GEORGE MORRIS' plantation some months ago.

C. S. KELLOGG vs. PETER W. LEATHERMAN   Land to be sold, bounded on the north by BURLING, on the west by JOHN THOMPSON, dec'd, and on the east and south by lands of ALEXANDER WALL. Same tract of 220 acres purchased by Leatherman from RANSON GRAHAM.

June 24, 1837
Married the 21st by the Rev. A. D. WOOLDRIDGE, Mr. J. C. DOUGHERTY, of Jackson, La., to Miss MARY LOUISA, daughter of Dr. S. ROBINSON, of Pinckneyville, Ms.

Died on the 19th, Mr. JEHU QUINE of this county.

Died on the 20th, Mr. MORDECAI QUINE of this county.

Died on the 20th, after a lingering illness, Mrs. SARAH E., consort of Mr. W. P. BURTON.

A fine bay mare has strayed or was stolen from HENRY L. CAMP at the new bridge over the Bayou Sara on the 7th or 8th, wearing a side saddle and a double reined brass bit bridle. Liberal reward is offered. (Originally from the LA. JOURNAL)

July 1, 1837
The partnership between JOHN H. READ & R. H. McDANIEL has been dissolved.

Drs. S. E. POTTS & C. J. THORNTON have associated themselves in the practice of Medicine.

Dr. ESAIAS KAIGLER has settled himself at his father's plantation on Dunbar's creed, 8 miles west of Woodville, on the lower Fort Adams road.

Dr. A. A. JONES practices the Botanic System of Medicine.

July 8, 1837
Attorneys in the area: JOHN NETTERVILLE, JOHN C. WATROUS, JOHN B. JONES, S. S. BOYD, W. H. DILLINGHAM, C. C. CAGE, N. SCUDDER, SHAUNCEY S. & H. D. KELLOGG.

Property now occupied by the Misses CALDER as a Female Seminary, is for sale by E. H. WAILES. Located nearly opposite the Planters Bank.

Additional candidates for the November elections: A. B. SAUNDERS, C. C. MASON, CHARLES NETTERVILLE,

Dr. SPENCER WOOD, JAMES A. VENTRESS, Capt. JAMES QUINE, H. M. FARISH, B. F. HERBERT, SAMUEL TURBEVILLE, ELISHA M'GRAW, WILLIAM T. JONES, VICTOR N. H. NETTERVILLE, and R. L. BONER.

Married in this town on the 28th of June, by Rev. JOHN F. FISH, Mr. ROBT. B. McALPHINE to Miss JENNETTE ANN ECCLES.

Died in this town on the 26th after a short illness of 10 hours, MARGARET ANN, only child of HENRY J. and MARGARET BASS, aged 15 mo. and 18 da.

July 15, 1837

Land belonging to the heirs of LEWIS DUBRILL to be sold for taxes due for 1836, $5.33.

160 acres belonging to the GEORGE McDUFFIE heirs to be sold for taxes due for 1836, $1.66.

Married the 11th by the Rev. Mr. FISH, Mr. ROBERT A. WILKINSON, of La., to Mrs. MARY F. GILDART, of this place.

Died on the 13th, CHAUNSEY S. KELLOGG, Esqr., member of the Bar of Wilkinson County.

JAMES HORNSBY claims an undivided 1/2 of 485 74/100 acres known as Sec. 22, T2, R3W, entered by JESSE ENLOW and JOHN BECK. Commissioners appointed to divide said land: WILLIAM HASLIP, WILEY WOODS and V. C. GROOMS.

July 22, 1837

Copartnership of JNO. L. WALL & NIC'S. NORWOOD has been dissolved.

ELIZABETH McCRAINE, adm'rx., & ARCH'D. McCRAINE, adm'r., of the HUGH McCRAINE estate

August 5, 1837

Wm. A. A. CHISHOLM vs. URIAH F. CASE. $1,500.00

FELLS & SAUNDERS vs. RANSON GRAHAM $81.00

August 12, 1837

Married on the 4th by Rev. B. SHAW, Mr. ELBERT G. DAVIS to Mrs. EMILY McKEY, both of this county.

The Rev. JESSE YOUNG & CHARLES FELDER will preach at the Baptist Church in Woodville on Wednesday.

Mrs. ANN RATLIFF has opened a boarding house for the accommodation of gentlemen.

DOUGLASS H. COOPER has taken up a stray mare.

August 19, 1837
Wm. B. WOODS has taken up two horses.

August 26, 1837
Died August 19th, Capt. PETER SMITH, 71 yrs. of age. He was a native of North Carolina and emigrated to Ms. as early as 1782 when this country was still a wilderness. (Extensive description of his character and personality)

Died Friday last, CHARLES RIDGELY LEWIS, in the bloom of life, and usefulness, aged 22 years, the youngest son of Major S. W. LEWIS. Fort Adams, August 19, 1837.

September 2, 1837
ABRAHAM ALEXANDER, adm'r., of the JOHN ALEXANDER estate, late of Warren County. (Originally from the NATCHEZ COURIER)

Died, the 18th at his plantation in Holmes County, Maj. B. W. EDWARDS.

Died on the 24th, at his residence in this county, JAMES MEEK, Esqr., in the 48th year of his age.

Died on the 25th at the plantation of Col. JOHN S. LEWIS, near Woodville, Mr. H. M. BURT.

Died the 25th in Woodville, FRANCES ANN VIRGINIA, the youngest child of THOS. F. GRAVIS.

The Rev. MANSFIELD BARLOW will preach in the Baptist Church in Woodville on Sunday, Sept. 3.

HIRAM FOWLER vs. JAMES SHROPSHIRE $231.00

September 9, 1837
Gen. E. L. ACEE, of Lowndes, declines being a candidate for congress, at the ensuing election in November.

SPENCER WALL does not believe his health will permit him to engage in his school before Oct.

September 16, 1837
Died of a wound in the abdomen given in an affray

by Mr. JOHN McDERMOTT, JAMES M. BRADFORD, Esqr., the senior editor ot the Louisiana Journal, the oldest editor and printer in Louisiana, thirty years a resident of the Territory and subsequently the State of Louisiana.

JOHN F. CARMICHAEL of Cold Springs, Wilkinson County, needs an overseer to take charge of a large plantation.

Mr. W. P. RUSSEL, Professor of Languages, has located in Woodville to teach.

September 23, 1837

ATKINSON & PITTMAN vs. THOMAS BROWN   Marion Co.Ms.

WM. B. DAVIS & Co. (HENRY H. BELL) vs. JAMES WOODS

Married the 21st, by the Rev. Mr. MARSHALL, Mr. AUGUSTUS W. FORSYTHE, to Miss MARY R. SHIELDS, both of this city.

Died at Fort Adams on the 5th Sept. 1837, JOHN OGDEN, Esqr., an old and respected citizen of Wilkinson County and for many years a member of the Baptist Church. He has left a wife and ten promising children.

Marion County, JAMES BOZEMAN vs. THOMAS BROWN
Wm.H. WHITE, OWEN VANVACTER. GEO B. COLLIER, adm'r., GEO. H. GORDON, ROBERT STANLEY, and STEPHEN JOHNSON against DAVID LEATHERMAN, DAVID ARMSTRONG & C. N. WOOD. 80 acres with a mill and gin thereon and bounded by FENNER's heirs, JOSHUA PRESLER, C. N. WOOD, and known as the HAYGOOD place near Fort Adams.

JESSE BANTER vs. JOS. T. CARR   Land is the same which Mrs. ELLEN CARR formerly lived and is now owned in part by JOHN MAYES, Esqr., Jos. T. Carr's interest is about 70 acres.

Lot to be sold bounded by lots of JAMES WALKER, V. N. HARRIS and HUGH CONNELL.

DAVID BRYANT vs. DAVID POOL   152 3/4 acres

WM H. SCOTT, adm'r., of the CHARLES L. HYATT estate

Received and for sale,"Memoirs of AARON BURR" by STONE & MARTIN.

September 30, 1837

E. T. FAISH, adm'r., vs. DAN. SLACK & EPH'M CAMPBELL

Lot belonging to ROBERT MILLER's to be sold bounded by lots of E. R. QUARTERMAN, T. MOLLEMAN, and by E. H. WAILES.

JEREMIAH D. BROWN, ex'r., of the JOHN GERMANY estate will present accounts for final settlement.

JOSHUA JOHNS has taken up as a stray, a mare mule.

J. A. KELLY, of Jackson, ordered to be shipped on board the steamboat Baton Rouge, a marble slab, which has never arrived. Reward is offered for its return.

October 7, 1837

Died on the 17th at Jerico, his residence, in Amite County, Mr. JACOB BOATNER, long a citizen of this state and South Carolina. He has left an aged, and amiable companion, and an only son to lament their misfortune.

Every Saturday after the next will be shot for at Bell & Davis store Pearcy Creek, one Beef and Mutton, for two months ensuing. Signed: JOHN A. WARREN, Woodville, Oct. 7th, 1837.

T. WISNER has lost, between Bayou Sara and Woodville, one piece of Kentucky Bagging containing 60 yards, and marked S. & C.   Reward offered.

October 14, 1837

ALEX'R. MITCHELL has lost a bay horse.

Died in Jackson, C. C. MAYSON, Esqr., a native of South Carolina. He was educated in New Haven, Connecticut and a member of the Legislature of South Carolina. About 6 or 7 years ago, he came to this state and established the "States Rights " paper.

We observe from the Vicksburg papers that CYRUS GRIFFIN, Esqr., died recently on his plantation in Washington County Miss. Mr. G. was the editor of the "Vicksburg Register" and other papers.

Married the 12th, by the Rev. BENJAMIN SHAW, Mr. HENRY E. SALE, Merchant of Woodville, to Miss MARIA E., daughter of the Hon. JOHN B. POSEY, of

Wilkinson County.

Departed this life on Tuesday the 26th ultimo, of Phrenetis, Doct. WM. BUTLER HOOKE, in the 24th year of his age. In the summer of 1836, he received with considerable eclat, the degree of M. D. from the Pennsylvania Medical School, one of the first institutions of the kind in the county. Soon he returned to his place of nativity in Wilkinson county......

October 21, 1837

M. M. PHARES & GEORGE MARTIN have entered into a copartnership in the clothing buisness.

BENJ. F. YOUNG, adm'r., of the JOHN T. SEMPLE estate presents his accounts for final settlement.

Married the 17th, by Hon. N. SCUDDER, Mr. E. A. KNOWLTON to Mrs. ANN RATLIFF, all of this place.

Died the 5th of October, ELIZA JANE WILLIAMS, aged 4 years, and 8 months, daughter of EBENEZER WILLIAMS.

Died at his residence near Pinckneyville, this morning, Oct.21st, Dr. JOHN F. CARMICHAEL.

C. P. SMITH, exec'r., of the PETER SMITH estate

SARAH ROACH will sell under the Royal Oak in Woodville, a tract of land lying 6 miles north of Woodville adjoining the land of HARTWELL STAFFORD, C. S. KELLOGG, and THOMAS HARRIS.

October 28, 1837

Died at his late residence in this town on the 24th, Dr. DICK H. EGGLESTON, in the 41st year of his age. He was a native of Amelia County, Virginia, receiving his medical degree in 1819 at the University of Pennsylvania and came to this state in the year 1820. Leaves a bereaved and sorrowing family.

Two horses stolen from DAVID BARLAND's plantation 5 miles below Natchez on the Mississippi river.

November 4, 1837

C. W. BANCKS, Chief Engineer W. F. Rail Road

Doct. JOHN F. CARMICHAEL died at his Cold Spring plantation on Saturday morning the 21, in the 74th year of his life. He was one of the oldest settlers of the State of Miss. After graduating at Philadelphia, he entered the army in 1789 as Surgeon Mate. In 1890 he was with Gen. HARMER, in 1791 with Gen. St. CLAIR, in 1793 he was commissioned by Gen. WASHINGTON as Surgeon in Gen. WAYNE's army , in 1798 he was ordered south under Gen. WILKINSON, where he finally settled.

November 11, 1837
Died on Friday last, 10th instant, Mr. JOHN BRYANT an old and respectable citizen of this town.

November 18, 1837
Contractors are wanted to make sealed proposals at the Rail Road Bank in Woodville until the 6th of November next, for grading Section 8, 9, and 10 of the first Division of the West Feliciana Rail Road. Signed by C. W. BANCKS, Chief Engineer.

LOZ. D. BROWN, ex'r., of the JOHN McCREADY estate

FRANCIS H. HOOKE, adm'r., of the WILLIAM B. HOOKE estate

ELIZA HORNSBY, adm'rx., & WILLIAM BAKER, adm'r., of the SAMUEL R. HORNSBY estate

JOHN H. RANDOLPH, adm'r., of the A. S. RANDOLPH estate

Married the 2nd by Wm. M. HELM, Esqr., Mr. Wm. TAYLOR of Adams County, to Miss ELIZABETH MCCULLCK of Wilkinson.(Printed index of Wilkinson County marriages state 11-16-37)

Taken through mistake from the Steamer Avalanch on the 24th between Vicksburg and Fort Adams, a leather trunk marked "RICHARD B. HOOK, Miss." Signed by FRANCIS H. HOOKE.

LOX. D. BROWN, ex'r., of the JOHN McCREADY estate will sell all perishable property of the estate.

The admininstrators of the SAMUEL R. HORNSBY estate, will sell on January 1st, 1838, the fine blooded stallion, ANTELOPE: Peedigree, "Antelope out of Mark, he by the truly renowned race horse and foal getter Virginia, he by the unequalled horse, old Sir Archy".

DANIEL HUFFMAN has lost two Bank Notes.

DAVID HOLT has given JOHN S. HOLT, at Woodville authority to collect his debts.

$400 reward offered by D. W. McCALEB of Jefferson County, for a group of runaway slaves. All were raised in this state by Capt. WILLIAM COLLINS, and finally fell into the possession of W. A. MISKEL by marriage. He moved from this county between two days for fear the property would be taken by their proper owner, to a village called Covington, in Tafitte Parish. McCALEB states that he was successful in getting most of the Negroes from him and the right of ownership is now in the courts. The Negroes, George, Nat, Little George, William, Thornton and Sarah, are aware of the situation and no doubt will make their way back to Covington, as his property with forged papers. (More detailed information of each individual is given)

HOWELL MORELAND offers his 282 acres of land for sale lying 6 miles east of Fort Adams.

November 25, 1837

B. R. COILE, the keeper of the Bayou Sara and Point Coupee Ferry, has now rented the Brick House, formerly occupied as the Atchafalaya Bank, as a tavern for the accommodation of travelers and others waiting for steam boats.

FOSTER & THERRELL vs. ALEXANDER SMITH $2,153

THEODORE MOLLEMAN offers his tavern in Woodville at auction on the 26th December to rent for three years.

JOHN HENDERSON, ex'r., of the ABRAM M. SCOTT estate will present accounts for final settlement.

RICHARD GARRISON of Magnolia Retreat, offers his plantation on the Seaboard, containing 1920 acres of land for sale. For further informaion, apply to WILLIS H. ARNOLD, Esqr., of Pearlington.

WILSON P. BURTON has taken up a gray horse.

December 2, 1837

Died on the 27th in this town, at the residence of Mr. J. A. SCOTT, Mr. A. J. GRAY.

Married the 30th by JOHN McCREA, Esqr., Mr. LEWIS A. YARBOROUGH, to Miss ELIZABETH HUMPHREYS, of Wilkinson county.

Died November 23rd, Dr. ALEXANDER M. KENNAN, native of Kentucky, in the 31st year of his age.

December 9, 1837
Married at Natchez, Ms. on the 1st, by the Rev. Mr. PAGE, WILLIAM HOWARD WEST, of this place and Miss SARA OLIVIA DUNBAR of Adams County.

Died Dec. 2nd, Dr. C. B. MAGOUN, a native of New Hampshire, but for several years past, a resident of this county and successful Practitioner of Medicine.

December 16, 1837
Died at his residence in this place on Sunday, the 3rd, after an illness of only three days, Doctor CALVIN B. MAGOUN, in the 39th year of his age. Leaves a young mother, widowed by the loss of an affectionate and indulgent husband. (Lengthy obituary)

Died the 11th December, 1837, AUGUSTUS D. HESTER of Wilkinson County, age 26 years., 29 days.

December 30, 1837
WOODVILLE FEMALE ACADEMY is conducted by Miss CHAPMAN from Tuskaloosa.

WM. B. CLUGSTON & ALEX. N. GALLOWAY, merchant tailors, have formed a copartnership.

On Friday night the 22nd., Lizzy, a 40 year old African Negro Woman, formerly the property of the late Wm. NETTERVILLE, left the new clearing of the subscriber, to return home and has not been heard of since. C. NETTERVILLE Jr., fears she was stolen and offers a liberal reward for information.

H. J. BASS offers for sale, a few acres of wood land within a mile and a half of town.

O. S. BREWSTER, cabinet maker.

GEORGE E. FRAZIER, adm'r., of the MICAJAH G. FRAZIER estate will sell all of the personal property of the estate.

DAVID HUBBARD, adm'r., of the JOHN HUBBARD estate will present accounts for final settlement.

The administrators of the GEORGE W. KELLER estate will present accounts for final settlement.

1838
January 6, 1838

WM P. GRAYSON, cashier of the" Bank West Feliciana Rail Road Co.",will purchase cotton at a fair price.

JEREMIAH D. GROWN, ex'r., of the JOHN GERMANY estate will present accounts for final settlement.

THOS. H. McGRAW, adm'r., of the PAUL McGRAW estate will sell all the personal property.

MARGARET COLE, adm'rx., of the MATTHEW COLE estate will sell property of the estate.

MARY A, JAMES, & ROBERT T. LESSLEY, executors of the SAMUEL LESSLEY estate will sell a sulkey, and all the household and kitchen furniture belonging to the estate.

MARIA OGDEN, adm'rx., of the JOHN OGDEN estate

Stolen from the premises of the Rev'd. JAMES SMILIE, a dark chesnut sorrel stallion. Reward is offered by CHARLES C. McKAY, or JAMES SMYLIE.

Married the 4th by the Rev. Mr. WINANS, CHARLES C. CAGE, Esqr., to Miss CATHARINE J. STEWART.

Married the 4th by the Rev. Mr. WINANS, Mr. J. W. BURRUS to Miss SARAH H. McGEHEE.

Married the 25th by the Rev. SAMUEL DAWSON, Mr. THOMAS McDONALD, to Miss D. (DARDENE) LEATHERMAN.

Married on the 28th by Judge SCUDDER, Mr. JAS. M. ILER to Miss CAROLINE GINN, all of this county.

ELIZABETH S. EGGLESTON, admr'x., & WILLIAM H. EGGLESTON, adm'r., of the DICK H. EGGLESTON estate.

V. C. GROON, adm'r., of the JOHN WILEY estate will present his accounts for final settlement.

SPENCER WALL has been well sustained as a teacher for a number of years in Woodville. The school will be resumed for the ensuing year. Jan. 1, 1838

MARGARET COLE, adm'rx., of the MATTHEW COLE estate will sell property of the estate.

ARCH'D McCRAINE, adm'r., of the HUGH McCRAINE estate will present the accounts as guardian of the minor heirs of CHARLES A. COON for final settlement.

DAVID ARMSTRONG, adm'r., of the EPHRAIM FLESHMAN estate will sell property of the estate.

January 13, 1838

JANE N. WILEY, adm'rx., of the WM. WILEY estate will present her accounts for final settlement.

V. C. GROOM, adm'r., of the JOHN WILEY estate will present his accounts for final settlement.

CYRUS S. MAGOUN & WM H. DILLINGHAM, adm'rs of the CALVIN B. MAGOUN estate

DAVID H. COURTNEY, was appointed administrator of the PETER LEATHERMAN estate at the January term, 1838, of the Probate Court of Wilkinson County.

BLAKE HOLLIMAN will sell to the highest bidder, under the Royal Oak, in Woodville, a tract of land containing 160 acres, lying on Beaver creek.

STAGE ARRANGEMENTS;--The Stages leave Woodville for Nachez and St. Francisville, on Tuesdays, Thursdays, & Saturdays, at 4 o'clock, A. M.
those wishing to engage passage for either of the above places will please apply to JOHN M'KEY who is appointed our agent.
                                    WM. RULE.
                                    WM. SCOTT
Woodville, January 6th, 1838.
(Example of advertisement)

Married the 28th by the Rev. SAMUEL DAWSON, Mr. SYLEVESTER C. ESTESS, to Miss EMELINE MURPHY, all of this county.

Married the 11th January, by the Hon. N. SCUDDER, JOHN SLADE, Esqr., to Mrs. LOUISA HAYES, all of this county.

PETER A. PRESLER Esqr., of Fort Adams is my authorised agent to receive and receipt for taxes for me at said place....WM. T. JONES, T. C. W. C.

JOHN OGDEN & SON are anxious to close their business in Fort Adams and will sell out their goods at a very moderate prices.

JOHN C. JENKINS, adm'r., of the JOHN F. CARMICHAEL estate

JOHN H. RANDOLPH, exec'r., of the A. S. RANDOLPH estate

China Grove For Sale! The subscriber offers for sale, that pleasant House and Lot formerly owned by Wm. T. LEWIS, Esqr., situated in the most delightful part of the town of Woodville. For a Physician, Lawyer, Merchant, or Planter, who wishes a Village Mansion for the purpose of Educating his Children, this place possesses all the requisite accommodations. The West Feliciana Rail Road terminating near this place will eventually very much enhance its value......
E. A. KNOWLTON. (Example of advertisement)

I. H. STANWOOD has the best quality of Sperm Oil.

JOHN B. JONES, Mayor, C. C. WEST, Wm. P. GRAYSON, A. G. FOSTER, and JACOB KELLER, Aldermen, GEO. L. POINDEXTER, Constable.

Bank West Feliciana Rail Road Co. Directors for 1838: JOSEPH JOHNSON, EDW'D. McGEHEE, JOHN S. LEWIS, JAMES L. TRASK, MOSES LIDDELL, F. R. RICHARDSON, E. H. WAILES, GEO. H. GORDON, and C. P. SMITH.

MOSES LIDDELL, adm'r., of the Wm. S. GRIFFIN estate

January 20, 1838
W. J. HODGE wishes to sell his interest in land lying on the Big Sand Creek in Carroll County.

Cloe will be sold by Special Appointed Trustee GEO H. GORDON, to clear DOUGLASS H. COOPER and Wm. M. HELM for their endorsement of a promissory note given on February 7, 1837 by M. W. CALLICOATE.

JOHN H. RANDOLPH, adm'r., of the A. S. RANDOLPH estate will sell all the furniture of the estate.

A horse has strayed from Judge McGEHEE's near Woodville. He will probably undertake to make his way back to R. M. NEWMAN's place near Fort Adams. $5 reward.

A. G. BATCHELOR, guardian of CHARLES M. STEWART will present his accounts for final settlement.

THOMAS DEVINE has commenced his tailoring buisness near the north west corner of the Public Square.

January 27, 1838

E. H. BROWN, adm'r., of the JESSE BROWN estate will sell property of the estate.

Died at his plantation in this county, the 16th, after a short illness in the 35th year of his age, Mr. WM. W. KAIGLER, a useful and respectable citizen, leaving a wife and child, and numerous relative and friends to regret his untimely exit.

Married the 16th, by JOHN McCREA, Esqr., Capt. HENRY H. RICE to Miss MARY McGRAW, all of this county.

Married the 18th, by JOHN McCREA, Esqr., Mr. SAMUEL F. GAULDEN to Miss ELIZA D. COLLINS, both of East Feliciana Parish, La.

Married the 17th by the Rev. SAMUEL DAWSON, Mr. JESSE G. SWAYZE to ELIZABETH BARNET, both of this county.

Married the 21st, by the Hon. N. SCUDDER, Mr. BENJAMIN M. HUBBARD to Mrs. ANNA N. VOSE, all of this county.

February 3, 1838

WILLIAM W. IVES, County Surveyor, offers his services. His residence is at ALEXANDER C.DUNBAR's Ashwood Place, on the St. Francisville road, four miles south of Woodville.

JOHN A. SCOTT, adm'r., of the WILLIAM HAILE estate will sell property belonging to the estate.

Died the 19th October of conjestive fever, CLEMENT BIDDLE PENROSE, Esqr., aged 35 years. On his visit to the Balize, fell victim to its pestilential marshes and sunk. Vale, Vale, requiesce in pace.

Married in Woodville, 23rd January, 1838, by the Rev. Mr. COLLINS, Rev. WILLIAM H. TAYLOR to Miss H. A. JACKSON, all of Massachusetts.

February 10, 1838

WM. M. WHITEHEAD cautions against trading for a certain note of hand given to the subscriber with (HUGH CONNELL & DANIEL WOODARD, as securities) to WILLIAM ILER, adm'r., of ABRAM ILER, deceased, for the sum of $1800.00 dated 17th January, 1837 and payable the first day of January, 1838.

JEHU KNIGHTEN, adm'r., of the JAMES MEEK estate will sell all personal property.

GERALD C. BRANDON, President of the Board of Police of Wilkinson County.

WM. A. A. CHISHOLM vs. URIAH F. CASE

WILEY DELOACH has taken up a grey horse.

The real estate of both DICK H. EGGLESTON, dec'd., and JOHN OGDEN, dec'd., will be sold.

February 17, 1838
ELIZABETH WARD will sell her tract of 130 acres at an auction under the Royal Oak. Land lying on the head waters of Percy's Creek, adjoining the lands of STEPHEN O. CHAMBERS & S. (SAMUEL) LEATHERMAN.

C. M. SHEPHERD, adm'r., of the HARRIETT BROWDER estate

FIELDING DAVIS vs. HENSHAW & BELL $3300

The Ragged Hill Place where ALEXANDER J. SCOTT now resides, being the undivided third part of said tract which JOHN A. SCOTT purchased of ALEXANDER J. GRAY, is to be sold. 160 acres.

EZER E. WOODS, B. F. SCOTT, J. J. LANDRUM, JOHN NETTERVILLE, against WILLIAM EVANS, & etc.

C. C. WEST, A. DUNBAR, J. B. & J. E. THERREL, JOHN L. WALL, vs. JOHN A. WARREN

J. A. MONTGOMERY has opened a new Dry Goods store on Commercial Row.

February 24, 1838
J. B. BULLOCK, adm'r., of the WM. QUINE estate

CAROLINE S. FARISH wishes to dispose of her place situated one half mile from Woodville on the Natchez road, opposite Mr. A. DANIEL, containing about 70 acres of good land, spring, out houses and a dwelling house.

W. B. ORR has in his possession a calf skin pocket book found on the road. Belongs to Franks &

Laverick of Natchez, to whom he has written.

NOLAND STEWART, FIELDING DAVIS, T. JONES STEWART & FRANCES M. STEWART, the administrators of WILLIAM STEWART's estate will present their accounts for a final settlement.

REBECCA STEPHENS, adm'x., of the FELIX E. STEPHENS estate will present the accounts for final settlement.

CATHARINE F. KAIGLER, adm'rx., & JOHN D. KAIGLER, adm'r., of the WILLIAM W. KAIGLER estate

W. H. SCOTT, adm'r., of the C. L. HYATT estate will sell all the personal estate of Hyatt.

Deed of mortgage made by HUGH CAIN & WILLIAM CAIN, to secure JESSE JONES & WILLIAM HALL, coadministrators of the ALLEN CAIN estate, for the sum of $4,280.25. Hugh and William Cain's 163 acres was deeded to them by ALLEN CAIN, out of his 205 acres and bounded by lands of Mrs. PENELOPE STEWART, JAMES A. VENTRESS. Also, a share of an undivided 85 acre tract on which Wm. CAIN Sr., lived at the time of his death -- all to be sold to clear debt. LEWIS CASON, Trustee

BENJAMIN KILLGORE vs. EDWARD H. STROTHER $150

March 3, 1838
Married the 1st, by the Hon'ble N. SCUDDER, Mr. Wm. HAYES, to LEVINA ILER, all of this county.

Died on Monday night the 26th, in this town after a protracted illness of several months, Miss L___ YOUNG.

WM DODD will attend to the duties of Auctioneer. He will use a part of Mr. C. FRAISSE's store as an Auction Room.

March 10, 1838
WOODVILLE LYCEUM ASSOCIATION was formed. Dr. C. S. MAGOUN--President, J. W. BURRUS-- Vice President, WM. HALSEY--Secretary, and C. S. MAGOUN--Chairman.

Married on the 3rd, by the Rev. S. DAWSON, Mr. JOHN WISNER, to Miss TEBITHA ELLSBERRY, all of this county.

March 17, 1838

Dr. S. E. POTTS, Dr. C.J. THORNTON, Dr. ESAIAS KAIGLER, Dr. T. P. HARRISON, and Dr. R. H. McDANIEL offers their professional services to the public.

JOSEPH A. HENDERSON, adm'r., of the JOSEPH HENDERSON estate

R. T. OGDEN, adm'r., of the Dr. A. M. KENNAN estate, will offer under the Royal Oak, all the personal estate of Dr. Kennan.

HIRAM G. RUNNELS, President of the MISSISSIPPI UNION BANK, located in Jackson, the place prescribed for the location of the Mother Bank.

MARGARET COLE, adm'rx., of the MATTHEW COLE estate will present her accounts for final settlement.

JOHN L. WALL, adm'r., of the ELIZA ANN GINN estate and the EDMUND GINN estate, will present his accounts for final settlement.

CHAS. NETTERVILLE, WILLIAM HENDERSON, A. MITCHELL & MARK ANDERSON against JAMES W. SMITH & C. P. SMITH.
1/6 of undivided parcel of land in the town of Woodville, bounded by A. M. FELTUS, which was purchased of the estate of PRESTWOOD SMITH, by W. W. WHITEHEAD, JOS. JOHNSON which was formerly owned by A. W. ALLEN, JAS L. TRASK, being a part of the real estate of of PRESTWOOD SMITH, dec'd., and the father of said J. W. SMITH, also the undivided 1/6 part of ten lots which are in the cases of P. G. PARHAM, adm'r., and SAM'L. W. LEWIS against PRESTWOOD SMITH 's adm'r.

JOHN D. WHITE vs. MOSES STEWART $152.95

ARMSTRONG & PARKER vs. JACOB HOWE $90.04

PETERSON G. PARHAM, adm'r. of THOMAS KELSEY, & SAMUEL W. LEWIS vs. PRESTWOOD SMITH's adm'r.

Land of MICHAEL COTTER & Wife, formerly owned by PRESWOOD SMITH, to be sold to cover court cost.

Died the 11th, at the residence of Wm. F. PAQUINETT, WILLIAM G. POINDEXTER, eldest child of JOHN G. POINDEXTER, in the sixth year of his age.

DANIEL BARTLET was found dead on Thursday the 8th, near the residence o Mr. THOS. WHITE, on Buffaloe. It is supposed he died in a fit.

JAMES FERGUSON, NANCY GAY, JESSE MABRY, SAMUEL BELL, A. M. WALSH, MARY S. OGDEN, A. LEFFINGWELL, ALANSON FERGUSON, THOMAS NETTERVILLE, LYDIA DOWELL, GEORGE EVANS, C. C. WEST, ANNA S. McCOMAS and JOHN A. FRANKER, per officers against DANIEL WOODARD, et als. Total of 980 acres to be sold to satisfy plaintiffs debts and cost of suit.

March 24, 1838
The well known steamer, BAYOU SARA, Captain C. LAURENT, will run a regular packet between New Orleans and Bayou, and all intermediate landings.

J. J. LANDRUM vs. WM. EVANS & THEODORE MOLLEMAN

SAM'L W. LEWIS vs. ANDREW REA, THOS. BELL, JNO. McALPINE, M. BRYAN & ANDREW REA

JESSE BANTER vs. JOSEPH CARR

LYONS & BLEDSOE vs. JACOB BUNCH

March 31, 1838
Died on Saturday night, the 17th in this town, after a long and painful illness, Mrs. ELIZABETH HERBERT.

NOLAD M. LUCKETT, JAMES CALVIT, ISRAEL T. BROWNING against A. R. FOSTER's adm'r., and GEORGE P. FOSTER

PLANTERS BANK MISS, vs. ALEXR. SMITH & others., JASPER S. M. COON, vs. ALEXR. SMITH, JOHN I. AMOS vs. ALEXR. SMITH

ALEXR. MITCHELL vs. A. J. GRAY, B. F. HARDIN vs. T. W. RADFORD & A. J. GRAY

THOMAS H. McGRAW vs. FELIX McGRAW $115

JOHN W. SCOTT vs. JAMES WOOD $132

April 7, 1838
EPHRAIM ESTESS, grardian of MARTHA KING, will present his accounts for final settlement.

JOHN HENDERSON, ex'r., of the ABRAM SCOTT estate will present his accounts for final settlement.

JOHN A. SCOTT wishes to be released as adm'r., of the WILLIAM HAILE estate.

JANE CIZZIE, adm'rx., of the HARRIS ANDERSON estate

Married the 1st April, by the Rev. S. DAWSON, Mr. LEATH MILLER to Miss LACKEY T. PARMER, all of this county.

R. W. HARRIS has lost 10 head of cattle.

LYONS & BLEDSOE vs. JACOB BUNCH   220 acrs being the same place on which Mrs. STEVENS now lives and bounded by ISRAEL SMITH, WILLIAM HASLIP, and Dr. N. E. RAYMOND WM. T. LEWIS, Sh'ff, and THO'S NETTERVILLE, Dp. Sh'ff.

April 14, 1838

DAVID BRYANT, use CADE HAVARD vs. ABRAM POOL

Married April 12th, by the Rev. Mr. COLLINS, Mr. EDWARD STEVENS to Miss ELIZABETH HUBBARD, all of this place.

H. HOOTSELL's horse has strayed.

Commissioners appointed to examine claims against the estate of THOS. J. HAMILTON, dec'd., J. P. HARRIS, J. B. THERREL, and A. G. FOSTER.

BENJAMIN WHITE, adm'r., of the ROBERT WHITE, Sr., will present accounts for final settlement.
He also will present same for ROBERT WHITE, Jr., both deceased.

P. E. H. LOVELACE offers $20 reward for the return of his sorrel horse.

H. E. SALE, clothing merchant in Woodville, Ms.

Wm. H. WHITE, Wm. McMUTRY, BANNISTER STONE and A. G. FOSTER, adm'r., against SAML. McMURTRY

April 21, 1838

JOHN H. TURBEVILLE has taken up a black gelding as a stray, and appraised at $50.

An Ordinance "to regulate the time and manner of improving the side walks in the Town of Woodville, and to prescribe the penalty for any failure to perform such improvements," passed the 11th day of

April, 1838.

A. T. WELSH has taken up a sorrel mare as a stray.

C. M. STEWART has taken up a gray horse as a stray.

Wanted 20 or 25 sober, industrious and skillful carpenters to go upon the West Feliciana Rail Road. Apply to Judge McGEHEE or JOS. JOHNSON, Esqr.

April 28, 1838

L. D. BROWN, adm'r., of the JOHN McCREADY estate will present accounts for final settlement.

Commissioners appointed to examine claims against the estate of ISRAEL T. BROWNING, dec'd., WM. H. SCOTT, J. B. THERREL, and G. L. POINDEXTER.

JOSEPH A. HENDERSON, adm'r., of the JOSEPH HENDERSON estate

R. T. OGDEN, adm'r., of the Dr. A. M. KENNAN estate, will offer for sale, under the Royal Oak, the personal property belonging to the estate.

503 arpents of land conveyed to WILLIAM W. KAIGLER, by SAMUEL McCUTCHENS and REBECCA, his wife, by deed, 18th of April, 1833, will be sold.

To those who are interested in the lands, tenements and heredetaments of PETER LEATHLITER deceased, Greetings:---(On January 13, 1838, the entry stated that DAVID H. COURTNEY was the adm'r., to PETER LEATHERMAN).

MATTHEW RAMSEY of Centreville, Amite County, offers a reward for a strayed mule.

R. RATLIFF of Jackson, La. has lost a horse.

BRISBAND MARSHALL vs. DAVID ARMSTRONG   983 acres to be sold near Pinckmeyville, and bounded by lands of JOHN BELL's heirs, JOHN F. CARMICHAEL, SAMUEL W. LEWIS and others.

HENRY SMITH vs. JOHN G. POINDEXTER   164 acres

In consequence of the unusual pressure of the times, the want of money and the impossibility of obtaining it upon any kind of terms, we give notice, that after this date, it will be entirely out of our poser to advance Cash, except for Freight that may be Consigned to us, the bills for which are to be considered due whenever presented. D. & D. I. ARMSTRONG, & CO.   March 31, 1838

Married on the 19th, by the Hon. N. SCUDDER, Mr. B. W. WRIGHT to Miss REBECCA J. WATKINS, all of this county.

May 5, 1838

C. S. MAGOUN will be absent for a few weeks, and Doct. Wm. STOCKBRIDGE will attend to my business.

Gen. JACKSON's FAREWELL ADDRESS." I leave this great people prosperous and happy."

JNO. B. THERRELL, adm'r., of the A. J. GRAY estate

Married the 26th April, at the residence of Mr. JAMES N. BROWN, by the Rev. A. T. SIMMONS, Mr. GEORGE R. DRAUGHAN to Miss MARY L. D. WINNINGHAM, all of West Feliciana Parish, La.

Married the 3rd, by the Hon. N. SCUDDER, Mr. JAMES ONEAL to Miss PRISCILLA FOGLEMAN, of La.

The Rev. GEORGE ROGERS, a Universalist Preacher will preach in the Court House on Friday evening next, at early candle light.

THOMAS ROWAN vs. JAMES A. KNIGHTEN, Franklin County Circuit Court, April Term, 1838- In Chancery.

500 acres of ROBERT DAWSON & GILDART's estate to be sold for taxes. 1837-$7.97

JOHN H. TURBEVILLE has taken up a black gelding.

500 acres of ROBERT COCHRAN's estate to be sold for taxes. 1837-$7.97

Lot in Woodville belonging to THO'S SIMPSON to be sold for taxes. 1837-$1.59

160 acres and also 1100 acres of JOHN SMITH to be sold for taxes. 1937-$43.45. Bounded by lands of GEO. ADAMS, the estate of JOHN JOOR, JOSEPH J. SCOTT, THOS. H. OSWALD, HUGH CONNELL, H. A. MOORE, JA'S CALLIHAM and Wm. T. MAYES.

May 12, 1838

We learn with the deepest regret, by passengers from Charleston that one third of the city of Charleston was laid in ashes at 6 o'clock and the fire was raging as if it would consume at least one third more.

Mr. J. C. DODGE, Tutor of the "Mabry Morris Seminary situated about four or five miles west of Woodville, had to retire due to ill health.

J. A. VENTRESS, JESSE EDWARDS, JOHN McCREA, WM. F. DYSON, A. G. CAGE, trustees of schools in T1, R1 East, 16th Secton, will lease land for the term of 99 years.

Married the 17th by the Rev. B. SHAW, STANHOPE POSSEY, Esqr., to Mrs. REBECCA B. KELLOGG, all of this town.

Married the 14th, by the Rev. SAMUEL DAWSON, Mr. JOHN FORBES to Miss LUCINDA C. BROWN, all of this county.

100 acres belonging to JOHN CRAWFORD and bounded by lands of the Wm. A. LUSK estate, & Wm. SWAYZIE, to be sold for taxes. 1837- $1.59.

JOHN P. SMITH respectfully announces to his friends and the public, that he has taken the hotel formerly occupied by the late ELIJAH BELL, and known as the "Mansion House". (Originally from the "Natchez Courier")

Married the 17th by the Rev. B. SHAW, STANHOPE POSEY Esqr., to Mrs. REBECCA KELLOGG, all of this county.

Married the 14th by the Rev. SAMUEL DAWSON, Mr. JOHN FORBES to Miss LUCINDA C. BROWN, all of this county.

May 26, 1838

CESSAR FRAISSE has just opened a Public House in this place, at the House formerly occupied by T. MOLLEMAN, opposite the Court House.

JOHN F. COURTNEY has taken up a horse as as stray.

Married in Kingston, N. H., April 30th, Doct. C. S. MAGOUN of this place to Miss SARAH B. SANBORN, daughter of J. H. SANFORN, Esqr. of the former place.

Married the 24th, by JOHN McCREA, Esqr., Mr. H. M. BUTTON to Miss ADALINE CAIN, all of this county.

June 2, 1838
Married the 30th, by the Rev. Mr. FISH, Mr. NICHOLAS NORWOOD to Mrs. M. A. HAMILTON, all of this county.

JOHN TIMON vs. MATILDA TIMON: Bill for divorce. Matilda resides out of the state; this order must be published for three months.

A. DANIEL, adm'r., of the Wm. UHLMAN estate will present his accounts for final settlement.

DAVID THOMPSON recaptured a blood bay horse at the Cold Springs Hotel on the 22d.

D. W. HAXALL has lost a four year old colt from his plantation four miles east of Woodville.

Wm JOHNSON claims a 2/11 part of 450 acres bounded by the DELOACH lands, G. C. BRANDON land and the Wm. L. BRANDON land. Commissioners to divide the land are: CALEB HALL, JOHN A. FELLS and ROBERT M. YERBY.

The estate of JAMES CAIN will be examined by commissioners, DANIEL McGAHEY, WM. F. DYSON, and IRWIN MURPHY.

June 9, 1838
Married the 7th, by C. C. WEST, Esqr., Mr. SAMUEL DEARMOND to Miss SARAH FAIRCHILD.

MARGARET P. FOLEY, adm'x., of the JAMES W. FOLEY estate will present her accounts for final settlement.

HIRAM FRAYARD has taken up a horse as a stray.

June 16, 1838
J. L. JONES, adm'r., of D. F. COON estate, and FELIZ EMBREE, of Wilkinson County, claim the first 2/7ths, and the second 5/7ths, of 750 acres of undivided land formerly owned by WM. CAIN, senior, being the same land on which he resided and known as the CAIN TRACT. Commissioners to divide land are WM. F. DYSON, PETER McKENZIE & Wm. VAUGHAN.

June 23, 1838

Married the 21st of June, 1838, by the Rev. Mr. COLLINS, Mr. WILLIAM HALSEY to Miss M. S. CHAPMAN, all of this place.

Married the 26th at Tuscombia, Alabama, by the Rev. C. RICHARDSON, Rev. JOHN C. BURRUSS of Ms. to Miss EMILY L. NUTTING, of Massachusetts.

D. H. COURTNEY, adm'r., of the PETER LEATHLIGHTER estate will sell a 41 acre tract of land.

SILAS PERRY, adm'r., of the DAVID C. PERRY estate will sell all the personal property of the estate.

June 30, 1838

M. P. FOLEY, adm'r., of the JAMES W. FOLEY estate will present her accounts for final settlement.

L. D. BROWN, guardian of ELIZA L. BRUCE will present his accounts for final settlement.

CHARLES HESTER, guardian of LEWIS H. BRYAN, will present his accounts for final settlement.

PETER CONRAD cautions anyone against crediting his account without his direct order.

WM. M. HELM has at his plantation at Cold Springs, a large quantity of bagging and rope which he will sell at the Natchez and New Orleans prices.

WM. W. IVES, County Surveyor will survey and establish the boundary lines between D. H. COOPER and T. S. EASTON.

JOSHUA FINDLAY vs. WILLIAM E. WILLIAMS & HENRY H. RICE

WM. W. IVES, County Surveyor will survey and establish the boundary lines between W. M. HELM & THOMAS ELLIS, whose lands ajoin.

July 7, 1838

M. P. FOLEY, admr'x., of the JAMES W. FOLEY estate will present her accounts for final settlement.

BENJ. RAWLINS cautions any person against trading for two notes given to him by THOS. WISNER.

ARCHIBALD McCRAINE, adm'r., of the HUGH McCRAINE estate

Commissioners appointed to examine claims against the WM. S. GRIFFIN are; CHAS. LANCASTER, WM. P. GRAYSON and GEORGE MARTIN.

DANIEL QOODARD appointed T. DAVIDSON as his trustee, since C. S. KELLOGG is now deceased. Davidson will sell 493 acres bounded by A. P. SLOCOMB's land, and JAMES HOLMES, being the same tract purchased by LEWIS HYNOR of A. P. SLOCOMB, adm'r., of CHARLES C. SLOCOMB, deceased. $2,837.

Married the 3rd July, 1838, by the Hon. N. SCUDDER, Mr. VICTOR N. H. NETTERVILLE to Miss CAROLINE DUNCKLEY, all of this county.

July 14, 1838

All persons indebted for letters and papers are requested to pay. J. RIDDLE, P. M.

MARIA OGDEN, adm'rx., of the JOHN OGDEN estate will sell 100 shares of stock in the Bank of the West Feliciana Rail Road and 50 shares of stock in the Planters Bank in Woodville.

BENJ. FERGUSON, guardian of Fielding Davis Wright, subject to the dower of MARY WRIGHT, will sell a tract of land.

ELIZA S. WILLIAMS, guardian of the heirs of ISAAC WILLIAMS, will sell 260 acres of land bounded by land of Mrs. NANCY PINSON and land of JOSEPH JOHNSON.

WALTER SHROPSHIRE, adm'r., of the JONATHAN DAY estate will sell all the personal property.

MARY JOHNSON, adm'rx., & RICHARD INMAN, adm'r., of the WILLIAM JOHNSON estate

GEO. B. COLLIER, adm'r., of the HALLET POTTER estate will present his accounts for final settlement.

SARAH SIMPSON, adm'x., of the WM. SIMPSON estate will present her accounts for final settlement.

JOHN S. HOLT & J. A. MONTGOMERY, Collecting Committee, serves notice to subscribers to the Presbyterian Church to be built in Woodville to pay fifty per cent, or more of the amount of subscription.

HENRY SMITH vs. JOHN G. POINDEXTER

July 21, 1838

Died near Woodville on the 14th of congestive fever, Mr. PLINEY TOWER, of Springfield Vermont, aged 25 years.

Died at Fort Adams on the 12th, Master JAMES MILLER, aged 13 years.

ADA MORNING STAR vs. EWING CHAMPMAN $135

RICHARD CLAMPITT has a house and lot for sale in Woodville.

July 28, 1838

The Rev. CHARLES FELDER will preach in the Baptist Church in Woodville, on Tuesday the 7th day of August.

WILLIAM M. HELM, executor of the JOSEPH W. MILLER estate will present his accounts for final settlement.

August 4, 1838

SUDDEN DEATH.-- SAMUEL GWIN, Esqr., Cashier of the Union Bank of Mississippi, died in New Orleans on Saturday last. His death was occasioned by drinking ice water. This is the second death among the officers of the Union Bank since their election, Mr. GILDART, the Bank Attorney having recently deceassed. (Originally from the NAT. COU.)

Married on the 29the July by Rev. SAML. DAWSON, Mr. Wm. WOODS to Miss MARY A. MOSLEY.

Married on the 26th July, by Rev. SAML. DAWSON, Mr. BENJAMIN F. SIBLEY to Miss ELIZA H. HORNSBY, all of this county.

Married on the 2nd., by the Rev. Wm. WINANS, Mr. W. D. POSTHLEWAITE to Miss SOPHIA T. CARTER, all of this county.

R. T. OGDEN, adm'r., of the A. M. KENNAN estate requests that all who are indebted to the estate come forth by September 1st, or the accounts will be found in the hands of JNO. B. JONES, Esquire.

THOS. H. QUARTEMAN has lost 18 sheep.

The copartnership in the planting business between DANIEL WOODARD and GEORGE H. SWIGART is dissolved.

J. E. THERREL, Ord. Serg't ordered all Citizen Volunteers to parade on Saturday the 4th day of August, at 3 o'clock P. M.

Partnership dissolved between JAMES VARNELL, P. A. PRESLER, JAS. F. THOMPSON and JNO. REES.

August 11, 1838
M. P. FOLEY, adm'r., of the JAMES W. FOLEY estate will present her accounts for final settlement.

F. R. RICHARDSON, guardian of AMANDA THOMPSON (late AMANDA SINGLETON) and RICHARD SINGLETON will present his accounts for final settlement.

WILEY DELOACH vs. J. A. LILLEY   Oct Term 1838 Attachment for $258 against real estate of Lilley. If the defendent does not appear, give special bail, and plead in said case, on or before the first day of our next October Term of said court, judgement will be entered against him and the goods and efects so attached, will be sold.

WM. W. IVES, County Surveyor will establish boundry lines between THOS. J. LENIER and JOHN PHIPPS.

August 18, 1838
Married on Sunday last, by C. C. WEST, Esqr., Mr. WILLIAM B. KELLER, of Louisiana, to Miss MARGARET ANN ROGERS, of this county.

Died on the 13th, after a short illness, ANN WILSON, daughter of Mr. THOMAS ELLIS, aged five years, seven months and thirteen days.

CHARLES MERRILL, adm'r., of the ALEXANDER MORGAN estate wishes to sell an undivided half of 600 arpens of land, situated on Pearl river in Hancock County.

August 25, 1838
Died in this county the 13th, Judge JOHN B. POSEY.

Died the 11th at the residence of Capt. MULFORD, in this Parish. Mrs. ANN KNOWLTON, daughter of the late CHRISTIAN BINGAMAN, age 45 years. (Originally in the LA. JOUR.)

A murder was committed last Monday on the person of NATHANIEL MEEK. One person has been committed for the offence, and others are standing their trial as being concerned in the crime.

We are sorry to see the death of the Hon. JAMES PHILLIPS, our worthy State Treasurer, announced in the Jackson papers.

Died in Wilkinson County on the 23rd, Mr. JAMES LESSLEY.

Obituary from the NATCHEZ FREE TRADER: The venerable Col. ANDREW MARSCHALE, a veteran of the US army, near the close of the revolution, between the years of 1791 and 1796, departed this life at his residence at Washington, Adams County. He was a member of the Masonic lodges, and the oldest member of the Society of Odd Fellows in the United States, having joined that over which the Prince of Wales, since George the Fourth, presided in London more than fifty years ago. We represent him as the Father of Typographical Art in Mississippi. He will be deeply lamented by a large circle of friends, neighbors, and relations.

WILLIAM DAVIS of Marshall and WILLIAM DYRE of Choctaw, have resigned their seats in the House of Representatives. (Originally from the MISSISSIPPIAN)

September 1, 1838

M. M. PHARES & GEORGE MARTIN have purchased a portion of Mr. Wm. H. SCOTT's stock.

C. HALL of Pinckneyville, has lost a bay horse.

September 8, 1838

GEORGE H. GORDON & STANHOPE POSEY, have associated themselves in the practice of law.

C. P. SMITH & T. LEIGH, attorneys

WILLIAM H. DILLINGHAM & JOHN B. JONES, have associated themselves in the practice of law.

JOHN NETTERVILLE & TRUXTON DAIVIDSON, attorneys

N. E. J. GODLEY has taken up a horse as a stray.

Married the 30th, by the Rev. S. DAWSON, Mr. HENRY PHIPPS to Mrs. SUSAN WILEY, all of this county.

Married the 29th, by the Rev. S. DAWSON, Mr. Wm. J. WELLS, of La., to Miss LEAH ANN LEATHERMAN, all of this county.

September 15, 1838

WILLIAM M. HELM, executor of the JOSEPH W. MILLER estate will present his accounts for final settlement.

Died the 11th, at Laurel Hill, Louisiana in the 5th year of his age, CHRISTOPHER ASHLY, only son of C. W. BANCKS, Civil Engineer.

Died the 14th, CHARLES C., youngest son of Maj. THOS. C. WEST.

Died 9th September of congestive fever, ISAAC SMITH, son of D. BASS, Esqr., aged 11 years.

Land of JONATHAN DAY is to be sold.

Land of JOHN S. WHITNEY is to be sold.

Land of SAMUEL D. WOODS, a minor, to be sold.

NATHANIEL HUBBARD vs. AMOS P. READ & HORACE BROWN. JAMES J. ROWAN vs. same; A. L. YEIZER vs. same and JOHN L. WALL; P. H. McGRAW, R. T. OGDEN vs. A. P. READ. A one half part of five lots lying in Fort Adams to be sold. Same lots purchased by said Read from ELENOR A. MONKS, 28th Oct., 1835.

BENJAMIN F. SCOTT vs. ALEXANDER J. SCOTT One third of undivided part of land on which A. J. GRAY formerly lived, usually called Ragged Hill, being the same purchased by JOHN A. SCOTT from A. J. GRAY, and sold to BENJAMIN F. SCOTT, to be sold.

WESLEY REILY has taken up a horse as a stray.

JOHN B. THEREL, by virtue of a deed of trust exectued by JAMES M. MILLER and JAMES WARD, on 24th of Feb., authorizing Therrel to sell land. Same land conveyed by CAROLINE M. & CORNELIA BURROUGH to said Miller and Ward.

September 22, 1838

HENRY L. CASON, adm'r., of the LEWIS CASON estate

DAVID BRYANT vs. ABRAM POOL

Died the 19th Sept. after a short illness, HARRIET ANN ALLEN, daughter of W. D. ALLEN, aged ten years and eight months, leaving a beloved father and mother to morn her exit.

September 29, 1838
October 6, 1838

WM. B. CLUGSTON & ALEX. N. GALLOWAY, Merchant Tailors, have formed a copartnership.

BASS &LEWIS, EZER E. WOODS, JANE M. SPEAR, ARCHIBALD McCRAINE & LOZ. D. BROWN vs. MICHAEL COTTER and wife. One undivided sixth part of ten lots in Woodville, to be sold.

WILLIS HUNTER, adm'r., of the CLAIBORNE TICKELL estate will present his accounts for settlement.

NOEL NORWOOD & ELIAS NORWOOD, adm'rs., of the MARTHA NORWOOD estate

October 13, 1838

MARY A. LEEK & JOHN WHEELER vs. THOMAS LEEK An undivided interest in 500 acres lying on Buffaloe creek, bounded west by SPENCER WOOD, THOS. G. ELLIS's heirs, being the same land on which FREDERICK A. LEEK, possessed and since his death and at this time occupied by MARY A. LEEK.

Died in this place on Wednesday, the 10th, after a long and painful illness in the 22nd year of his age, Mr. J. M. KERCHEVAL.

Married the 2nd by the Rev. Wm.WINANS, Mr. JAMES J. GRAVES, late editor of the "Liberty Advocate" to Miss MARY A. A. ANDERSON, daughter of Capt. JOHN. B. ANDERSON, both of Amite County.

Married in Wooville on Wednesday evening last by JOHN B. JONES, Esqr., Mr. PETER KELLEY to Miss JANE LESSLEY, both of this town and county.

DIVISION ORDER #3, Possum Castle, 18th September, 1838. In the exercise of power, vested by law, I have appointed the following officers, members of the Division Staff of the 1st Division, M. M. --as follows: ROBT. SEMPLE, Division Inspector, to rank as Lt. Col., P. F. KEARY, Aids-De-Camp, and St. JNO. R. LIDDELL, rank Major. All offices and soldiers of the First Division, M. M. will respect and obey them accordingly. WILL. L. BRANDON, Major General Commanding the First Division, M. M.

The guardian of THOMAS A. SHEPPARD, a minor, will sell an undivided interest in a tract of land.

The guardian of SAMUEL D. WOODS, a minor, will sell a tract of land containing 490 acres and also a tract of 60 acres, all bounded by lands of Mrs. SARAH PETTIBONE, EDWARD McGEHEE, Dr Wm. H. EGGLESTON and ANDREW HARE's heirs.

Lands of JONATHAN DAY to be sold by WALTER SHROPSHIRE, administrator of the estate.

October 20, 1838

LEGRAND KILLGORE, adm'r., of the NATHANIEL T. MEEKS' estate

ELIAS FORD, adm'r., of the JAMES ARD estate in Hancock County, Ms.

Married the 16h by the Hon. N. SCUDDER, Mr. JOHN AME - - to Miss MARY A. FAVAND (FATAND)???
(This entry was unreadable due to too much ink)

Died in Woodville the 16th, Mrs. P. DeGRAFFENREID, consort of Gen. M. F. DeGRAFFENREID.

Died the 19th, Mrs. S. SLAUGHTER.

October 27, 1838

T. S. EASTON, adm'r., of the Wm.H. FAIRCHILD estate will present accounts for final settlement.

E. H. WAILES wishes to be released as exec'r., of the Wm. NEWELL estate.

Lands of JOHN S. WHITNEY is to be sold.

M. G. GAULDEN, executor of the ELIZABETH HATFIELD estate

Married the 18th by the Rev. Mr. COLLINS, Mr. THOMAS B. THORP to Miss ANN MARIA HINCKLEY.

WM. A. AUSTIN wishes to well his land of one section. Please enquire of Maj. L. D. BROWN or Wm. D. POSTLETHWAITE, Esquire.

A. B. THOMPSON, adm'r., of the CHARLES N. WOOD will sell all the personal property of the estate.

J. L. JONES, adm'r., of the HARVY JOHNSON estate will sell all the personal property of the estate.

November 3, 1838

Married the 21st of Oct. , 1838, by the Hon. N. SCUDDER, Mr. SAMUEL BELL to Miss ESTHER ANN FENNER, all of this county.

P. H. JOOR, adm'r., of the WILLIAM HAILE estate

WILEY DELOACH, adm'r., of the JESSE DELOACH estate will at the next December Term of the Probate Court of Wilkinson county, present his accounts as Administrator of said Estate, for final settlement and allowance--at which time all who are interested can attend. Oct. 27, 1838

WM. AUSTIN, near Fayette in Jefferson County, has lost a bay horse.

H. Y. COLLINS, JOHN McKEE & I. H. STANWOOD, were appointed as commissioners for the WILLIAM BROWN estate.

November 10, 1838

WILLIS HUNTER, adm'r., of the CLAIBORNE TICKELL estate will present his accounts for final settlement.

Wm. W. IVES, County Surveyor will lay off and divide a tract of land belonging to the estate of ANDREW WHITE, deceased.

November 17, 1838

Died the 8th of pleurisy, Mr. HENRY QUINE.

ELIZABRTH POSEY, adm'rx., of the JOHN B. POSEY estate

$1000 reward will be paid by the undersigned for the apprehension of JOHN STEP and SOLOMAN STEP, who murdered MARTIN FRALEY, Sen'r' on the 8th of October, near Wolf's Ferry in Hardin, County, Tennessee. The Steps formerly resided in the Cherokee country in Georgia, and it is thought they will either make their way back to Georgia or strike for Texas. SALLEY FRALEY, BENDERSON G. FRALEY, JACKSON FRALEY, and SAMUEL LENOX. Forward information to SALLEY FRALEY, Humburg, P. O. Hardin County, Tenn. (Description of the two Step men is included in the advertisement)

November 24, 1838

JOHN S. LEWIS, ex'r., of the LUCY YOUNG estate will sell all the personal property of the estate.

ELLIS T. ROGILLIO of Jackson, La., wishes to sell his plantation containing 240 acres, a dwelling house, gin-house, corn mill and etc.

J. PHILBRICK, adm'r., of the C. C. PHILBRICK estate will present accounts for settlement.

C. S. MAGOUN & WM. H. DILLINGHAM, adm'rs., of the CALVIN B. MAGOUN estate will sell the remaining part of the personal property of estate.

JAMES QUINE & JAMES B. BULLOCK, adm'rs., of the HENRY QUINE estate

LEWIS HYNOR loaned a horse, saddle and bridle to ISAAC RATCLIFF, to be returned in three days. He has absconded with the same and a $100 reward is offered for his apprehension. (Originally in the NATCHEZ COURIER)

W. T. LEWIS, Sheriff of Wilkinson County, will attend, with a jury of twelve men, on the lands of STEPHEN DUNCAN, Esquire, to assess any damages sustained by said Duncan, in consequence of the passage of the Homochitto Turnpike and Bridge through his land.

NOEL NORWOOD & ELIAS NORWOOD, adm'rs., of the MARTHA NORWOOD estate will sell a tract of 361 acres and a tract of 466 acres of land. Also on the same day they will sell all personal estate belonging to the estate.

December 1, 1838

A persons indebted to F. S. MAYES are requested to call on Mr. D. F. LEWIS in Woodville, and make immediate payment.

JOHN STAMBRIDGE vs. JAMES CAIN's admr.   155 acres

Commissioners of the JOHN S. WHITNEY estate: H. Y. COLLINS, W. S. BRADSTREET, and JOS. E. THERREL.

WM. W. IVES, County Surveyor, will attend at the house of Mrs. White to divide a tract of land belonging to the estate of ANDREW WHITE.

MARY WHITE vs. JOHN STROTHER $192

Married the 22nd by JOHN McCREA, Esqr., Mr. JOSEPH S. JAGERS of Madison, to Miss MARY MARTIN, of this county.

JEREMIAH YATES has bought out E. R. QUARTERMAN in the "TIN" business.

Died the 25th, Mrs. LEONORA SEMPLE, consort of Col. ROBT. SEMPLE, in the 20th year of her age.

Mrs. M. C. MARSHALL's boarding house, 127 Canal Street, New Orleans, is now open for the convenience of members of the legislature.

Capt. JORDON, of the steamer, HUNTSVILLE, will carry cotton during the balance of the season, at seventy five cents per bale.

December 8, 1838
JOHN H. GREADY offers his 160 acre plantation near Whitesville, and also his possessions, for sale.

WILLIS HUNTER, adm'r., of the CLAIBORNE TICKELL estate will present his accounts for final settlement at the next December term.

December 15, 1838
P. E. H. LOVELACE, guardian of THO'S A. SHEPPARD, a minor under 21 years of age, will sell a portion of the land known as the Rock Hill plantation near Fort Adams. 1/5 and 1/3 of 1/5 part of sections.

JAMES M. MILLER claims an undivided 2/6 of ten lots in the town of Woodville.

Land of ELIZABETH HATFIELD, deceased, to be sold.

ELIZABETH A. KAIGLER, widow and relict of WILLIAM KAIGLER, petitions the court for her 1/3 dower part, besides the distributive ahare of 1/7 part of the personal estate of said deceased.

December 22, 1838
JOHN STEMBRIDGE vs. JAMES CAIN'S adm'r.

Married the 13h by the Hon. N. SCUDDER, Mr. J. J. STOCKETT to Miss MARY OLIVIA McKENZIE, all of this county.

MASONIC NOTICE...The St. Albans Lodge, No: 28, will celebrate the ANNIVERSARY OF ST. JOHN THE EVANGELIST on the 27th Dec'r. instant , at Jackson. The neighoring Lodges, and all transient Brethrea, are invited to attend at our Lodge Room, at 9 o'clock, on said day. By order of said Lodge, PARKER SMITH, Sec'ty., Jackson, La.

A. S. McCOMAS wishes to lease the plantation formerly occupied by JAS. LEE.

MARY JOHNSON, adm'rx., & RICHARD INMAN, adm'r., of the WILLIAM JOHNSON estate will sell 78 acres of land and on the next day will sell a pair of Timber Wheels and Mill Irons, and etc.

December 29, 1838
H. F. SIMRALL, late of Kentucky, attorney and counsellor at law, has located in Woodville.
Refer to Hon. DANIEL MAYS, Judge T. P. WILSON and Hon. Wm. J. GRAVES of Lexington, Kentucky and H. D. MOSLEY of Natchez, Mi.

The steamer "Brian Boroihme" now runs a regular packet between New Orleans and Fort Adams. GEORGE SWENEY, Master.

Lands of WILLIAM CONNELL to be sold.

JAMES Mc'DONALD & ELENOR Mc'DONALD, adm'rs., of the GEO. W. KELLER estate will sell all personal property of the estate.

WALTER SHROPSHIRE, adm'r., of the JONATHAN DAY estate will sell land belonging to the estate.

JOS. BROWN, guardian of the minor, ELIZABETH L. BRUCE, will sell personal property of the estate.

Married the 27th by the Rev. SAMUEL DAWSON, Mr. JAMES M. HOLMES to Miss MARY CARSA, both of this county.

WM. W. IVES, County Surveyor will attend the house of Mr. Wm. M. HELM to establish the boundries of JAS. NICHOLSON, JAS. STEELE, LYMAN HARDING and the THOMAS CUMMING's tracts of land.

1839
January 5, 1839
JOANNAH McREADY, adm'rx., of the JOHN McCREADY estate

Married the 3rd by the Hon. N. SCUDDER, A. M. STAR, of this place to Miss ELIZABETH PARKER, of Cincinnati, Ohio.

B. STONE vs. SAMUEL McMURTRY

MICHAEL H. SULLIVAN is not responsible for any

debts contracted by P. G. TIGNER.

MATHEW G. GAULDEN, executor of the Mrs. ELIZABETH HATFIELD estate will sell at her residence, all the personal property of said estate.

W. SOWELL of Jackson La., has lost a bay horse.

January 11, 1839

I. H. STANWOOD is an agent for piano fortes, manufactured by J. Gilbert & Co. of Boston.

THOMAS WHITE has a horse which was stolen or strayed from BENJAMIN WHITE. A reward is offered.

J. A. STEWART & MOSES LIDDELL, trustees, were given a deed of trust by PHILIP N. NORRIS, the 20th of May, 1836. They will sell 640 acres of land bounded by lands of JESSE DELOACH's estate, JNO. W. LEATHERMAN, JNO. C. SIMS, and S. E. POTTS.

Married the 9th by the Hon. N. SCUDDER, Mr. SIMEON H. BROCKWAN of St. Francisville to Miss AMANDA A. LEATHERMAN of this county. (Published Wilkinson County marriage records state SIMEON H. BROCKWAY)

Married the 10th, by the Hon. N. SCUDDER, Mr. JAS. D. PATE of this county to Mrs. (Miss) ELEANOR E. CONNER of Adams County.

January 19, 1839

WM. HAMMOND has taken up a stray mare.

Commissioners appointed for the insolvent estate of JOHN S. WHITNEY will continue to meet for the ensuing six months.

JESSE OGDEN, exec'r., of the Mrs. REBECCA OGDEN estate

STEPHEN G. SMITH killed four hogs in the month of December, 1838. If the owners can prove his marks, he will be compensated for the hogs.

J. B. THERRELL, adm'r., of the Doct. S. E. POTTS estate.

Married the 17th by N. SCUDDER Esqr., Mr. BENJAMIN C. STUART to Miss MARTHA C., daughter of Maj. F. S. MAYS, all of this county.

Died on the 8th, Mrs. REBECCA OGDEN.

Died on the 17th, Mrs. LANEHART, consort of Mr. ABRAHAM LANEHART.

The next public meeting of the Woodville Lyceum Association will be held at the Methodist Episcopal Church on Monday evening the 28th. Lecture by Mr. L. L. BREWER on the history of Poland and an essay by the Rev. H. DWIGHT.

JOHN P. HARRIS, adm'r., of the CHARLES S. COSBY estate

W. SOWELL of Jackson, La., has lost a horse and a small yellow mule. Reward offered

January 26, 1839
February 2, 1839

CHARLES NETTERVILLE, Jr., has lost a horse which was stolen or has strayed from his field east of Woodville near the Liberty road.

52 acres of land belonging to LYDIA WHITE, THOS. WHITE, and JACKSON WHITE, minors, to be sold. The land is bounded on the north by E. J. LANIER, south by A. JETER, and on the west by THOMAS ELLIS.

ROBERT T. LESSLEY, executor of the JAMES LESSLEY estate

JESSE CARTER has taken up a mare and a colt.

JAMES F. CONNER claims an undivided 1/3 part of the 160 acre tract of land known as the "Ragged Hill" tract, about 3 miles south west of Woodville. Commissioners JAMES QUINE, FRANCIS GILDART and GEORGE MORRIS will divide the land into equal shares.

February 9, 1839

E. R. QUARTERMAN & J. RYDER have bought out the Steam Saw Mill on Buffaloe.

Died Feb. 5th at his late residence in Woodville, Mr. JAMES C. WEEKLEY, in the 59th year of his age.

February 16, 1839

Married the 15th by the Rev. R. A. STEWART, Mr. GEORGE MARTIN, merchant of this place, to Miss MARGARET DICKSON, of this county.

Married on the 2nd, by JOHN MCREA, Esqr., Mr. F.

BRINDLEY to Miss HARRIET BUTLER, both of East Feliciana Parish, Louisiana.

Died on the 25th, Mrs. MARIA LOUISE FRASER, wife of Mr. Wm. T. FRASER, merchant of this place, aged 20 years and 8 months, after an illness of thirty days. She has left two small chidren, one an infant daughter, whose existence was coeval with the disease, which deprived her children of a mother, and an affetionate husband of the wife of his bosom, and the partner of his cares. She had been but little more than a year a resident here, in which time she had formed acquaintances who universally esteemed, and regret her. (Example of an obituary from the NATCHITOCHES HERALD, Jan. 31)

Died near Woodville on the 12th, CHARLES RAD-CLIFFE, infant son of JAS. and MARY P. BELL, aged seven months.

February 23, 1839

C. W. MILLER, adm'r., of the S. A. FREEMAN estate will present his accounts for final settlement.

JOHN ROUTH, MARY M. ELLIS, & ELIAS OGDEN, adm'rs., of the THOMAS G. ELLIS estate will sell 600 acres of land which adjoins Dr. C. F. MERCER, Dr. WOOD and the Elliston plantation. Probate Court of Adams County.

In consequence of an unjust judgment rendered against me at the last session of our District Court, it appears that the sheriff is authorized to sell a part of my personal property, say bricks to the amount of about four hundred dollars, to pay a most unjust and not deserved account against me. I will sell 150,000 first rate bricks. On the same day, he will also sell 210 acres of land on which is situated a most splendid Brick Yard, near the West Feliciana Rail road, and a new patent machine for making, with little cost, 6,000 bricks per day......... E.H.SKILLMAN

EVELINE D. McNULTY vs. GEORGE H. SWIGART amd
ARCHIBALD McCRAINE vs. GEORGE H. SWIGART

T. W. DYER, Att'y., will sue anyone who owes Wm. H. Scott if not cleared by 20th of March.

M. M. PHARES' Boarding House on Commercial Row in Woodville, Mississippi. Travellers accommodated.

March 2, 1839

Died in this place on the 23rd of February, Mr. FREDERICK O. JENKINS, late of Baltimore, Md. aged about 24 years.

Mrs. VIRGINIA POINDEXTER will be prepared on Monday to give instruction to Young Ladies in the science and practice of MUSIC.

Due to the death of FREDERICK O. JENKINS, the firm of Hickley & Jenkins was dissolved. THOMAS HICKLEY

DANIEL WOODARD, exec'r., and LOUISA SWIGART, exec'x., of the GEO. H. SWIGART estate

Sheriff's sale: GEORGE PHIPPS, use A. BUCKNER vs. ELEANOR STEVENSON, adm'rx.

Sheriff's sale: S. W. OAKEY & Co. vs. HENRY CONRAD

200 acres of land to be sold as well as the undivided interest of MORGAN S. REILEY in a tract of land on which SAML REILEY, his father lived at the time of his decease, about 3 miles east of Mount Pleasant, and adjoining he lands of H. & A. CAGE, Mrs. GORDON and others.

March 9, 1839

Died at the house of Wm. D. ALLEN in this county, on the 4th of consumption, JAMES JACKSON LANDRUM, in the 25th year of his age.

Died in this town on the 8th, after a short illness, Mr. GEORGE L. POINDEXTER.

March 16, 1839

FRANCIS B. HAYNES, adm'r., of the ARMSTEAD HAYNES estate will present his accounts for settlement.

WM. W. IVES, County Surveyor will establish the lines between the Wm. GILBERT tract and the JAS. NICHOLSON, the HENDERSON and DUNBAR tracts.

JOHN C. JENKINS, adm'r., of the estate of JOHN F. CARMICHAEL, and guardian of RICHARD HOOKE, MOSES HOOKE, FRANCIS HOOKE, HARRIETT HOOKE, and WILLIAM HOOKE, will present his accounts for final settlement.

JOHN D. KAIGLER, adm'r., of the SAMUEL HOLLIMAN estate will present his accounts for final settlement.

CATHARINE F. KAIGLER, adm'rx., & JOHN D. KAIGLER, adm'r., of the WILLIAM W. KAIGLER estate, will present their accounts of said William W. Kaigler as admininstrator to the estate of SAMUEL HOLLIMAN, for final settlement.

Married the 7th March, by Rev. S. DAWSON, Mr. JOHN LYONS to Miss JULIA ANN SAPP, all of this county.

Married on the 14th by TRUMAN POWELL Esqr., Mr. ROBERT T. OGDEN, to Miss AMANDA CAROLINE TIGNER, both of this county.

H. H. BELL, adm'r., of the JAMES C. KENNER estate will sell all the personal property of the estate.

SARA FENNER, adm'rx., of the JAMES FENNER estate

MARY WEEKLEY, adm'rx., of the JAMES C. WEEKLEY estate

FRANCIS S. MAYES vs. SARAH ROACH   40 acres purchased from W. W. ROACH and SARAH ANN ROACH.

EXSEM LEWIS vs. JOSIAH JETER   136 acres bounded by lands of ISAAC KING, lands of ISRAEL SMITH, and lands of N. E. RAYMOND to be sold to satisfy plaintiff's debts, and cost of suit.

J. B. & J. E. THERREL, JOHN HOLMES, DAVID POOL, H. J. BASS & Co. SUSAN HART use & Co. and P. & W. SMYDER vs. ROBERT MILLER

T. DAVIDSON & A. G. FOSTER, commissioners of the estate of WILLIAM HAILE, report is extended.

March 23, 1839

Died in this place on 22nd, after a short illness, Mrs. SARAH B. MAGOUN, wife of Dr. C. S. MAGOUN, and daughter of JACOB H. SANBORN, Esqr., of Kingston, N. H. Mrs. Magoun left her connection with Miss Grant's celebrated Female Academy, Ipswich, Mass. about one year ago to become the companion of he now widowed husband. She leaves an infant child.

M. E. SAUNDERS forwarns all persons from trading for a note of hand by him, given to N. M. LUCKETT.

Sheriff's sale: J. B. & J. E. THERRELL vs. DAVID HOLT. Same land Holt purchased from J. A. THOMS, attorney for ROBT. S. THOMS on 21, May, 1831.

Faculty of JEFFERSON COLLEGE, WASHINGTON MISSISSIPPI: Rev. CHARLES W. HACKLEY, Rev. A. STEPHENS, Doctor LEONARD D. GALE, JACOB AMMEN, SETH EASTMAN, J. A. T. MIDDERHOFF, Mr. WILLIAM WHIELDEN, and Mr. JOHN W. LANGSTAFF.

FRANCIS S. MAYES vs. N. M. TURNER 126 acres of land bounded by lands of Col. JOHN S. LEWIS, and BLAKE HOLLOMAN.

March 30, 1839

RICHARD CLAMPITT offers for lease a two story dwelling house in Woodville, formerly owned and now occupied by WM. EVANS, bounded south by Jail Lot, north by Water street, west by ------street, and east by property of C. C. WEST, Esqr. The property is now in complete repair with a good Well in the yard.

GEO. E. FRAZIER, adm'r., of the MICAJAH G. FRAZIER estate, will present his accounts for final settlement.

F. H. HOOKE, adm'r., of the WILLIAM B. HOOKE estate, will present his accounts for final settlement.

MARY STEWART, ex'rx., of the CHARLES STEWART, Sr. estate, will present her accounts for final settlement.

PATRICK O'BRIEN, Tailor, is located nearly opposite the Royal Oak.

April 6, 1839

GEORGE H. GORDON, given a Deed of Trust by JOHN PHILBRICK to sell 184 acres of land patented to LYMON HARDEN dated 3d Feb., 1823, the same land conveyed by R. M. GAINES, attorney for WINTHOPE S. HARDEN, decendent of said patentee, by deed of conveyance 15th Nov. 1834, to JNO PHILBRICK. Also, another tract being a part granted to JOHN CO9MMINGS which ajoins JNO. STEEL's tract.

WM. WEED has taken up a mare as a stray.

M. M. PHARES & GEO. MARTIN has dissolved their partnershop.

SUSAN PHILBRICK forewarns all persons from trading for two notes, viz: P. W. FARRAR's note for $5000, dated Feb. 22d, 1837, to HENRY MOORE, and by him and Wm. SCOTT, endorsed. The second note also is for $5000 dated the same, to F. S. MAYS, and endorsed by F. S. MAYS and WM. SCOTT. Both notes are her property and are wrongfully witheld.

EMANUAL AUSTIN informs the citizns that he is prepared to carry out the House Painting Business.

WM. W. IVES, County Surveyor will establish the boundry lines on the tract of land on which D. H. COOPER now resides.

April 13, 1839

GEORGE PHIPPS, use A. BUCKNER vs. ELEANOR STEVENSON, adm'rx.   364 acres

JOHN BAYNTON vs. JOHN PHILBRICK

JOHN F. WILLIAMS, THOS. A. G. BATCHELOR & J. L. D. SIMMONS vs. JOSEPH C. RILEY   JOHN H. BUTT vs. MORGAN S. RILEY & JOSEPH C. RILEY

Died at Payson, Adams County, Illinois, on the 25th of February last, Miss LUCRETIA OLIVIA ANN DODD, aged five years and three months.

H. QUINE, A. QUINE's ex'rs, ALEXANDER MITCHELL, J. D. NOLAND, R. T. OGDEN, surv'r. & SAM'L. BUDLONG, WM. STEWART 's adm'r., R. T. OGDEN, surv'r., vs. JOSEPP THOMPSON and Security
R. T. OGDEN surv'r and MARIA OGDEN vs. SINGLETON J. COOK & JOSEPH THOMPSON

JOHN BAYNTON vs. JOHN PHILBRICK

Commissioners will meet to make partitions of ten lots owned by the legal representatives of PRESTWOOD SMITH, dec'd., so that JAMES M. MILLER, will have his portion.

JOHN WISNER, adm'r., of the SOUTHARD ELLSBERRY estate will present his accounts at the next May Term for final settlement.

Dr. ESAIAS KAIGLER continues to practice his profession. His residence is at his father's plantation known as Magnolia Hill, on the Bluff road to Fort Adams, 8 miles from Woodville.

Wm. W. IVES, County Surveyor, at the request of Mr. C. G. FOSHEY, of Natchez, will establish the boundary lines of land belonging to Dr. W. N. MERCER of Adams County.

JEREMIAH YATES has lost a bay horse. $10 reward

A. LEFFINGWELL offers a liberal reward for the recovery of a small pair of pocket pistols, German silver mounted, and taken from his store.

Notice.---I hereby give notice that WILEY DELOACH is no longer agent for the undersigned, and he is required to deliver all papers belonging to him. Signed by Z. WALKER (ZACHARIAH) April 3, 1839

To all persons interested in the Real Estate of SAMUEL DELOACH, deceased,---Greeting:
By the next June Term, show if you can , why the real estate of said SAMUEL DELOACH should not be sold to pay the debts. His undivided interest, being the ninth part of a tract of Land lying in Wilkinson County, adjoining the lands of ALEXANDER DUNBAR and C. A. & C. J. THORNTON, containing 550 acres. Issued April 11th, 1839

Land of JAMES C. WEEKLY, on which he resided at the time of his death, is to be sold.

M. E. SAUNDERS forwarns all persons from trading for a note given to N. M. LUCKETT for $437. 07.

DANIEL BROWN vs. CALLICOAT & HUNTER; J. A. SCOTT vs. M. W. CALLICOATTE   April 12, 1839

FRANCIS BEVERLY has taken up a mare as a stray.

April 20, 1839
PLANTERS BANK vs. ELISHA McGRAW   Land bounded by lands of DANIEL McGAHEY, LEWIS CASON, JOAN BRYANT, and D. F. COON heirs, to be sold.

PLANTERS BANK vs. JAMES A KNIGHTEN

THOMAS E. SHANNON vs. JOHN L. WALL, NELSON, CARLETON & Co. vs. WM. TIGNER , WARREN KEMKBALL vs. same

April 27, 1839
CHARLES C. CAGE & HORATIO F. SIMRALL, have associated themselves in the practice of law.

Dr. C. G. TRASK offers his professional services and is located at Mr. Elliot's plantation.

Dr. S. BRADFORD offers his professional services in Woodville and resides at Mrs. S. DAVIS.

Dr. R. H. McDANIEL continues the practice of his profession in Woodville and vicinity. His residence is near the Baptist Church.

Dr. C. S. MAGOUN informs his patrons that he has moved nearly opposite Mr. THEREL's Boarding House.

Additional physicians in the area: Doctors CURRIER, STONE, STOCKBRIDGE, and MARTIN.

Copartnership dissolved between JOHN E. SMITH & A. N. SMITH in Fort Adams.

PERTHENY BURT, adm'x., of the HOLLIMAN M. BURT estate will sell all the personal property of said dec'd., at the plantation of JOHN S. LEWIS.

May 4, 1839

Married the 2nd, by T. POWELL, Esqr., Mr. JOHN D. KAIGLER to Mrs. CATHARINE F. KAIGLER, both of this county.

Departed this life, suddenly on the 3rd, Mrs. CAROLINE NETTERVILLE, consort of Mr. VICTOR N. H. NETTERVILLE.

Deed of Trust made by WILLIAM STAMPS to THOMAS HENDERSON, Trustee, 20th Nov. 1837, recorded in Book L, pages 289-291 of the records of Deeds of Adams County, to sedure to JOHN A. BROWN & Co. the payment of certain promissory notes. H. S. EUSTES, Substituted Trustee.

May 11, 1839

Married the 9th by the Rev. J. F. FISH, Mr. FRANCIS D. RICHARDSON, of Attakapas, Louisiana, to Miss BETHIA F. LIDDELL, daughter of MOSES LIDDELL, of this county.

Married the 2nd, Mr. CALEB SWAYZE to Miss NANCY JETER, both of Wilkinson County.

Died in this place of scarlet fever, on Monday morning, the 6th, LEMUEL, only son of Mrs. CELIA ANN PREWETT, aged 5 years and 6 months.

Copartnership dissolved between M. H. SULLIVAN and P. G. TIGNER, as P. G. TIGNER has removed from the state.

J. P. HARRIS has a house and lot to rent, last occupied by M. OVERMAN.

WM DOWTY has lost or mislaid a note of hand drawn in favor of BENJAMIN M. MAYS, JOHN L. WALL, WM. MAYES & MASON E. SAUNDERS, and endorsed by WM. DOWTY.

Married in Amite County the 16th, by the Rev. CHARLES FELDER, Mr. WILLIAM T. JONES, of Wilkinson, to the beautiful and interesting Miss MARY MAGDALENE, daughter of Col. HOLLOWAY HUFF, of the latter county.

Died at Louisville, Kentucky, on the 27th April last, Mr. JAMES C. DODGE, for many years a most worthy citizen of this county.

May 25, 1839

B. MARSHALL, J. P. HARPER, and JAMES BLACKBURN has dissolved their partnership.

SARAH WOOD will apply for her dower in property in Woodville and county of Wilkinson. Mentioned were GEORGE B. COLLIER, JEREMIAH NOLAND & wife, ASA SAPP & wife, WILLIAM L. COLLIER, and JAMES M. WOOD and SARAH WOOD.

Married the 21st, by the Rev. Wm. WINANS, Mr. JOHN WHITTAKER to Mrs. ROBIN ROGERS.

Married the 23rd, by the Rev. ELIJAH STEELE, Mr. WILLIAM P. DICKSON to Miss MARGARET L. C. WINANS.

Married on the 23rd, by the Rev. JOHN FISH, Mr. CHARLES A. THORNTON to Miss CORNELIA V. RANDOLPH.

Married on the 16th, by the Rev. CHAS. FELDER, Mr. WILLIAM T. JONES, of Wilkinson to Miss MARY MAGDALENE, daughter of Col. HOLLOWAY HUFF, of Amite County.

At the meeting of the Woodville Lyceum, FRANKLIN SOULE will lecture on the "Conscious Existence of Plants". Z. A. MUDGE, Sec'y.

Notice is hereby given that at the July term, 1839, of the Probate court of Wilkinson County, I shall present, for final settlement and allowance, my account, as administrator, of the estate of NATHANIEL SWAYZE, deceased.   STERLING JETER, administrator. May 25, 1839.

June 1, 1839

The partnership between J. RIDER and E. R. QUARTERMAN has been dissolved by mutual consent.

W. W. IVES, will establish the boundary lines of JAMES HILL.

Deed of Trust made by WILLIAM STAMPS to THOMAS HENDERSON, dated 1st Nov. 1837, recorded in Bk K, pp 476-78, of the records of deeds of Wilkinson County, to secure to JOHN A. BROWN & Co. Sale to be held 28th May, 1839, of the "Artonish Plantation" 1500 plus acres and 39 slaves. Also the "Lochleven" plantation containing 1571 plus acres and 47 slaves, along with all stock, farming utensils, crops, appurtenances, and privileges, unto said plantations. Also additional smaller tracts of land in a seperate sale.

Deed of Trust given by STEPHEN O. CHAMBERS to GERALD C. BRANDON & WM. M. HELM to sell land on which Chambers resided, situated on the waters on Percy's Creek, 175 acres. Recorded Bk 1, pp 603-4.

W. W. IVES will establish the boundary lines on land which JAMES HILL now resides.

June 8, 1839

All persons are cautioned against trading for a note given by SYLVANUS WALKER for Z. WALKER, to J. F. RAMSEY, for twenty-five dollars, dated sometime in May lat; as the consideration for which said note was given has failed, and I am determined not to pay the same unless compelled by law.
Signed: Z. WALKER   June 8, 1839

Married the 4th, by the Rev. B. SHAW, Col. WILLIAM T. LEWIS to Miss HARRIET ELIZA DAVIS, youngest daughter of Mrs. SUSAN DAVIS.

Died at her residence on Thursday night, the 31th, Mrs. ELIZABETH YERBY, relict of the late Col. WILLIAM YERBY of this county.

JESSE SAUNDERS vs. JOHN & HIRAM ASHLY   50 acres on which John Ashly not lives, bounded by lands of Thomas Ashley, SUSANA ASHLY, also a tract of 40 acres on which Hiram Ashly now lives, to be sold.

CESAR FRAISSE vs. JONES H. SMITH   An undivided 3rd of 3 acres in Woodville, bounded by lands of JOSEPH JOHNSON, JOHN NETTERVILL and GEORGE ADAMS.

WM. F. PAQUINETTE has 853 acres of land for sale.

The Woodville, Bayou Sara & Natchez Stages, will run regular three times a week, until further notice, leaving Woodville every Saturday, Tuesday and Thursday. J. L. HODGE, Agent

June 15, 1839

HARTWELL STAFFORD will sell his plantation on the lower Natchez road, 5 miles from Woodville, and one mile from the road containing 220 acres.

I. H. STANWOOD & C. A. BULKLEY have formed a copartnership.

EZER E. WOOD, adm'r., of the SARAH SMITH estate will present his accounts for final settlement.

June 22, 1839

THOS. B. NETTERVILLE, appointed adm'r., of the SAMUEL DELOACH estate in the June Term, 1839, will sell all the real estate belonging to Samuel Deloach, deceased, being the 1/9 part of a tract of land in the county of Wilkinson, adjoining the lands of ALEXANDER DUNBAR and C. A. & C. J. THORNTON, containing 550 acres. Sale to be taken under the Royal Oak. June 15, 1839

June 29, 1839

Died reently in Columbus Mi., B. W. BENSON, Secretary of the State of Mississippi.

Died in this town on the 20th, EMMA JANE, only child of Mr. CHARLES PASCOE.

THOS. C. WEST will sell his plantation containing 807 acres, lying 7 miles west of Woodville, and 11 from Fort Adams.

900 acres of land known as the "Burland" tract is to be sold for taxes. $48. 09

July 6, 1839

One lot in Woodville belonging to the FRANCIS KELLER estate is to be sold for taxes. $16. 25. Bounded by land of JOHN S. LEWIS, & JACOB KELLER.

W. H. LYNE has lost his large black Newfoundland dog, by the name of Euberto. Please return him to JOHN NETTERVILLE in Woodville or Dr. A. COOPER in Jackson, La., as a liberal reward is offered.

500 acres to be sold for taxes of $10.15, belonging to STEPHEN HENDERSON's estate.

H. C. EARLY has lost a cow with a red heifer calf.

840 acres to be sold for taxes of $24.00, belonging to LEWIS LAPORTE of Concordia, La.

Died in this place on the 29th, THOMAS LEIGH, Esqr., from a wound received in a recounter with FIELDING DAVIS, Esqr. Mr. Leigh was the son of the Hon. B. W. LEIGH, the late distinguished U.S. Senator.

Died at the residence of her son, Mr. JOSHUA PRESLER of this county, on the 9th, Mrs. JAEL PRESLER, relict of Mr. PETER PRESLER, dec'd in the 106th year of her age. She emigrated to this country with her husband in the year 1789.

L. P. PEETS forewarns all persons from trading for certain promissory notes payable in cord wood, to THOS. A. AVERY.

July 13, 1839

JOHN McKEE has sold out his establishment of groceries & etc., near the Royal Oak, to Mr. JAMES L. HODGE.

DOUGLAS H. COOPER, President of the stockholders of the Homochitto Turnpike and Bridge Company.

FELIX EMBREE, adm'r., & ELIZABETH SCUDDER, adm'rx., of the THOMAS SCUDDER estate.

MOSES LIDDELL, adm'r., of the WILLIAM YERBY estate.

July 20, 1839

Died in this county on the 25th of June, FRANCES MATILDA, aged 8 months and 5 days, daughter of Dr. P. E. H. LOVELACE, of Wilkinson.

Dr. WM. STOCKBRIDGE will present the "Influence of Philosophy" at the Woodville Lyceum meeting.

JESSE SAUNDERS vs. JAMES JONES & ELIZABETH, his wife. Superior Court states that the Jones couple lives out of state.

HUGH B. ESKEW vs. DON PEDRO ACQUILLA COOK Cook does not live in state.

July 27, 1839
Married the 25th, by the Hon. N. SCUDDER, Mr. ELISHA F. MORELAND to Miss CATHARINE F. CHAMBERS, all of this county.

THOS. J. LANIER offers his plantation for sale. 300 acres lying on Big Piney creek, 4 miles east of Cold Spring post office. It contains several springs of pure free stone water, and is considered as healthy as any situation in the county.

August 3, 1839
HYDE PARK plantation for sale. 1187 acres bounded by lands of E. J. LANIER and BENJAMIN KILGORE. Refer to THOS. ELLIS, WM. M. HELM. and DOUGLAS COOPER, Cold Springs. Mi. Signed by WM. TAYLOR

HENRY SMITH vs. JOHN G. POINDEXTER and surities House and lot offered for sale, under the Royal Oak, and bounded by a lot of T. MOLLEMANS, E. H. WAILES, and JOHN McKEE.

August 10, 1839
August 17, 1839
$215 note mislaid or stolen, given by J. B. RICHARDSON, to ROB'T R. RICHARDSON.

J. H. RANDOLPH, adm'r., of the A. S. RANDOLPH estate will sell personal property of the estate.

DANIEL WOODARD & WM. B. DAVIS, adm'rs., of the HENRY A. MOORE estate

MARY A. LEEK, adm'rx., of the FREDERICK LEEK estate will present her accounts for settlement.

NOTICE.---The undesigned, guardian of JNO. R. DELOACH, will, at the October term of the Probate court of Wilkinson County, surrender, or give up, the guardianship of his said ward, at which time, all who are interested, can attend. Signed by WILEY DELOACH, Guardian. August 17, 1839

Married the 11th by the Hon. N. SCUDDER, Mr. JESSE OGDEN to Miss CAROLINE E. POOLE, all of this county.

All who are indebted to JOSEPH RIDDLE, are requested to make payment. TRUMAN POWELL, J. P.

August 24, 1839
On Sept. 1st, Rev. WILLIAM WINANS will deliver a

discourse entitled, "Divinity of the Bible".

Married the 22nd by N. SCUDDER, Mr. JAMES F. BROWN to Miss SUSANNAH NETTERVILLE, daughter of CHARLES NETTERVILLE, Sr., of this county.

Died the 4th in Pike County, Mi., REBECCA C. KAIGLER, wife of Mr. JOHN KAIGLER, in the 59th year of her age.

Died in the town of Fort Adams on the 3rd, after an illness of eight days, Mr. CHARLES S. VENPORT, in the 36th year of his age, a native of the State of Virginia.

DAN'L WOODARD, adm'r., of the GEORGE H. SWIGART estate

WILEY DELOACH vs. JOSEPH LILLY WM. T. LEWIS, sheriff of Wilkinson County will sell 1/9 share of undivided 552 acres, it being the same tract of which JESSE DELOACH, died seized and possessed, bounded on the east by ALEXANDER C. DUNBAR, north by J. L. TRASH, west by SAM'L & JNO WL LEATHERMAN and south by _____ THORNTON, to satisfy plaintiffs debt and cost in the above stated case.

A. G. FOSTER, M. M. PHARES, & GEORGE MARTIN appointed commissioners for claims against the estate of WILLIAM BROWN, reported insolvent.

The O. S. BREWSTER & A. MORNINGSTAR firm has been dissolved on August 5th, by mutual consent.

August 31, 1839
Died in this town on Wednesday, Mrs. PRISCILLA MOISE, consort of Dr. E. W. MOISE, late of Charleston, South Carolina.

September 14, 1839
The Market House of the town of Woodville is now open and free of expense, to all persons desirous of supplying the market. T. POWELL, Mayor.

MARK CAWDITT, adm'r., of the JAMES B. WILDS estate

CHARLES MACKEY, adm'r., of the JOHN H. MACKEY estate will present his accounts for final settlement.

Died in this county on the 4th, Mrs. MARY MOORE, consort of A. T. MOORE, Esqr.

Died on the 11th, Mrs. _____ EARLY, consort of H. G. EARLY.

Died on the 12th, Mr. P. W. OGDEN.

Wm. F. PACQUINETTE vs. F. G. McGRAW $224

ERASTUS CASE vs. JAMES SHROPSHIRE $145. 52

A. T. MOORE wishes to sell the 300 acre plantation on which he formerly resided, nine miles east of Woodville on the Liberty road.

J. B. BULLOCK, adm'r., of the WILLIAM QUINE estate will prsent his accounts for final settlement.

AMOS B. THOMPSON, ex'r., of the LITTLEBERRY THOMPSON estate

M. DUBOSE of Mobile Ala., and J. W. RICHARDSON of Atlakepas, La., have formed a copartnership.

September 21, 1839
ELIAS ECKERT vs. FLEMING LITTLEFIELD $165

Married the 24th in Clement County, Ohio, Capt. GEORGE M. SMITH of this county to Mrs. MARY STEVEN of the former place.

Died at Donaldsonville, La., on the 9th, after 5 days illness, Col. P. G. TIGNER, in the 27th year of his age, originally from Georgia, but late from this county, brother to Capt. WILLIAM TIGNER, who has resided here for many years.

September 28, 1839
JAMES M. SHANNON vs. THOS. E. SHANNON $8194.66

MARK CAWBITT, adm'r., of the JAMES R. WILDS estate

BASS & LEWIS vs. M. M. SIMMONS; A. G. FOSTER use & Co. vs. M. M. SIMMONS; JOHN KNIGHTEN vs. same.

JOHN A. SCOTT vs. THOMAS CONKLIN; JOHN C. MORRIS vs. THOMAS CONKLIN

Married on Thursday last, by C. C. WEST, Esqr., Mr. THOMAS ALLEN to Mrs. LAVINA PEARCE, La.

Died in this town on the 27th, after 3 days illness, Mr. WALTER N. BARREL, of Bayou Sara.

PLANTERS BANK vs. DAVID HOLT

EXUM LEWIS, ERASTUS CASE & H. FOWLER vs. WILLIAM D. WHITE and Security. Interest in tract of land belonging to ANDREW WHITE heirs.

D.& D. I. ARMSTONG & Co., F. DAVIS et al. & W & P ILER, & Co. vs. L. SCARBOROUTH

PULASKI CAGE has taken up a stray ox, value $20.

JOHN BRYCE vs. HUGH DUNLAP $200.00

October 5, 1839
Yellow Fever! This fatal disease continues to rage with unabated violence in most of the cities of the south and south-west. Our neighboring city, Natchez, is still afflicted with it. We do not believe there is a more healthy spot on God's earth than Woodville,--so those who wish to seek a safe retreat from disease, could not do better than by spending their summers here.

We have seen a picture, by Mr. MOISE, of this place, of the Rev. WILLIAM WINANS, which is a very striking likeness. A lithographic print will be taken of it and the price per copy will be $6.

The real estate of ANDREW WHITE will be divided between his heirs and sold at the JOHN SLADE's hotel at Cold Springs on the 9th of November.

ROBERT GERMANY vs. RILEY FINDLEY

October 12, 1839
WM. ST. JOHN ELLIOT, A. M. FELTUS, & FIELDING DAVIS, commissioners for the JOSEPH RIDDLE, Senr., estate will sell personal property of the estate.

W. L. COLLINS, S. G. ROWAN, & W. S. BRADSTREET commissioners for the S. E. POTTS, insolvent, will continue meeting the first Saturday each month.

Appointment made by WILLIAM T. LEWIS & GEORGE H. GORDON to TRUMAN POWELL as special trustee to execute the trust given to CHAUNCY S. KELLOGG, dec'd.,in Feb. 1837, by JOSEPH THOMPSON and MARY, his wife, in trust for the benefit of said WILLIAM T. LEWIS & GEORGE H. GORDON. 300 acres (north-west corner of the 600 acres) of land bounded by lands formerly owned by Dr. BROWN and FRANCIS S. MAYES and south by lands of WILLIAM TIGNER. This land purchased by JOHN MAYES from an agent of said Dr. BROWN, but retaining one quarter of an acre on which Mrs. BROWN is buried.

October 18, 1839

SAM'L TURBEVILLE will lease his plantation of 247 acres from one to six years. It is located 4 miles from Woodville on the road to Natchez.

Persons listed in the sheriff's sales: THOS. WISNER, JAS. BALLAIRD, JAMES D. BEARDEN, WM. M. HELM, SAMUEL BUDLONG, A. L. GAINES, JAMES O. FARRELL, H. A. MOORE, JNO R. McMURDO, W. THORNTON, A. LEFFINGWELL, A. CALDER, JOSIAH LUNN, JAMES FERGUSON, A. MITHDELL, HIRAM CARVER, J. P. HARRIS, L. M. GARRETT, C. FRAISSE, H. N. MARTIN, C. C. WEST, A. T. MOORE and H. A. MOORE.

W. BOYDEN, D. P. A. COOK and Wm. ILER against JOS. THOMPSON

JNO. A. SCOTT, M. OVERMAN, and R. INMAN against THOS. H. QUARTERMAN.

M. E. SAUNDERS, adm'r., ot the G. D. D. FOSTER estate will present accounts for final settlement.

WM. O. GLASS, adm'r., of the JOEL GLASS estate will present accounts for final settlement.

The final settlement of guardianship of JNO. R. DELOACH, by WILEY DELOACH, is postponed until the next December term.

WALL & NORWOOD, and ELI MONTGOMERY vs. GEORGE H. SWIGGART

JOHN H. BUTT vs. M. S. & JOS. C. REILEY

ROBT. T. OGDEN, adm'r., of the P. W. OGDEN estate

D. W. HAXALL, adm'r., of the THOMAS LEIGH estate

R. M. NEWMAN, adm'r., of the JOHN E. SMITH estate will sell all the personal property of the estate.

WM. T. LEWIS vs. HENRY A. MOORE

J. H. DULANEY, adm'r., vs. C. P. SMITH & H. A. MOORE, ex'rs, JAMES M. SMITH, deceased.
J. G. SELPH vs. same and same, E. E. BRYANT vs. same and same.

B. MARSHALL will take charge of the establishment of Mr. WALTER N. BARRELL, deceased. Bayou Sara.

WILLIARD BOYDEN, JOHN A. SCOTT, J.R. THERREL, J. E. THERREL, WILLIAM H. SCOTT vs. P. W. FARRAR.

JOHN HOLMES, Commission, Receiving and Forwarding Merchant, Bayou Sara. All cotton is shipped by the subscriber, free of charge.

October 26, 1839

JOHN P. CARNY of Jackson, La. has lost 3 horses.

Died the 21st at the residence of her father, Mrs. LYDIA F. KING, wife of Captain SAMUEL KING, of Adams County, in the 31st year of her age.

Died at his residence in this county on the 23rd, Judge THOS. H. PROSSER.

JOHN H. HANNA and PHEBE HUNTER offers the "Hare tract" of 775 acres now in the possession and cultivated by Dr. Wm.H. EGGLESTON. Located 4 miles from Fort Adams on the road leading out to Woodville.

COLLINS W. MILLER will sell 450 acres lying on the Buffalo river, 7 miles above Fort Adams.

November 2, 1839

Sheriff's sale. BRANCH JORDAN, MARK IZOD, WESTERN MUSE, JESSE HUTCHINS, ROBERT BRADLEY, A. C. DUNBAR and others, vs. THOS. H. PROSSER and Securities.

Sheriff's sale. ELI MONTGOMERY and others vs. GEORGE SWIGGART, and J. BELL.

Died the 15th October, of yellow fever in Barker's settlement, Louisiana, Mr. JOHN A FELL, formerly of Fort Adams, and of the firm of FELL & SANDERS of this county, and a native of Hartford County, N. C., in the 42 year of his age.

Died at Cold Springs, Wilkinson County, Miss. on the 24th Oct. of the bilious fever, LUTHFR PARDEE, aged 22 years. Mr. Pardee was formerly from Livona, Livingston County, N. Y.

Died in Woodville on the 31st of October, Mr. ALEXANDER MITCHELL.

C. H. STONE has a supply of paper, quills and

other stationary supplies.

November 9, 1839

NANCY BARKLEY has a horse which strayed or was stolen from Major LORECZO D. BROWN's plantation, near Whitestown on the 26th of October. Reward

Married last evening at St. Marks Church, by the Rev. Dr. SCHROEDER, the Rev. J. F. FISH, of Watertown, Jefferson County, New York, to Miss JULIA ANTOINETTE, daughter of JOHN I. MUMFORD of that city.

Married in Woodville on Tuesday, by Col. C. WEST, Esqr., PIERCE N. DURANO, of Avoyles Parish, La., to Miss ELIZABETH BOMAN, of New Orleans.

GEORGE E. FRAZIER has 16 mules for sale.

DANIEL DUKE vs. BENJ. ATKINSON, Marion Circuit Ct.

November 16, 1839

Dissolution of partnership between C. J. THORNTON and C. A. THORNTON. Greenwood, Oct.11, 1839
Dr. C. J. THORNTON continues to practice his proffession.

C. H. STONE has a new invoice of new music.

4 to 500 dollars of County Warrants and Jury Certificates wanted. Tombigby money taken at par, for Groceries, and in payment of accounts, at the Royal Oak Exchange by JAS. L. HODGE.

Died the 24th October, at the residence of her husband, Mrs. SOPHIA BANCKS, consort of C. W. BANCKS, Engineer on the West Feliciana Rail Road. The deceased was a native of England and emigrated to this country and settled in this Parish some four or five years since with her husband, where she resided until her death. She has left one small infant and a kind husband to mourn her loss.

November 23, 1839

JOHN B. THERREL's boarding house is located on Main Street, Woodville, Miss.

MOSES M. PHARES' boarding house is on Commercial Row, Woodville, Miss.

E. H. WAILES, Agent of Protection Insurance Company of Woodville.

J. H. GREADY appoints Mr. F. M. RICHARDSON of Fort Adams as his agent while he is out of the state.

ADAM ROSE and JOHN ANKER have opened a boot and shoe business in Woodville.

November 30, 1839

We have not--perhaps never will receive full returns of the election for Judge and District Attorney of this Circuit--Enough however is known to render it certain that C. C. CAGE is elected Judge, and STANHOPE POSEY, District Attorney.

Died in this place on Thursday, the 28th, HENRY, the infant son of ADAM and ELIZABETH MORNINGSTAR.

Died of whooping cough at Harrodsburg, Kentucky, on the 29th of October, SARAH JANE, second daughter of Col. F. R. and S. M. RICHARDSON, in the 8th year of her age.

December 7, 1839

Married on Thursday last, by C. C. WEST, Esqr., Mr. FRANCIS BEST to Miss SARAH CONRAD, all of this county.

Died on Wednesday the 4th, near Fort Adams, Dr. WM. H. WINSTON, after a short illness.

Died last evening, DUNPAR (DUNBAR??) infant son of Mr. W. H. WEST, Esqr., aged 14 months.

ALEX. WALL, executor of the SARAH WALL estae will present his accounts for final settlement.

ELIZABETH EDWARDS, adm'rx., of the JOHN H. DAVIS estate will present her accounts for final settlement.

C. S. MAGOUN will file his request to be released as adm'r., of the C. B. MAGOUN estate.

F. M. HEREFORD's tract of land on which he now resides, in the parish of West Feliciana, on the Little Bayou Sara, thirteen miles from the town of St. Francisville, is for sale.

December 14, 1839

D. W. HAXWELL, adm'r., of the THOMAS H. PROSSER estate

N. N. McCARSTLE of Laurel Hill, La., has machinery

for sale.

WILEY DELOACH, guardian of JOHN R. DELOACH, will sell 1/9 interest in 550 acres of land on the 28th day of January.

PETER A. PRESLER, adm'r., of the JOHN REESE estate

PETER A. PRESLER, adm'r., of the JAMES VARNELL estate

ROBT. R. RICHARDSON, adm'r., of the WRIGHT B. ORR estate

PETER McKENZIE, adm'r., of the RICHARD D. WILLIAMS estate

END VOLUME 1

ABSHEAR, 22
ACEE, 201
ADAMS, 16 47 61 64 65 67 74 107
　121 139 160 164 184 188 218
　243
AILES, 50 72
AITSBURY, 182
ALEXANDER, 8 46 141 179 198
　201
ALFORD, 2
ALLAN, 120 127
ALLBRITTAINDEN, 29
ALLBRITTEN, 27
ALLEN, 27 48 96 107 120 214
　227 236 248
ALTER, 54 67
AMBROSE, 2 37 74 117 127
AME, 228
AMMEN, 238
AMMENS, 27
ANDERSON, 10 11 17 23 29 50 54
　70 91 94 107 118-121 127 159
　170 187 197 214 217 227
ANDREWS, 24 35 46 143
ANGELL, 49 177
ANKER, 253
ARBUTHNOT, 53
ARCHER, 123
ARD, 228
ARDREY, 31 85 134
ARDRY, 145
ARGUS, 79
ARIEL, 15
ARMAT, 184
ARMSTRONG, 21 32 42 47 73 91
　93 96 128 154 187 196 202 209
　214 217 218 249
ARNAUD, 69
ARNELL, 46
ARNES, 68
ARNOLD, 206
ASHLEY, 62 142 153 178

ASHLY, 77 142 166 226 243
ASPANALL, 49
ASPIN, 7
ASPINAL, 3 10
ASPINALL, 3 16
ATKINSON, 202 252
AUSTIN, 74 146 168 186 228 229
　239
AVERY, 245
BACHELOR, 153
BACOT, 182 190
BAGGET, 125 130
BAGLEY, 111
BAILEY, 12 17 28 53 54 62 88 89
　108 114 172 182 184
BAILLEY, 64
BAILLIE, 61
BAILY, 64
BAIRD, 90 114 168
BAKER, 9 121 122 127 205
BALLAIRD, 250
BAMBER, 14 23
BANCKS, 141 177 204 205 226
　252
BANK, 240 249
BANTER, 202 215
BANYAN, 13
BARKLEY, 108 252
BARLAND, 157 204
BARLOW, 169 201
BARNARD, 74 91
BARNES, 4 33 123
BARNET, 211
BARR, 93
BARREL, 248
BARRELL, 192 251
BARROW, 1 70 80
BARRY, 14 70
BARTLET, 215
BARTLETT, 65
BARTON, 119 182 192
BASCOMB, 77

BASS, 22 46 61 64 65 76 78 80 81 96 113 120 129 134 140 148 175 200 207 226 227 237
BASSETT, 34
BATCHELOR, 160 177 183 210 239
BATEMEN, 130
BATROW, 74
BATTERSON, 2
BAUM, 175
BAY, 74 86
BAYETT, 147
BAYNTON, 239
BEADLES, 59
BEARD, 176
BEARDEN, 250
BEARDIN, 161
BEASELEY, 6
BEASLEY, 21 35 49
BEASLY, 37 49
BECK, 40 58 200
BECKEM, 90
BEDFORD, 16
BEECH, 49
BEIDLER, 51
BELL, 2 8 10 26 33 36 45 48 56-58 60 74 92 99 102 112 114 115 119 127 133 139 142 168 176 182 190 192 196 202 203 212 215 217 219 229 235 237 251
BENDER, 67
BENNET, 92 144 153
BENNETT, 40
BENOIST, 1
BENSON, 244
BENTHAL, 14 35 103
BENTHALL, 51
BENTLEY, 89 103 126
BENTON, 11
BERAVER, 48
BERRY, 21 28 31 61 73 81 82 110 122 175
BERTRON, 90 113
BEST, 253
BETHANY, 20
BEUFORD, 7 19
BEVERLY, 240
BIGGS, 136
BILLS, 171
BINGAMAN, 19 30 224

BIRMINGHAM, 34 60
BIRNEY, 96
BLACKBURN, 242
BLAKE, 128 193
BLEDSOE, 59 215 216
BLOUNT, 166
BOATNER, 50 104 106 147 153 159 203
BODLEY, 151
BOHANON, 81
BOLAND, 93
BOMAN, 252
BONE, 52
BONER, 74 152 195 200
BONNEER, 13
BOOK, 48
BOON, 74
BOOTH, 12 56
BORRELLA, 28
BOSWELL, 153 154 156
BOUIS, 69
BOURGH, 90
BOWDEN, 69 74
BOWMAN, 27 40
BOWREN, 75 111
BOYCE, 2 23
BOYD, 14 23 48 50 56 60 73 74 76 79 80 83 85 87 97 100 106 111 114 118 120 127 138 143 168 175 199
BOYDEN, 250 251
BOZEMAN, 202
BRADDOCK, 80
BRADEN, 14
BRADFORD, 32 77 105 138 140 196 202 241
BRADLEY, 9 12 251
BRADSHAW, 58
BRADSTREET, 230 249
BRADY, 76
BRANCH, 69
BRANDON, 6-8 19 23 43 58 63 74 80 81 83 94 96 115 117 137 138 146 165 178 183 212 220 227 243
BRANNON, 39 166
BRATCHER, 50
BRECKENRIDGE, 91
BRENT, 2
BREWER, 234
BREWSTER, 119 207 247

BRICE, 19
BRIDGES, 66
BRIGGS, 104 123
BRINDLEY, 234 235
BRISCOE, 68
BROADWAY, 70
BROCKMAN, 233
BROCKWAY, 233
BROEN, 83
BROOKS, 36 57 63 72 92 98 130 132 146
BROOM, 27
BROWDER, 22 27 35 60-62 78 80 88 130 170 183 194 212
BROWN, 19 20 30 46 54 59 61-63 65 68-70 72 76 79 81-83 86 87 89 90 93 94 97-99 101 102 104 108 114-116 119 122 125 137 138 141-143 145 147-151 154 155-157 159 160 162 164 168 171 178 182 185 189 192 197 198 202 203 205 211 217-219 221 226-229 232 240 241 243 247 249 250 252
BROWNE, 116
BROWNING, 154 176 182 188 189 215 217
BRUCE, 4 11 14 23 33 45 50 51 53 60 63 69 76 81 82 85 88 93 97 108 115 125 129 221 232
BRYAN, 49 50 79 123 126 215 221
BRYANT, 55 64 95 96 131 145 147 198 202 205 216 226 240 250
BRYCE, 49 52 57 249
BUCKHOLT, 191
BUCKHOLTE, 21
BUCKHOLTS, 175 183 188
BUCKNER, 66 236 239
BUDLONG, 175 239 250
BUFFALOE, 119
BUFORD, 78 87 106 107 157 165 180
BUFORE, 57
BULKLEY, 244
BULLITT, 150
BULLOCK, 114 212 230 248
BUNCH, 4 8 215 216
BURK, 193

BURKE, 25 101 104 134 178
BURLING, 199
BURNELL, 55
BURNET, 55 56
BURNETT, 56 115 175
BURNEY, 147
BURNS, 73 170
BURR, 23 41 69 99 181 202
BURRIS, 86 87
BURROAS, 148
BURROUGH, 41 226
BURROUGHS, 174 182
BURRUS, 44 47 48 50 60 69 74 208 213
BURRUSS, 81 93 126 131 152 156 221
BURRVSS, 88
BURT, 201 241
BURTON, 17 30 40 59 92 93 97 102 124 132 133 140 199 206
BURTRON, 106
BUSH, 21 33 34 36 49 75 93 114 121 122 182
BUSHNESS, 133 140
BUTLER, 83 99 123 130 139 147 154 235
BUTT, 175 239 250
BUTTON, 229
BYNAM, 171
BYNUM, 88 90 124 125 157 195
CAGE, 6 7 20 38 46 69 71 85 153 169 171 180 185 189 199 208 219 236 240 249 253
CAIN, 24 50 91 153 213 220 230 231
CALBE, 59
CALDER, 118 154 166 173 199 250
CALLAHAM, 43
CALLAHAN, 26
CALLEHAN, 3
CALLENDER, 7 12 16 29
CALLFIELDS, 193
CALLICOAT, 240
CALLICOATE, 210
CALLICOATTE, 157 197 240
CALLIHAM, 16 43 54 56 81-83 95 99 106 107 167 218
CALLIHAN, 42 99
CALVIT, 215

CAMP, 199
CAMPBELL, 75 79 86 102 116 203
CANFIELD, 20 66 109 124
CAPELL, 81
CAPEZ, 32
CARLETON, 240
CARLILE, 107
CARLIS, 165
CARLISLE, 137
CARMICHAEL, 124 194 196 202 204 210 217 236
CARMICHEL, 78
CARNY, 251
CARPENTER, 71
CARR, 4 5 10 34 42 88 147 202 215
CARRAWAY, 9 15 32 58 68 100
CARROLL, 28 41
CARSA, 232
CARSON, 17 51 73 110 137
CARTER, 7 26 40 58 65 83 105 150-152 160 166 186 223 234
CARTWRIGHT, 3-5 8 24 30 189 192
CARVER, 250
CASE, 144 200 212 248 249
CASON, 2 6 7 19 22 25 26 54 114 148 193 213 226 240
CASSEALES, 92
CASSELLS, 87
CASSIDY, 186
CASTELL, 113
CASTLEMAN, 196
CASTON, 104 150 153 177
CATCHING, 96
CATLETT, 98
CATOE, 71
CAUSEY, 146
CAWBITT, 248
CAWDITT, 247
CAWSEY, 95 110 123
CHALFANT, 153
CHALMER, 2
CHAMBERS, 16 35 49 54 55 73 76 82 100 113 141 145 146 165 170 179 198 212 243 246
CHAMPMAN, 223
CHANDLER, 97
CHAPMAN, 207 221
CHEATHAM, 52 62 76
CHICKERING, 101

CHINN, 53
CHISHOLM, 1 17 39 54 73 91 125 128 150 200 212
CHOTARD, 2
CHRISTMAS, 96 97 141
CHURCH, 19
CIAN, 198
CIZZEE, 159
CIZZIE, 216
CLAIBORNE, 184
CLAIRBORNE, 194
CLAMPET, 120
CLAMPIT, 82
CLAMPITT, 2 76 223 238
CLARESON, 37
CLARK, 39 42 55 131 182 186
CLARKSON, 16 32 35 38 56 114 121 130
CLARKSTON, 19 43
CLAY, 22 23 68
CLAYTON, 37
CLELAND, 16
CLENDENIN, 119
CLOUD, 29
CLUGSTON, 207 227
CO-MMINGS, 238
COATES, 127
COATS, 97 166
COBB, 16 24 83
COBBETT, 153
COCHRAN, 2 189 192 218
COFFIN, 22
COILE, 206
COLE, 29 33 54 57 106 153 187 208 214
COLEMAN, 17 68 90 110 128 140 146
COLFAX, 47
COLLAER, 16
COLLES, 135 169
COLLIER, 11 36 43 56 73 94 114 144 148 190 196 202 222 242
COLLINGS, 42 43
COLLINGSWORTH, 57
COLLINS, 26 62 66 84 91 103 126 206 211 216 221 228-230 249
COLVER, 61 63 89
COMB, 11
COMBS, 4 23 141 158 195
COMER, 154
COMFORT, 91

CONEY, 5
CONKLIN, 176 178 181 248
CONNELL, 7 13 19 31 36 38 43
    46 51 63 67 87 90 104 106 110
    117 122 142 155 156 162 169
    202 211 218 232
CONNELLY, 62
CONNER, 46 90 105 109 110 112
    114 233 234
CONNOR, 34
CONRAD, 34 87 134 153 221 236
    253
CONROD, 144
CONSTANTINE, 2
CONWAY, 147 151
CONY, 150
COOK, 2 19 47 58 75 79 85 134
    162 181 182 190 198 239 245
    250
COOLEY, 168 170 173 175 176
    195 196
COON, 14 24 27 53 56 73 89 92
    97 125 154 160 172 194 196
    209 215 220 240
COOPER, 9 10 14 28 59 128 131
    157 162 201 210 221 239 244-
    246
COPE, 86
CORLEY, 73
CORNEL, 4
CORNELL, 2 15
CORP, 181
CORY, 107 141 157 179 187
COSBY, 47 59 66 90 148 172 234
COTTEN, 132
COTTER, 89 103 137 139 143 145
    181 186 190 214 227
COULTER, 2 9 26 34 116
COURSEY, 68
COURTNEY, 50 159 172 209 217
    219 221
COURTS, 115
COVINGTON, 71
COX, 70 84
CRAFT, 18
CRAIG, 153
CRAWES, 8
CRAWFORD, 131 219
CREATE, 38
CREATH, 26 29 38
CRESP, 175

CREWS, 18-20 32 70
CROPPER, 97
CRORY, 27
CROSS, 64
CROW, 159 189
CRUTCHER, 70
CRUZAT, 10
CULATH, 26
CULLEN, 116 118
CULLIN, 116
CUMMING, 232
CUMMINGS, 149
CUMMINS, 149
CUNNINGHAM, 115
CUNNINGS, 58
CURRIER, 241
CURRY, 28
CURTIS, 20 36 112 124
CURTISS, 166
CURTS, 12
DAIVIDSON, 225
DALLEY, 49
DAMON, 151
DANCER, 175
DANIEL, 16 19 31 37 39-42 47-
    49 56 72 78 80 81 93 119 126
    128 132 148 178 198 212 220
DAOGHERY, 138
DARES, 10
DARWIN, 79
DATER, 60
DAVENPORT, 26
DAVIDSON, 198 222 237
DAVIS, 1 3 5 7 13 15 17 19 21-25
    28 29 33 36-38 42 45-47 61 68
    69 71 75 79-82 87 91 102 107
    115 116 122 127 128 133 134
    140 147 148 153 163 164 167
    168 174 181 189 191 192 194
    198 200 202 203 212 213 225
    241 243 245 246 249 253
DAWSON, 3 7 18 34 57 72 75 91
    94 123 139 154 156 158 165
    172 176 185 186 208 209 211
    213 217-219 223 225 226 232
    237
DAY, 22 144 222 226 228 232
DEAL, 103 1128 132 139 143 145
    180 193
DEARMOND, 220
DECKER, 184

DEEVINE, 211
DEFRAFFENREID, 8
DEGRAFENREID, 198
DEGRAFFENREID, 19 160 169 228
DEGRAPHENREID, 147
DELOACH, 6 31 32 46 58 80 87 108 109 113 114 122 132 134 136-138 160 168 189 191 195 196 212 220 224 229 233 240 244 246 247 250 254
DENNIS, 123
DERBIGMY, 54
DEVALCOURT, 5 28
DGAHAN, 1
DICKERSON, 99
DICKS, 112
DICKSON, 31 86 180 234 242
DILLAHUNTY, 19 58 91 102 156 177 180 198
DILLINGHAM, 116 130 199 209 225 230
DIXON, 4 54 82 85 88 94 124
DODD, 89 97 111 115 155 174 213 239
DODGE, 219 242
DOLES, 196
DONELSON, 69
DORSETT, 2
DORSEY, 181
DORSHE, 31
DORSSETT, 8
DOUGHERTY, 61 87 199
DOUGHTY, 124
DOUGLASS, 87
DOVE, 9
DOWELL, 101 215
DOWNING, 21 24 25 37 67 69
DOWNS, 9 141 159 196
DOWTY, 33 84 85 242
DRAKE, 5 41 62 64 70 71 84 91 96 122 124 131 133 140 167
DRAUGHAN, 218
DREAR, 93
DRESLER, 78
DRURY, 12
DUBERTRAND, 69
DUBOSE, 2248
DUBRILL, 189 196 200
DUFF, 65
DUGAS, 80
DUHY, 10
DUKE, 28 39 65 252
DUKES, 47
DULANEY, 250
DUNBAR, 2 26 43 86 101 105 136 160 207 211 212 236 240 244 247 251
DUNCAN, 230
DUNCKLEY, 53 98 101 108 167 169 176 193 222
DUNLAP, 151 249
DUNN, 29 36 59 81 89 97 98 106 120 125 130 140 142 150 169 172 176 184 185
DUNPAR, 253
DURANO, 252
DURANT, 102 107 137
DUTY, 142 197
DUVALL, 189 192
DVIS 170,
DWIGHT, 234
DYER, 235
DYRE, 225
DYSON, 219 220
EACLES, 9
EARLY, 245 248
EASTMAN, 238
EASTON, 150 154 179 180 221 228
ECCLE, 12
ECCLES, 2 16 19 22 23 26 36 68 200
ECKERT, 248
EDGAR, 154
EDNEY, 11
EDWARDS, 7 12 29 45 52 72 100 104 115 119 180 181 201 219 253
EFLEESON, 17
EGGLESTON, 42 46 51 54 58 65 92 112 120 125 133 139 140 145 149 164 168 183 204 208 212 228 251
EILER, 16
ELLESBERRY, 61
ELLINGTON, 2 30 51 57 60 101
ELLINGTONS, 86
ELLIOT, 140 240 249
ELLIS, 36 40 74 119 149 163 168 193 221 224 227 234 235 246
ELLSBERRY, 4 6 7 41 156 171

ELLSBERRY (continued)
  213 239
ELSBERRY, 161
EMBREE, 220 245
EMOCH, 13
EMRY, 25
ENDT, 119 139 143
ENLOW, 48 86 178 186 195 200
ENOS, 158 160
ERWIN, 26
ESKEU, 143
ESKEW, 245
ESTESS, 209 215
ESTIS, 163
EUSTES, 241
EVANS, 51 67 82 98 108 126 128
  143 147 174 177 179 180 182
  186 191 212 215 238
EVELETH, 73 89 97 106 139 149
EVENS, 15
EVERETT, 88 170
EWELL, 2 17
EWING, 59
FAIR, 188
FAIRCHILD, 27 179 180 220 228
FAIRWELL, 182 186
FAISH, 203
FANNER, 19 25 41 89
FANNING, 112 119
FAREWELL, 88 198
FARISH, 2 17 20 58 85 98 104
  106 117 121 128 146 163 169
  177 200 212
FARMER, 8
FARNANDIS, 66
FARR, 65
FARRAR, 35 57 70 83 89 93 106
  129 146 169 173 188 198 238
  251
FARRELL, 250
FARWELL, 81
FATAND, 228
FAUSE, 151
FAUST, 107 128 136 142 151 157
FAVAND, 228
FELDER, 200 223 242
FELL, 251
FELLS, 114 148 149 220
FELTUS, 1 11 18 23 26 52 92 112
  167 176 180 214 249

FENNER, 85 186 229 237
FERGUSON, 94 115 143 169 195
  215 222 250
FERIS, 24
FERRELL, 61 119 128 141 143
FINCH, 39
FINDLAY, 221
FINDLEY, 249
FINUCANE, 98
FISH, 200 220 241 242
FISHER, 22
FITZ, 31
FLEASON, 74
FLECHEUX, 193
FLEESON, 18 37 86
FLEMING, 5
FLESHMAN, 114 209
FLESON, 31
FLOWER, 40
FLOYD, 59 105 153
FOGLEMAN, 218
FOLEY, 19 23 25 57 74 90 98 139
  220 221 224
FOOLEY, 25
FOOTE, 77 78
FORBES, 219
FORD, 95 96 149 157 179 228
FORDON, 39
FOREHAND, 11
FORNEQUET, 144
FORSYTHE, 202
FORT, 129
FORTER,
FOSHEY, 239
FOSTER, 4 5 15 17 23 34 39-42
  47 51 52 57 69 76 90 94 102
  103 107 114 130 131 133 135
  140 143 149 158 164 170 171
  187-189 191 194 196 198 206
  210 215 216 237 247 248 250
FOULER, 110 112
FOWLER, 139 201 249
FOX, 9 13 15-17 21 22 28 42 120
  137 168
FRAISSE, 167 185 213 219 243
  250
FRALEY, 229
FRANKER, 215
FRASER, 181 235
FRAYARD, 176 220

FRAZER, 10 37 111
FRAZIER, 5 10 15 37 43 48 52 55 61 106 163 207 238 252
FREEMAN, 160 235
FREIOT, 4
FULLER, 64 181
FULSON, 67
FUQUA, 2 71 181
FURGUSON, 159
GADBERRY, 66
GAILLARD, 20
GAINES, 238 250
GAINS, 149
GALE, 238
GALLOWAY, 207 227
GARFLEY, 30
GARNER, 27 75 79 130 135 151
GARRETT, 52 94 115 117 250
GARRISON, 206
GARTLEY, 30
GASTIN, 12
GAULDEN, 119 131 133 157 211 228 233
GAY, 215
GAYDEN, 185
GAYLAN, 183
GAYLE, 151
GEORGE, 64
GERALD, 86
GERMANY, 8 47 168 203 208 249
GETER, 100
GETTER, 100
GIBBS, 24
GIBSON, 15 47 160 170 187 194 198
GILBERT, 34 53 57 64 83 85 91 173 233
GILDART, 17 34 38 41 42 47 50 65 66 73 74 79 89 103 106 120 132 133 140 168 173 177 178 200 218 223 234
GILDHART, 42
GILES, 59
GILHAM, 77
GILL, 3 4 46-48 55
GILLILAND, 137
GILMORE, 129
GINN, 21 38 39 64 66 88 90 105 114 164 179 208 214
GIRAULT, 54 70

GLASS, 5 14 19 25 75 93 115 125 127 132 137 164 179 181 188 191 250
GLOVER, 3 45 50 91 145 165
GLOWER, 37
GOBLE, 59
GODLEY, 225
GOFF, 75
GOLLIFER, 27
GOMBALL, 146
GOODRICH, 49 54 58 95 155
GOOLEY, 118
GOOLSLY, 83
GORDON, 5 7 13 16 60 63 64 69 72 75 100-102 106 111 118 131 146 149 161 169 174 202 210 225 236 238 249
GOTTSCHALD, 186
GOULDING, 8
GOVERNEUR, 80
GOWER, 13 49 74
GRAHAM, 65 154 199 200
GRANT, 237
GRAVES, 31 33 43 50 153 177 193 227 232
GRAVIS, 116 118 120 151 154 178 201
GRAY, 24 29 34 49 112 117 119 206 212 215 218 226
GRAYSON, 4 44 174 208 210 222
GREADY, 145 231 253
GREEN, 15 51 76 89 144
GREENLIES, 51
GREER, 30
GRIFFIN, 101 106 124 127 128 152 155 156 167 169 184 203 210 222
GRIMBALL, 96
GRIMKE, 134
GRISSAN, 5
GROOM, 123 197
GROOMS, 6 200
GROON, 208
GROWN, 208
GRUNDY, 20
GUALDEN, 119
GUIBERT, 162
GUIDAV, 28
GUIGNARD, 20
GUIN, 129

GUINN, 96
GUION, 69 94 168
GULLEDGE, 82
GUNLY, 83
GUNN, 130
GUTHRIE, 198
GWIN, 104 223
HACKLEY, 238
HADEN, 28
HADLEY, 18 48 56 79
HAILE, 11 19 28 31 73 84 111 116 143 174 198 211 216 229 237
HALL, 8 10 14 17 25 28 30 93 127 133 139 140 153 157 179 180 186 188 213 220 225
HALSEY, 213 221
HAMBERLIN, 185
HAMILTON, 9 85 150 156 167 169 192 195 197 216 220
HAMMETT, 2 4 6 17 21 58 60 62 74
HAMMOND, 233
HAMPTON, 25 26 29 35 37 41 78 90 97 143 180
HANCOCK, 59
HANDY, 61
HANES, 23
HANEY, 91
HANNA, 18 251
HANNAH, 93 191
HARDEN, 238
HARDIN, 215
HARDING, 232
HARDSEY, 80
HARDWICK, 70
HARE, 228
HARLEP, 101
HARLESS, 107
HARMER, 205
HAROLDSON, 58
HARPER, 143 163 242
HARRELL, 75
HARRIS, 14 15 28 29 31 50 59 69 77 118 131 135 148 151 167 169 171 172 174 175 178 184 186 187 190 202 204 216 234 242 250
HARRISON, 21 40 42 43 51 214
HARSON, 54 149 185 193 194

HART, 24 29 68 75 164 166 185 193 237
HARVARD, 121
HARVIN, 45
HASLEP, 179
HASLIP, 95 200 216
HATCH, 55
HATFIELD, 172 198 228 231 233
HATHORN, 80
HATTON, 143
HAVARD, 142 149 172 175 216
HAVORD, 175
HAWTHORN, 85
HAXALL, 171 220 250
HAXWELL, 253
HAYES, 13 29 35 81 92 94 102 209 213
HAYGOOD, 43 108 202
HAYNES, 47 69 86 93-95 107 113 114 123 138 139 143 162 164 170 175 236
HAYS, 61 91
HAZARD, 134
HAZLIP, 27
HEADY, 30 108 113 120 158 179
HEARTT, 133 171
HELM, 114 149 152 155 190 197 205 210 221 223 226 232 243 246 250
HELMER, 176
HELON, 148
HENDERSON, 20 39 41 58 60 72 93 96 100-102 104-107 111 112 120 121 126 138 147 157 162 175 196 206 214 215 217 236 241 243 245
HENLEY, 30 72 73 93 100 152 168
HENRY, 84
HENSHAW, 212
HERBERT, 22 29 50 63 78 97 128 173 180 184 198 200 215
HEREFORD, 253
HERFORD, 44
HERRING, 173
HERRINGTON, 49
HERSON, 52
HESTER, 49 111 122 137 147 160 162 179 207 221
HICKLEY, 236

HICKS, 81 93 120 123 126 133
  136 138 143 147 179
HIGGINS, 169
HILL, 21 60 102 137 243
HILLS, 82
HINCKLEY, 228
HINSO, 37
HINSON, 36 37
HODGE, 210 244 245 252
HODGEN, 160 173 174
HODGES, 10 23 165
HOLLAND, 146 165 178
HOLLEMAN, 190
HOLLIDAY, 87 115
HOLLIMAN, 8 56 67 90 110 112
  134 142 161 209 236 237
HOLLOMAN, 238
HOLLOWAY, 44
HOLMES, 82 89 100 149 156 164
  171 176 187 190 222 232 237
  251
HOLT, 13 126 133 140 142 179
  188 206 222 237 249
HONOR, 49
HOOK, 22 60 138 205
HOOKE, 27 48 78 204 205 236
  238
HOOTSELL, 181 216
HOPE, 36 52 72 76 82 97 100 165
  170 178 179
HOPKINS, 31 145 169
HORGOOD, 45
HORNSBY, 200 205 223
HORTON, 9 13 26 69
HOSACK, 181
HOWARD, 104
HOWE, 214
HOWELL, 93 133 140 166
HOWIE, 103
HUBBARD, 129 173 179 180 187
  207 211 216 226
HUDRY, 58 145
HUDSON, 133 140 147
HUFF, 39 56 111 165 242
HUFFMAN, 205
HUFFMANN, 117
HUGES, 2
HUGHES, 13 15 22 70 75 76 92
  134 164 186
HUGHEY, 122 126 145
HUGHS, 75
HULL, 3 5
HUMBLE, 26
HUMPHREYS, 160 194 196 206
HUMPHRIES, 125
HUNGERFORD, 175
HUNT, 15 121 130 152
HUNTER, 2 4 35 45 47 57 58 66
  68 83 107 110 128 131 146 152
  156 164 185 188 196 227 229
  231 240 251
HURST, 77
HUSTON, 169
HUTCHINS, 98 251
HYATT, 173 192 202 213
HYDE, 133
HYLAND, 68
HYNOR, 222 230
ILER, 18 45 46 64 67 84 88 94
  124 141 145 148 151 158 178-
  181 183 191 198 208 211 213
  249
INGRAHAM, 73
INMAN, 222 232 250
IRION, 15 23 29 34 39
IRON, 16 18 33
IRWIN, 14 94
ISLER, 24 99 156
IVES, 74 85 211 221 224 229 230
  232 236 239 243
IZOD, 251
JACKSON, 16 17 35 117 180 211
  218
JAGERS, 230
JAMES, 59 69 75 76 78 99 117
  145 170 178
JAQUESSS, 4
JAYNE, 38 133 137 140
JEETER, 193
JENKINS, 66 77 107 127 150 210
  236
JENKS, 117 190 196
JETER, 35 36 41 42 49 51 54 100
  234 237 241 242
JEWELL, 69 163
JIMASON, 41
JINKS, 90
JOHNS, 203
JOHNSON, 2 10 19 30 35 36 40 77
  91 105 107 111 112 120 135
  145 147 148 156 160 172 187
  198 202 210 214 217 220 222

JOHNSON (continued)
   228 232 243
JOHNSTON, 154 187
JOHNSTONE, 161
JONES, 18 20 25 26 32 34 36 37
   39 42 43 46 50 69 76 81 82 88
   95 100 109 110 112-114 116
   129-133 136 142 143 145 148
   153 161 169 173 176 181 188
   196 199 200 209 210 213 220
   223 225 227 228 242 245
JONTE, 156
JOOR, 12 17 21 22 28 47 50 56 69
   70 103 115 117 172 178 218
   229
JORDAN, 130 194 251
JORDON, 231
JOURDAN, 120
JULL, 87
JUMEL, 99
KAIGLER, 11 28 46 66 89 90 115
   119 150 161 190 199 211 213
   214 217 231 236 237 239 241
   247
KARY, 64
KEAGAN, 146
KEAGY, 96 104 106
KEARY, 126 227
KEEN, 131 135 136
KEITH, 23
KEITHLEY, 2
KEITHLY, 61
KELER, 115
KELLER, 3 8 11 12 33 38 51 81
   87 120 128 133 140 148 154
   185 187-189 194 198 207 210
   224 232 244
KELLEY, 140 227
KELLOG, 37 41 86 87 91 133 140
KELLOGG, 19 31 73 84 106 122
   128 135 140 145 166 169 177
   199 200 204 219 222 249
KELLY, 133 203
KELSEY, 18 47 214
KELSOE, 23
KEMKBALL, 240
KENNAN, 207 214 217 223
KENNER, 237
KERCHEVAL, 227
KETCHUM, 49

KIDD, 14 20
KILBOURN, 139
KILGORE, 57 70 74 117 184 194
   246
KILLGORE, 44 91 114 213 228
KIMBALL, 51 57 65 66
KING, 1 7 17 26 29 36 37 39 42
   53 71 74 109 111 137 175 177
   215 237 251
KIRKBY, 156
KIRKHAM, 20 51 142 175
KNEHTEN, 81
KNIGHT, 6 30 32 118 121 167 171
KNIGHTEN, 180 212 218 240 248
KNOWLTON, 204 210 224
KNOX, 91 96 99
LABARTHE, 45
LABAUVE, 80
LABONE, 80
LAMMOND, 23
LANCASTER, 222
LAND, 83 126 137 139 158 168
   174
LANDERUM, 27
LANDLY, 45
LANDRUM, 29 115 125 164 168
   169 212 215 236
LANDSEY, 2
LANE, 41
LANEHART, 6 46 48 86 162 166
   234
LANGDON, 39
LANGFORD, 52 185
LANGLEY, 5 115 120
LANGSTAFF, 238
LANIER, 156 234 246
LAPICE, 20
LAPORTE, 245
LARD, 86 92 113 116
LARKSTON, 19
LAROCHE, 183
LATTIMORE, 134
LAURENT, 215
LAURET, 7
LAW, 114
LAWRENCE, 154
LAYSON, 67 115 117 148
LEA, 9 11 12 31 32 37 51
LEAK, 39
LEAKE, 159

LEATHERBERRY, 44
LEATHERMAN, 34 49 65 75 94 97 105 114 117 132 134 151 154 179 199 202 208 209 212 217 226 233 247
LEATHLIGHTER, 221
LEATHLITER, 217
LEE, 66 67 111 148 175 232
LEECH, 51 88 109 117 168 168 170 173 176
LEEK, 48 227 246
LEFFINGWELL, 167 172 181 215 240 250
LEFINEIL, 135
LEIBY, 21
LEIGH, 225 245 250
LELAND, 5
LENIER, 224
LENNEX, 191
LENNOX, 86 103 139
LENOX, 145 229
LEOD, 130
LESLEY, 51
LESLIE, 195
LESSLEY, 90 116 158 198 208 225 227 234
LESTER, 24
LEVIN, 91
LEWIS, 2-5 21 22 27 30-32 39-41 44-46 49 53 55-58 62 63 73 78 79 81 86 89 94-96 100 101 112 114-116 119 120 123-125 132 133 145 147-149 152 154-156 160-163 167 169 172 181 182 186 191 196 198 201 210 214-217 227 229 230 237 238 241 243 244 247-250
LIDDEL, 5
LIDDELL, 3 5 12 25 39 120 124 145 155 162 168 173 183 195 210 227 233 245
LIGON, 19 31 36 42 60
LILLEY, 130 132 157 224
LILLY, 80 247
LINDSAY, 57
LINDSEY, 2 18 48 68 73
LINEBAUGH, 46
LIPSCOMB, 95 155
LITTLEFIELD, 248
LOCKIE, 72
LOMBARD, 74 119 128

LONDELL, 44
LONG, 72 89
LONGIMIRE, 144
LOVE, 3 10 44 105
LOVELACE, 6 31 33 44 61 77 92 112 119 179 216 231 245
LOWRY, 78 144 153
LOYD, 45
LUCAS, 173
LUCKETT, 95 215 237 240
LUNN, 250
LUSK, 45 144 147 186 219
LYNE, 20 62 109 111 113 116 126 144 145 168 194 244
LYONS, 215 216 237
LYTLE, 96 187
M'ALPINE, 58
M'CONNELL, 54 59 64
M'CORRLES, 165
M'CRANE, 177
M'CREDY, 38
M'CULLOCH, 152
M'GEHEE, 60
M'GRAW, 153 200
M'INTOSH, 155
M'MGRAW, 61
M'MORRIS, 61
M'NEELY, 163
M'PHARISON, 11
M'REA, 38
M'VEA, 80
M'WHORTER, 166
MABRY, 121 124 143 215
MACKEY, 47 183 193 247
MACMURDO, 85
MADISON, 84
MAFFIT, 159
MAGDALENE, 51 242
MAGEE, 198
MAGOFFIN, 16
MAGOUN, 90 207 209 213 218 219 230 237 241 253
MAGRUDER, 4
MAHE, 191
MANSFIELD, 21
MARBLE, 68
MARLEY, 28
MARLOW, 4
MARSCHALE, 225
MARSCHALK, 15 73
MARSH, 25 69 77

MARSHALL, 18 27 36 41 60 62 72 74 80 99 103 116 124 154 164 171 197 202 217 231 242 251
MARTIC, 11
MARTIN, 2 27 38 75 170 174 202 204 222 225 230 234 238 241 247 250
MASON, 170 199
MASSY, 104 106 129
MATHEWS, 28 72 86 88 90 104
MATTHEWS, 6 46 55 80
MAURY, 60 71
MAVES, 47
MAXWELL, 15 45 119
MAY, 12
MAYES, 33 40 45 54 57 65 73 74 103 110 113-115 119 126-128 133 140 144 148 149 157 159 174 181 188 197 198 202 218 230 237 238 242 249 250
MAYRANT, 129
MAYS, 145 232 233 239 242
MAYSON, 94 203
MC'DONALD, 232
MC'GEE, 194
MCALES, 67 68
MCALPHINE, 200
MCALPINE, 3 19 215
MCCALEB, 206
MCCALOP, 167
MCCARNEY, 2
MCCARSTLE, 10 14 56 79 108 115 184 192 253
MCCARSTLES, 4
MCCARTHY, 145
MCCARTNEY, 8 20 78 138
MCCASTLE, 26
MCCAULEY, 52
MCCAUSLAND, 187
MCCJULLOUGH, 27
MCCLEARY, 105
MCCLLOCH, 98
MCCOMAS, 2 95 215 232
MCCONNELL, 48
MCCRADY, 22
MCCRAINE, 128 172 189 200 209 221 227 235
MCCRANE, 97
MCCRANEY, 7 87
MCCRAY, 67
MCCREA, 157 197 198 206 211 219 220 230
MCCREADY, 196 205 217 232
MCCREARY, 104
MCCROSSON, 27 31
MCCULLCK, 205
MCCULLOCH, 36
MCCULLOCK, 10
MCCULLOUGH, 27
MCCUTCHENS, 217
MCCUTCHIN, 50
MCDANIEL, 197 199 214 241
MCDERMOTT, 69 202
MCDONAL, 148
MCDONALD, 187 188 194 208
MCDOWEL, 9 147
MCDOWELL, 144 190
MCDRAINE, 26
MCDUFFIE, 6 28 67 189 200
MCDUGAL, 71
MCFADEN, 55
MCGAHEY, 35 66 122 176 177 220 240
MCGAMEY, 19
MCGANEY, 14
MCGEE, 34 36
MCGEHEE, 8 35 47 107 145 169 208 210 217 228
MCGHEE, 34 51 90
MCGRAW, 3 26 33 43 82 92 93 112 138 187 208 211 215 226 240 248
MCINTOSH, 71
MCKAY, 208
MCKEE, 180 229 245 246
MCKENSIE, 117
MCKENZIE, 220 231 254
MCKEY, 200
MCKNIGHT, 119
MCLEOD, 1 119
MCMANUS, 75
MCMICKEN, 35
MCMILLAN, 91
MCMORRIES, 35 37 124 175
MCMURDO, 184 250
MCMURTRY, 74 127 216 232
MCMUTRY, 114 216
MCNABB, 34
MCNAIR, 126

MCNEELEY, 195
MCNEELY, 55 87 89 94 117 121 127 148 155 194
MCNULTY, 102 127 140 141 143 146 235
MCPHEATERS, 5
MCRAE, 96
MCREA, 234
MCREADY, 232
MCSHEE, 38
MCVEA, 42
MCWHORTER, 72 139 159 167 194
MCWILLIAMS, 27
MCWORTER, 168
MEDKIFF, 83
MEED, 100
MEEK, 18 46 88 181 184 201 212 225
MEEKS, 228
MELLEN, 79
MELLON, 27
MELTON, 30 36 89 114
MERCER, 35 83 235 240
MEREDITH, 25
MERRILL, 4 149 224
MERSEILLES, 33
MESSENGER, 141
METCALF, 67 108 116 121 166
MICOUD, 113
MIDDERHOFF, 238
MILES, 15 23 28
MILIKIN, 184
MILLER, 12 22 23 32 79 100 114 160 161 165 171 173 177 197 203 217 223 226 231 235 237 239 251
MILLS, 3
MISKEL, 206
MITCHELL, 56 62 98 109 114 154 203 214 215 239 251
MITHDELL, 250
MIXON, 111 116
MOCK, 184
MOISE, 174 247 249
MOLLEHAN, 143
MOLLEMAN, 60 86 167 203 206 215 219
MOLLEMANS, 41 118 173 177 246
MOLLMAN, 145

MONETT, 121
MONK, 56
MONKS, 21 28 55-57 119 150 175 226
MONROE, 80
MONTGOMERY, 83 99 212 222 250 251
MOON, 186
MOOR, 171
MOORE, 1 8 39 44 70 124 150 168 176 218 239 246-248 250
MORANCY, 184
MORE, 121
MORELAND, 8 34 43 206 246
MORGAN, 224
MORNINGSTAR, 133 177 247 253
MORRIS, 6 16 32 34 37 39 42 65 101 109 120 121 158 167 168 171 178 198 234 248
MORTON, 92
MOSLEY, 223 232
MOSS, 15 108 132 166
MUDGE, 242
MULFORD, 224
MULLER, 29
MUMFORD, 10 89 164 192 252
MURCH, 97
MURPHEY, 69
MURPHREY, 37 104 107 141 143
MURPHY, 90 123 143 168 209 220
MURRAY, 15 66
MURSROUGH, 119
MUSE, 104 124 154 251
MXWELL, 174
NANN, 108
NEELEY, 91
NEELY, 146 153
NELSON, 2 18 42 48 79 93 159 182
NERSON, 34 88 99 110 112 115 149 152 156
NESMITH, 25 27 72 185
NETERVILLE, 169
NETTERVILL, 243
NETTERVILLE, 9 10 15 39 44-46 55 57 76 92 105 108 109 113-116 124 129 132 133 135 140 141 144 150 153 155 165 166 173 177 178 183 189 191 199 200 207 212 214-216 222

NETTERVILLE (continued)
225 234 241 244 247
NEVILL, 104
NEWELL, 36 86 106 122 138 148 176 197 228
NEWMAN, 26 61 93 109 158 185 210 250
NEWSHAM, 81
NEWSON, 90
NEWTON, 145
NICHOLSON, 4 36 54 58 72 82 86 101 143 232 236
NILES, 84
NIMON, 12
NOBLE, 70
NOLAN, 18 57 126
NOLAND, 1 7 71 73 84 106 110 123 142 146 165 172 178 183 196 239 242
NORMAN, 134
NORMENT, 51
NORRIS, 157 164 233
NORTH, 151
NORTON, 1 78
NORWOOD, 10 21 23 24 44 47 64 86 97 110 123 140 149 172 179 188 200 220 227 230 250
NUTT, 144
NUTTING, 221
O'BRIEN, 238
O'CONNER, 40
O'CONNOR, 13
O'DONALD, 34
O'LEARY, 194
O'NEAL, 174
OAKEY, 236
ODUM, 98
OGDEN, 11 17 21 45 47 50 55 70 72 75 76 89 91 100 102 105-107 109 117 118 122 126 136 145 161 162 164 169 170 172 179 183-185 191 202 208 209 212 214 215 217 222 223 226 233 235 237 239 246 248 250
OGLESBY, 156
OLD, 156
OLDS, 43
ONEAL, 153 218
ORMSBY, 39
ORR, 22 59 60 147 194 212 254
OSWALD, 49 56 158 160 161 167

OSWALD (continued)
172 218
OVERMAN, 77 160 169 193 242
OWENS, 65 166
OWINGS, 53
P--UETT, 129
PACQUINETTE, 248
PAGE, 207
PALMER, 4 72 101 137
PANNELL, 141
PAQUINETT, 62 132 174 214
PAQUINETTE, 244
PARDEE, 251
PARHAM, 7 47 214
PARK, 246
PARKER, 58 63 65 74 173 182 186 187 214 232
PARMER, 216
PARROT, 18
PASCOE, 197 244
PATE, 233
PATRICK, 77 88 106 136 198
PATTERSON, 4 6 20 72 95 134 141
PATTON, 78 116
PATTREY, 27
PAXTON, 48
PAYNE, 129
PEABODY, 132
PEARCE, 156 248
PEARSON, 75 90 111
PEBBLES, 86
PECK, 60 99
PEEBLES, 113 117 140
PEETS, 245
PELARA, 32
PELL, 82
PEMBLE, 129 153 155
PENNIMA, 85
PENNIMAN, 16 40 134
PENNISTON, 22
PENNY, 137
PENNYMAN, 134
PENROSE, 184 211
PERCY, 61 80 163 176
PERDUE, 92 93
PERKINS, 15 69 74 143 169
PERRY, 221
PERRYMAN, 24
PETERSON, 81
PETTIBONE, 3 83 228

PHARES, 94 134 155 180 204 225 235 238 247 252
PHELPS, 53 76 104
PHILBRICK, 64 75 77 129 195 230 238 239
PHILIPS, 125 130
PHILLIPS, 36 46 225
PHIPPS, 10 41 79 149 150 193 224 225 236 239
PICKEN, 28 120
PICKENS, 29 65 109 113
PICO, 132
PIERCE, 20
PIETY, 82
PILLET, 140
PILLETT, 110 111 128 132 133
PILMORE, 6
PINSON, 17 35 222
PIPES, 59
PIPKIN, 30
PIRAM, 89
PITCHER, 4 11 13 31 36 37 50 120 168
PITTMAN, 202
PLATNER, 43 55 94
PLUMMER, 192
POINDEXTER, 14 61 75 76 109 125 178 183 198 210 214 217 223 236 246
POOL, 42 57 92 121 127 170 196 202 216 226 237
POOLE, 57 58 98 246
POPE, 13
PORCHE, 73 103
PORTER, 35 63 67 78 81
POSEY, 42 43 100 120 186 203 219 224 225 229 253
POSSER, 178
POSSEY, 219
POST, 12
POSTHLEWAITE, 223
POSTLETHWAITE, 15 228
POSWELL, 156
POTTER, 71 112 114 222
POTTS, 22 61 93 158 162 199 214 233 249
POURCHE, 154
POURSH, 32
POWE, 71
POWELL, 37 44 171 176 181 237 241 246 247 249
POYNER, 113
PRESBURY, 157
PRESLER, 7 11 13 154 202 209 224 245 254
PRESSLER, 110
PRESTON, 137 139 145
PREVOST, 181
PREWETT, 6 8 17 43 116 129 132 241
PRICE, 39 75 136
PROSSER, 22 24 25 70 116 132 133 160 251 253
PURDEW, 132 133
QOODARD, 222
QUARTEMAN, 223
QUARTERMAN, 129 150 203 231 234 243 250
QUICK, 54
QUIN, 24 27
QUINE, 55 74 90 119 145 161 168 191 192 199 200 212 229 230 234 239 248
QUINN, 67 71
QUITMAN, 132 180
RABB, 58 140 189 192
RADCLIFFE, 235
RADFORD, 122 141 144 215
RAIFORD, 90
RALPH, 104 177
RAMAPO, 7
RAMSEY, 26 217 243
RANALDON, 95
RANALDSON, 17 59 74 79 80 84 117 130 153
RANDAL, 150
RANDALDSON, 79
RANDALL, 156
RANDELL, 70
RANDOLPH, 1 7 8 13 17 25–27 34–38 44 48 58 59 74 83 89 96 103 106 120 124 132 133 145 166 172 197 205 210 242 246
RAOUL, 153 177
RATCLIFF, 25 29 39 52 113 130 230
RATLIFF, 84 94 201 204 217
RAWLINS, 167 174 221
RAYMOND, 4 13 31 148 154 156 216 237
RAZER, 14
REA, 38 215
READ, 121 126 128 197 199 226

REAMS, 87
REAVES, 59
REAZEALE, 29
RED BIRD, 40
REED, 27 55 59 92 103 118 126 140 143 166
REES, 224
REESE, 254
REID, 6 45 63 82 92 95 109 118 157 166
REILEY, 7 236 250
REILY, 39 43 136 226
REYNOLDS, 38 77
RHEA, 79 80
RHODES, 104 175
RICE, 12 43 103 105 107 119 128 147 211 221
RICHARDS, 15 28 101
RICHARDSON, 1 2 3 12 16 21 27 30 37 48 62 63 91 105 106 125 131 133 141 145 147 149 157 210 221 224 241 246 248 253 254
RICHMOND, 106 157
RIDDLE, 40 166 194 222 246 249
RIDER, 243
RILEY, 239
RIST, 163
ROACH, 2 19 29 30 36 204 237
ROACHE, 169
ROBERT, 125
ROBERTS, 68 89 117 147 190
ROBERTSON, 52 70
ROBINSON, 16 38 75 76 79 91 98 103 114 127 134 139 192 199
ROBSON, 148 175
RODGERS, 38
ROGERS, 20 41 149 218 224 242
ROGILLIO, 230
ROLLINS, 2
RORCK, 69
ROSE, 253
ROSS, 61 83 163
ROUNTREE, 38
ROURKE, 9
ROUSE, 71
ROUTH, 40 235
ROWAN, 218 226 249
RUELL, 2
RUFFIN, 24 25 51 120 168 195
RULE, 209

RUNNELLS, 68
RUNNELS, 214
RUSSEL, 202
RUSSELL, 47 116
RUTLEDGE, 2 18 37 44 46 132 173 176
RUTZELL, 74
RYDER, 234
SALE, 140 159 170 174 203 216
SANBORN, 219 237
SANDERS, 48 251
SANFORN, 219
SAPP, 49 67 70 99 110 112 124 161 162 184 237 242
SATTERWHITE, 177
SAUNDERS, 1 41 48 52 68 77 97 108 115 132 135 138 139 145 149 153 159 164 170 172 175 187 198-200 237 240 242 243 245 250
SAVAGE, 4
SCARBOROUGH, 158
SCARBOROUTH, 249
SCARLETT, 9
SCHROEDER, 252
SCOTT, 2 3 7 8 19 30 47 56 57 60 65 75 76 79 87 93 94 95 106 107 114 121 129 140 143 144 148 155 159 162 165 168 170 172 173 178 182 184 188 194 198 202 206 209 211-213 215-218 225 226 235 239 240 248 251
SCRIPPS, 121 126 128
SCUDDER, 24 45 48 114 116 117 121 122 124 125 127-129 137 169 171 180 181 184 187-189 196 199 204 208 209 211 213 218 222 228 229 231-233 245-247
SEAGARS, 23 76
SEALE, 99
SEEBER, 26 138 153
SELLERS, 95
SELLIER, 64
SELPH, 250
SEMPLE, 107 110 114 146 156 169 204 227 231
SEVERSON, 9 12 48 50
SEWELL, 148
SEYMOUR, 121 127

SHAFER, 13
SHAFFER, 3 124 131 145 154 170 177 193 194 198
SHANNON, 83 88 90 95 144 162 240 248
SHAW, 2 21 166 172 182 200 203 219 243
SHELBY, 8 17
SHEPARD, 110
SHEPHARD, 48
SHEPHERD, 33 40 113 212
SHEPPARD, 31 228 231
SHIELDS, 63 66 202
SHIPP, 150
SHOPE, 126 130
SHORT, 175
SHROPSHIRE, 27 187 189 201 222 228 232 248
SIBLEY, 21 223
SIDEBOTTOM, 46 79
SIKES, 122
SILVEY, 176
SIMMONS, 70 86 148 218 239 248
SIMONTON, 67
SIMPSON, 68 218 222
SIMRALL, 232 240
SIMS, 11 32 62 80 81 87 95 97 113 114 132 154 182 233
SINGLETON, 5 44 50 52 58 67 69 91 94 105 106 224
SIX, 47 69 71
SKILLMAN, 61 118 235
SLACK, 14 23 33 34 36 86 198 203
SLADE, 45 52 120 145 161 168 187 191 249
SLAUGHTER, 228
SLEEPER, 157
SLOCOMB, 158 222
SLOCUMB, 53 114 171 175
SMILIE, 208
SMITH, 2 5 7 12 17-19 21 23 25 29 31 33-36 39 42-44 49 51 53 54 61 63-65 70 72 74-76 79 85 87-93 97 100 104 109 111 112 114 115 117-120 122 127 128 130 133 134 139 140 143-145 147 148 152 153 157-159 161 165 171 172 174 177 178 180 181 185 190 197 198 201 204 206 210 214-219 223 225 226

SMITH (continued) 231 233 237 239 241 243 244 246 248 250
SMITY, 2
SMYDER, 237
SMYLIE, 126 174 175 208
SNODDY, 143
SOCKETT, 126
SOJOURNER, 8 20 24 25
SOLOMON, 108
SOULE, 242
SOUTHERLAND, 68
SOWELL, 233 234
SOWER, 30
SPADE, 179
SPAIN, 174
SPEAR, 227
SPEARS, 18 19 26 39 48 56 57 62 70 71 84
SPENCER, 134
SPURLOCK, 2 101 105 110 116 124 130 131 135 136 151 198
STAFFORD, 190 204 244
STAMBRIDGE, 230
STAMPS, 3 49 79 106 133 135 169 173 196 241 243
STANLEY, 202
STANTON, 6
STANWOOD, 163 197 210 229 233 244
STAR, 223 232
STARK, 13 38 40 53 65 83 84 85 120 133 140 144 168 185 186
STARKE, 133
STARNS, 102
STEEL, 238
STEELE, 156 232 242
STEEN, 21
STEMBRIDGE, 231
STEMDRIDGE, 187
STEP, 229
STEPHENS, 10 19 94 151 213 238
STEPHENSON, 91 120 189
STERLING, 44 132 198
STEVEN, 123 248
STEVENS, 7 13 43 55 96 103 110 112 116 120 124 128 130 133 135 140 216
STEVENSON, 236 239
STEWART, 4 7 13 25 28 41 46 58 70 74 77 92 93 97 98 100 103

STEWART (continued)
116 117 120 129 137-139 141
144 150 151 153 154 156 160
166 167 169 174 177 178 183
185 191 195 197 208 213 214
217 233 234 238 239
STIDGER, 33
STOCKBRIDGE, 218 241 245
STOCKET, 30
STOCKETT, 7 90 197 231
STOCKILL, 58
STOCKTON, 19 83
STOCKWELL, 59
STONE, 24 93 164 168 202 216
232 241 251 252
STOUT, 160
STOVALL, 84
STREET, 118 119 144 154 157-
159 163 165 166 169 175 183
STRIBLING, 157
STRICKLAND, 99
STRONG, 60 99 126 174
STROTHER, 213 230
STUART, 40 105 107 184 233
SULLIVAN, 232 241
SUTTIN, 2
SWAYSE, 144
SWAYZE, 107 122 125 141 179
181 211 241 242
SWAYZEY, 65
SWAYZIE, 219
SWEARINGEN, 117 122
SWENEY, 232
SWIGART, 108 158 179 224 235
236 247
SWIGGART, 250 251
SWINGLE, 182
TANNER, 21
TARBE, 69
TARKINSON, 159
TARQUIS, 82 83
TARVER, 91 135 138 155
TAYLOR, 76 87 109 147 151 181
205 211 246
TEKEL, 146
TEMMON, 190
TEMON, 78
TEMONS, 34
TERRELL, 30 69 151 183
TESTARD, 70
TEW, 179

THEREL, 226 241
THERILL, 32
THERREL, 7 143 151 154 155
183 193 198 212 216 217 224
226 230 237 251 252
THERRELL, 19 20 90 97 128 178
206 218 233
THERRIL, 45
THERRILL, 44 49 61
THIRLKILL, 25
THOM, 3 133
THOMAS, 37 85 197
THOMLINSON, 50
THOMPSON, 20 21 25 31 39 41
45 47 78 79 85-87 97 103 111
115 117 122 134 187 198 199
220 224 228 239 248 249
THOMS, 237
THOMSON, 65
THORN, 140
THORNTON, 69 199 214 240 242
244 247 250 252
THORP, 228
THROOP, 28
TICKELL, 53 66 141 156 157 188
227 229 231
TIDWELL, 67
TIGNER, 63 70 89 95 117 146 162
179 182 233 237 240 241 248
249
TILDON, 97
TILLER, 141
TILLERY, 175
TILLOTSON, 91 116 152
TIMON, 173 220
TINGEY, 48
TISON, 17 41
TOLLES, 59
TOMPKINS, 181
TOMS, 195
TOOL, 76 81 176 183
TOOLE, 93 115 133 182
TOOLEY, 39
TORANCE, 84
TORRANCE, 183 186
TOWER, 223
TOWNSEND, 93 96 97 122 161
181
TRASH, 247
TRASK, 27 28 66 67 82 103 112
117 120 124 140 160 168 176

TRASK (continued)
 178 188 210 214 240
TRAVIS, 110
TRENTHAM, 157 180
TRENTHAN, 157
TRIPP, 44
TUELL, 13 88 137
TUFTS, 69
TULANE, 69
TULAVE, 69
TULLIS, 119
TURBEVILLE, 43 85 98 161 200
 216 218 250
TURNANN, 58
TURNER, 34 80 83 99 113 134
 145 152 156 162 188 238
TURNMANN, 74
TURSEVILLE, 155
TUTTLE, 147
TUTTY, 39
TYSON, 40 119
UHLMAN, 178 220
UNDERWOOD, 98
UNTER, 131
USHER, 94
VAHAMONDE, 44
VANBUREN, 177
VANHOUTEN, 69
VANKENREN, 70
VANMETER, 59
VANNORMAN, 135
VANVACTER, 138 202
VARNELL, 26 39 59 107 115 141
 143 147 254
VAUGHAN, 55 109 116 125 220
VAUGHN, 122
VEAL, 42
VENPORT, 247
VENTRESS, 1 11 24 38 69 114
 200 213 219
VICTOR, 33
VINING, 143 182
VOSE, 55 126 176 188 195 211
VOUSDEN, 179
WADDELL, 10 148
WADDILL, 33 38 86 87 148 172
WADE, 36
WAIDE, 8 11 31 37 40 47 49 50
 56 57 84 86 111 115
WAILED, 112

WAILES, 36 106 117 118 122 133
 135 139 169 197 199 203 210
 228 246 252
WAIT, 88 100
WALKER, 4 15 39 65 70 93 102
 112 118 122 132 137 146 148
 174 192 202 240 243
WALL, 38 52 56 105-107 112 114
 127 130 131 136 137 140 143
 146 148 154 164 176 179 180
 182 186 199-201 208 212 214
 226 240 242 253
WALLACE, 91
WALLER, 14 16 40 140
WALSH, 215
WALTON, 107 137 197
WAMACK, 3 4
WARD, 212 226
WARREN, 203 212
WASHINGTON, 141 205
WATAROUS, 196
WATERS, 157
WATKINS, 58 99 100 107 128 145
 146 155 189 192 218
WATROUS, 169 199
WATSON, 177 181
WAYNE, 205
WEATHERSBY, 92 133 153
WEBB, 98 100 127 128 173 184
 190
WEED, 195 238
WEEKLEY, 234 237
WEEKLY, 119 180 240
WEEKS, 117 122
WELCH, 169 182 188 189
WELLER, 68 91
WELLS, 74 155 226
WELSH, 217
WESBROOK, 10
WEST, 46 58 89 91 92 95-97 103
 117 133 135 140 143 145 148-
 150 161 169 174 195 197 207
 210 212 215 220 224 226 238
 244 248 250 252 253
WESTBROOK, 30
WHEELER, 103 227
WHETSTONE, 62 174
WHIELDEN, 238
WHITAKER, 31
WHITE, 8 13 14 20 38 49 53 55

WHITE (continued)
56 58 62 68 75 77 80 81 98 102
103 121 123 135 137 140 143
145 155 163 168 174 179 193
202 214-216 229 230 233 234
249
WHITEHEAD, 5 40 45 58 101
211 214
WHITNEY, 93 129 130 144 198
226 228 230 233
WHITTAKER, 242
WHITTINGTON, 193
WIGLEY, 126 171
WILCOX, 30 68
WILDER, 101
WILDS, 247 248
WILES, 167 168
WILEY, 123 188 197 208 209 225
WILKINS, 47 95 160
WILKINSON, 18 40 143 183 200
205
WILLIAM, 64
WILLIAMS, 1 12 17 20 24 34 36
41 66 71 104 105 135 144 164
165 181 190 195 198 204 221
222 239 254
WILLIRSON, 65
WILLIS, 82
WILLS, 144
WILSEY, 40
WILSON, 14 19 25 35 36 43 48 49
52 53 56 58 74 77 88 134 224
232
WINANS, 13 19 27 33 47 107 148
149 166 176 182 208 223 227
242 246 249
WINCHESTER, 38
WINNINGHAM, 218
WINNS, 136
WINSTON, 6 253
WINTERS, 83
WIRT, 119
WISEMAN, 8

WISNER, 167 191 193 203 213
221 239 250
WITHERSPOON, 150 153
WOMACK, 36
WOOD, 69 78 80 82 85 88 97 115
130 143-145 152 156 170 183
200 202 215 227 228 235 242
244
WOODARD, 52 102 103 149 174
188 211 215 224 236 246 247
WOODRUM, 54
WOODS, 58 74 83 94-96 112 113
115 124 128 131 135 137 153
156 169 172 174 181 185 193
200-202 212 223 226-228
WOODSIDE, 96 118 121 122 145
159
WOODSIDES, 53 77
WOODWARD, 97 101 110
WOOKARD, 37
WOOLDRIDGE, 169 199
WOOLDRIGE, 161
WOOLFOLK, 38
WOOSTER, 94 97
WORMLEY, 74
WORMLY, 83
WREN, 174 183 184
WRIGHT, 4 41 54 146 165 193
218 222
WYATT, 144
WYSE, 80
YARBOROUGH, 197 206
YATES, 231 240
YEISER, 4 63
YEIZER, 28 63 226
YERBY, 4 5 9-11 16 18 22 28 53
58 72 84 88 99 103 146 148
173 183 220 243 245
YOUNG, 8 17 35 59 110 112 119
146 161 165 169 200 204 213
229
ZIPPORAII, 5

www.ingramcontent.com/pod-product-compliance
Lightning Source LLC
Chambersburg PA
CBHW070726160426
43192CB00009B/1327